ED BEGLEY, JR.'S
GUIDE TO
SUSTAINABLE
LIVING

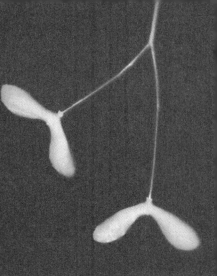

Also by Ed Begley, Jr.

Living Like Ed

ED BEGLEY, JR.'S
GUIDE TO
SUSTAINABLE
LIVING

**Learning to Conserve Resources
and Manage an Eco-Conscious Life**

Clarkson Potter/Publishers

New York

This book is printed with soy-based inks on 100-percent
postconsumer recycled paper.

Copyright © 2009 by Ed Begley, Jr. and Brentwood
Communications International, Inc.

Published in the United States by Clarkson Potter/Publishers,
an imprint of the Crown Publishing Group, a division of
Random House, Inc., New York.
www.crownpublishing.com
www.clarksonpotter.com

CLARKSON POTTER is a trademark and POTTER with
colophon is a registered trademark of Random House, Inc.

Library of Congress Cataloging-in-Publication Data is available
upon request.

ISBN 978-0-307-40514-2

Printed in the United States of America

Design by Amy Sly

10 9 8 7 6 5 4 3 2 1

First Edition

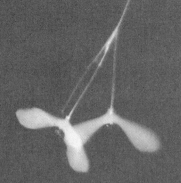

THIS BOOK IS DEDICATED

To Jackson Browne and Dianna Cohen, for living off the grid and living a life that we could all aspire to.

To Don Henley, for saving Walden Woods—and me, on more than one occasion.

To Carrie Fisher for inspiring me to write a book.

To Glenne Headly and Byron McCulloch, for being one of the greenest couples in town, and (like Jackson and Dianna) never making a big deal about it.

To Gavin DeBecker, for helping me be a better writer, and for going solar so many years ago.

To Peter Falk and Shera Danese, for their incredible friendship toward me and countless other mutts.

To Bill Nye for being the best neighbor a guy could have.

And finally, to my wife, Rachelle, and my three perfect children—Amanda, Nicholas, and Hayden—for giving me the very best reason to do all that I do.

CONTENTS

FOREWORD

I first met Ed Begley, Jr., in 1974. It was at a show called "Dean Martin's Comedy Shop." We were doing the program together. Ed was doing this "disappearing man with a necktie" bit. I think he continued to do stand-up comedy for several more years before making the decision to focus on acting.

During an appearance on *The Tonight Show* last year, Ed told me that he struggled a bit to find acting work in the late 1980s and 1990s. One of his agents felt it might have been due to his environmentalist lifestyle. I have to admit, many of us used to make fun of Ed and call him a wacko back then. Of course, many of those same people have now jumped on the "green" bandwagon, as if they'd been doing these things all this time too. I give people like Ed a tremendous amount of credit—this guy was right.

A lot of the things Ed does in his life really wouldn't work for me. He lives in a house that is, like, seven square feet—I think it's a converted Fotomat booth or something. He rides his bike a lot—I think it takes him twenty-eight hours to ride across town to work. He has a solar oven in his backyard that he uses to cook food. It's sort of like frying ants with a magnifying glass. When his family asks "When will dinner be ready?" his reply is "Tuesday."

But Ed and I also have some things in common. We both had fathers who would yell "Turn that crap off" when we left the lights or the TV set on. Ed reminded me that this was a form of energy conservation, so I guess my father was an environmentalist. Who knew? Ed and I both believe in leaving this planet in no worse shape than we found it. Ed says to "live simply so that others can simply live." I think of it as "do no harm." Ed's focus is very much on conservation, and I think that's good for many people. Since I've been lucky enough to have some success, I've tried to make sure that if I'm going to use more electricity than the average guy, then I should be committed to produce that power myself in a sustainable way.

As many people know, I'm quite passionate about automobiles and motorcycles. I have a fairly large garage where I keep cars and work on them. Ed has been over to the garage several times in the last year or two for visits. The first time Ed visited Jay Leno's Garage, I was a little nervous—it was like having your mother-in-law giving your place the white-glove test. But Ed was very encouraging to me as I told him I wanted to make the garage green and get it off the power grid. He advised me on utilizing nontoxic cleaning products for the garage and installing a new high-efficiency water heater.

When we installed 54 kilowatts of solar panels on the roof to help power the garage, Ed helped me partner it with a 10-kilowatt wind turbine for additional power.

I also enjoyed sharing with Ed all of the classic alternative fuel vehicles we have at Jay Leno's Garage. We looked at my 1916 Owens Magnetic Hybrid, one of the earliest gas/electric hybrids designed by Westinghouse. We checked out my 1925 Doble steam car, which is so efficient that it can still pass California emissions standards today. We even took a ride in my 1909 Baker electric car. This country really has a history of doing great things, which I think is why both of us are hopeful for the future.

There's no question that Ed is a bit of an oddball, as well as a little cheap. But he has also turned me on to a lot of this stuff, and Jay Leno's Garage is a better, greener, and more efficient place because of it. I'm a great admirer of what Ed's done over the years and he's inspired a lot of deadbeats like me. I hope he can inspire you, too.

Jay Leno
Jay Leno's Garage
www.jaylenosgarage.com

Answering all of your questions about making your home—and your lifestyle—greener

INTRODUCTION

THE LAST TWO YEARS OF MY LIFE HAVE been unbelievable. I've been filled with hope, watching Americans from all walks of life embrace the environmental challenges of today with action and optimism. Getting e-mails from red-state Republicans that say things like, "I may not always agree with you politically, Mr. Begley, but where do I get one of those barrels to catch rainwater?" makes me realize that this is a challenge we all understand and want to overcome.

Although I think many people give me way too much credit, if the example I've set in my life has been the inspiration for some people to make positive changes in their homes and businesses, then I'm eternally grateful.

In my first book, *Living Like Ed,* I tried to summarize my thirty-nine-year eco-journey and all of the things I had done in various areas of my life—including my home, my transportation choices, my efforts to recycle and save energy, and much more.

Since that book came out, I've received incredible feedback from people all over the country, including an avalanche of advanced questions on various green subjects. People are hungry for answers, and I feel that since I started this green journey for my readers, I'd better join them on the ride.

If the first book was a map, I tried to give everyone the correct ZIP code for Ecotopia. We even visited some of my favorite points of interest along the way.

Now with this new book, *Ed Begley, Jr.'s Guide to Sustainable Living,* I want to really turn on that green GPS unit and take a very specific look at my entire journey so that I can answer all of your great questions.

AS MY FRIEND PAUL CONNETT LIKES TO SAY, there are two kinds of thinkers today: back-end thinkers and front-end thinkers. Imagine your bathtub faucet is stuck and water is pouring onto the floor. Back-end thinkers start to bail water using a cup. When they find the cup is too small, they switch to a bucket. When they find the bucket still isn't keeping up, they bring in a pump to bail the water. When that's not enough, they bring in an even larger pump in an attempt to keep up.

The front-end thinker, on the other hand, turns off the tap to the bathtub, and then begins the process of cleanup. In this book, I've tried to take a front-end thinker approach to going green. If you make the right decisions and do things in the proper order, you can put money in your pocket, reduce waste and pollution in the city where you live, reduce our overall dependency on Mideast oil, and lead a healthier and more toxin-free life. And who isn't for all of those things?

Please join me on this journey to make your home—and your lifestyle—greener and healthier and better overall in so many ways.

SECTION I
CONSERVE

**Reducing Our Needs for Energy—
& Water—Before We Even
Consider Producing Our
Own Energy**

Conservation is our ultimate goal. From 1970 to 1985, the vast majority of the environmentally friendly things I did in my life were based on conservation. The fact is, we practice conservation in almost every aspect of our lives . . . especially in business. When businesses become wasteful, they generally become less profitable.

The great environmentalist David Brower once said, "Capitalism is a great idea. We ought to try it." By that he meant we should stop using unsound business practices when it comes to our natural resources. We should stop liquidating those resources like an enterprise having a fire sale.

Our natural resources—the forests, arable land, minerals, water, aquatic life—are assets that we own. We own the forests just like we own the buildings that house the Smithsonian Institution. It would be crazy to demolish the Smithsonian just because we had a good market for bricks. We need to value our forests and our other natural resources the same way.

Similarly, we need to make good choices about how we use our resources in our own lives. The energy efficiency of our home is an exercise in conservation. A kilowatt *saved* is always cheaper and easier than a kilowatt *produced.* Putting solar panels on the roof of a home that's energy-inefficient would be like walking in the rain with an umbrella filled with holes. You need to create an environment of energy efficiency *before* you begin to *produce* energy in the environment.

Conservation is where the big savings are. Less really is more. So let's get started.

1

THE GREEN
HOME AUDIT

Measuring Your Carbon Footprint

I KNOW, FOR A LOT OF FOLKS, IT'S REALLY TEMPTING to go straight to the shiny, sexy stuff, like installing solar panels or a whole-house fan or geothermal heating and cooling. But before you mount solar panels on your roof, before you invest in a residential wind turbine, before you buy new windows, before you install more insulation—in fact, before you spend a dime on changes to your home and your lifestyle—you'll want to have someone perform a green energy audit on your home.

This audit will identify the areas where you can *conserve* energy, where you can become more efficient. This type of audit will establish a baseline: It'll give a snapshot of where you are right now. I promise you, the time and money you invest in an energy audit will pay off several times over.

In order to take your level of green up a notch, *first* you want to conserve. Establish a baseline, see the challenges you face with your home, and see where you can improve the situation. Then go from your baseline to a lower energy-usage position *before* you do anything else. First you want to work to get your use of electricity down to the lowest possible level. Only then can you start to think about creating your own electricity on-site. Otherwise, you're just going to be overproducing electricity, and that's wasteful in many, many ways.

Let's begin with some ways to establish that all-important baseline.

DIFFERENT TYPES OF GREEN AUDITS

The best way to figure out your home's energy performance is to perform a *green home energy audit*. This term is used a lot these days. Some people call it a green home audit. Some call it an energy audit, but the terms are not always used to describe the same types of activities.

Actually, there're all different kinds of green home audits and energy audits. Some audits look at your electricity use. Some look at your natural gas use. Some look at your water use. Some look at all of the above. Some also consider your recycling habits and your waste management. And some go so far as to consider your overall carbon footprint.

For simplicity's sake, we can break down the offerings into three levels of green home audits. From the most basic to the most detailed and involved, you can

1. use an online resource to get a general idea of your home's energy use
2. contact your local utility company for an audit, which is often free
3. get a professional green audit, in which a company sends representatives to your home to evaluate your energy usage, water usage, and more

Another really valuable type of home audit is a green home health issues audit. Many professional energy auditors will address potential health threats from your home during their audits, too.

TAP INTO FREE RESOURCES FIRST

When you look at the different levels of green home audits, the first two typically are free—at no cost to you, the consumer. So start with the free options and consider the results.

A great example of a free audit is on the Energy Star website (see Resources, page 340). In the website's section on home improvement, you'll find the interactive Energy Star Home Energy Yardstick. You'll need to have your last twelve months of utility bills (or ask your utility company or companies to get you a twelve-month summary). Plus, you'll have to enter some basic information about your house, including the following:

- your ZIP code
- your home's age
- its square footage
- the number of occupants

The site will tell you how your home's energy efficiency compares with similar homes across the country, and it provides recommendations for energy-saving home improvements.

If you want more detail, another great free resource online is ENERGY Guide (see Resources, page 340). Check that site to see if your electric or gas company offers a "personalized energy center." Many utilities from all across the United States are included. Once you choose the link for your utility, you can get some pretty helpful information.

YOUR HOME CONTRIBUTES TO
THE QUALITY OF OUR ENVIRONMENT
U.S. Environmental Protection Agency · U.S. Department of Energy

ENERGY STAR

About ENERGY STAR · News Room · FAQs · KIDS   Search [ ] Go

Products | **Home Improvement** | New Homes | Buildings & Plants | Partner Resources

Home Improvement

Common Home Problems

Home Energy Yardstick

Home Energy Audits

Air Seal & Insulate

Heat & Cool Efficiently

Home Performance with ENERGY STAR

Home Improvement FAQs

For Contractors

For Insulation Manufacturers

Join ENERGY STAR

Home > Home Improvement > **Home Energy Yardstick**

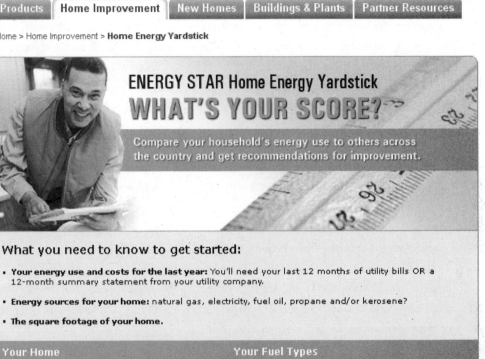

ENERGY STAR Home Energy Yardstick
WHAT'S YOUR SCORE?

Compare your household's energy use to others across the country and get recommendations for improvement.

What you need to know to get started:

- **Your energy use and costs for the last year:** You'll need your last 12 months of utility bills OR a 12-month summary statement from your utility company.

- **Energy sources for your home:** natural gas, electricity, fuel oil, propane and/or kerosene?

- **The square footage of your home.**

Your Home	Your Fuel Types
What is your zip code? [ ]	In addition to electricity, which fuel type(s) does your home use? Select all that apply. **Maximum 2.**
How many people live in your home? [ ]	
What is the square footage of your home, including the basement? [ ]	☐ Natural Gas ☐ Propane
More information	☐ Fuel Oil ☐ Kerosene

Your Energy Use

Would you like to use **annual** or **monthly** billing information to enter your household's energy use?

◉ Annual

○ Monthly

Select the Start Date for the year covered: [Select Month ▼] [Select year ▼]

Enter Totals for the year: [ ] kWh [ ] dollars

SUBMIT

UTILITY COMPANY AUDITS

Another option for a free audit is to contact your local utility company directly and see if it offers home-inspection-type audits for its customers. Many utility companies will do this to help you conserve energy and to help you better understand your utility bills, too.

Naturally, these types of audits focus specifically on the service provided by the particular utility company. So if the utility provides both natural gas and electricity, the audit will cover both.

These audits can be very helpful. For example, Silicon Valley Power (see Resources, page 340) in Santa Clara, California, will send a specialist to customers' homes for free. The audit is quick and painless. It takes just an hour or less. The specialist will walk through your home and evaluate your refrigerator (or refrigerators), your dishwasher, your washer and dryer, and your lighting. The specialist also will ask questions about your energy habits, how many people live in your home, and other important information.

The specialist will come armed with copies of two years' worth of your utility bills. They're looking for any trends in usage, including seasonal shifts with your winter heating and summer air-conditioning.

"The auditor usually will give recommendations for ways to save energy right at the audit," says Leslie Mackenzie of Silicon Valley Power. And it includes information on ways to save money when you invest in newer, more efficient appliances and other items. "We talk to people about our rebate programs at the time, if we feel that they're appropriate. We have rebates for attic insulation, whole-house fans, refrigerator purchase and recycling, LCD monitors, and recently added solar attic fans, ceiling fans, and the new energy-efficient pool pumps."

To encourage customers to get these free audits and take steps to conserve energy use, some utility company auditors also give homeowners compact fluorescent lightbulbs and other useful items to help them save energy—all part of the package.

A free audit may not be the most in-depth energy audit available, but it's obviously well worth sixty minutes of your time.

HOUSEHOLD IMPACT CALCULATOR

Free utility company energy audits are really useful, and so are some of the quick

An infrared gun measures the amount of heat coming in and out of your home.

and easy online tools. When you're ready to investigate even further, there's one other great and still free tool: the most in-depth free resource I've run across, which is on Low Impact Living's website.

So before you have someone visit your house, I highly recommend using this site's free household impact calculator (see Resources, page 340). It covers all the environmental impacts for your household—carbon emissions, energy usage, water usage, trash production, water runoff on your property, and even more.

To get you thinking about things you might want to change, the calculator asks some really valuable questions about:

- ❏ the age of your heating and cooling systems
- ❏ how often you use your air-conditioning
- ❏ how many loads of laundry you do each week
- ❏ how many times you run the dishwasher
- ❏ how many refrigerators you have, how old they are, and how large they are
- ❏ how many of your lightbulbs are compact fluorescent lightbulbs (CFLs)
- ❏ your recycling habits
- ❏ information about your yard
- ❏ how many vehicles you have, including their year, make, model, and annual mileage
- ❏ how many short, medium, and long airplane flights you take each year

The site then gives you a LILI—that is, a Low Impact Living Index number. This score lets you know how you compare with other homes in your area, and it reflects not just your carbon footprint but your entire environmental footprint. The average score is 100. The lower this number is, the better.

The site then provides many suggestions regarding how to lower your Low Impact Living Index number. Some of the relatively simple suggestions include, for instance,

- installing low-flow showerheads
- installing ultraefficient toilets
- installing a high-efficiency dishwasher
- replacing your incandescent lightbulbs
- increasing ceiling insulation
- planting shade trees
- reducing the temperature setting on your water heater
- buying carbon offsets for airplane travel

Alongside each suggestion, you'll find a number indicating how much the change will lower your LILI score. I find this to be a really helpful resource. It goes into considerably more detail than the other free resources I've found.

A PROFESSIONAL GREEN HOME AUDIT

Once you've taken advantage of all the free resources and you've gotten a general idea of your home's energy consumption, the next step is to hire a professional to visit your home to perform a thorough green audit. I can't emphasize enough the importance of getting an expert to come out and do a home energy audit.

Duct-pressure testing can show if there are any leaky ducts in your home.

Performing green home audits is a pretty new field, and different companies within this field do things differently. Some will mostly look at your heating and cooling systems. Some will bring out some fancy equipment—duct testers, blower door testers—to figure out how well your home is sealed and insulated. Some will look at your appliances and your lighting, both indoors and out. Some will look at your water usage and your carbon footprint as a whole.

There's one specific tool that you want to make sure these folks have, and that's an infrared gun that can measure heat. If your home auditor doesn't have an infrared gun, tell them thanks, but the audit isn't worth a penny

without it. This infrared gun is a heat-sensing camera, basically. It will tell you where your home is losing heat in the wintertime and where it's letting in heat in the summer.

The prices for these services range from $100 or $200 for a basic audit to $1,500 or more, depending on the size of your house and the size of your property. Naturally, an audit of a 1,200-square-foot home on a quarter-acre of land will cost a lot less than an audit of a 6,000-square-foot home on fifteen landscaped acres.

The extent of the analysis also affects the price. And speaking of analysis, some companies will give you your audit results and also take the next step: analyzing what various changes will cost and how much money you'll save as a result. This cost/benefit analysis is incredibly valuable, since it basically provides a road map for you to follow as you make the types of changes that will help you conserve energy and water and make your home even more efficient.

FINDING A COMPANY TO PERFORM AN AUDIT

It's not difficult to find a company that performs green audits or energy audits (you can do a Google search).

Low Impact Living, which is based in the Los Angeles area, has associates all around the country, and if you visit their website (see Resources, page 340), you can search for reputable, highly skilled individuals in the energy audit realm near you.

Before you get too concerned about the money you'll spend with this audit, think of it as an investment, rather than a cost. If your electricity and gas bills combined come to more than $100 each month, having a professional perform an energy audit will pay for itself in a very short time—maybe even within the first year.

Remember all the benefits this audit will give you—beyond the financial. You may be able to improve your health and the health of your family by performing a green audit. If you were able to reduce allergies and reduce other health issues, how much would that be worth to you? It's invaluable, isn't it?

LOW IMPACT LIVING'S APPROACH

So what do you get when you pay a green home auditor to work for you? If you've been watching my TV show, *Living with Ed,* you've seen Jason Pelletier and Jessica Jensen, the folks from Low Impact Living, in action. When Low Impact Living performs an audit, the team members leave no part of your home unexamined:

- They look at energy and water and utilities and recycling.
- They look at indoor air quality.
- They look at your *behavior* and how it affects the overall picture at your home.
- They even look at your transportation habits.

- They look over your utility bills.
- They go through your home and your property and do a detailed evaluation.
- They look at your overall carbon footprint.
- And then they play "what if" using sophisticated computer models, so they can tell how much of a difference it will make in *your* house—on *your* energy bills—if you make a particular change.

They also bring in high-tech equipment to detect leaks or to find places where the insulation may have settled in your walls, if the indicators point to that type of a problem, and finally they provide a useful report to you.

THE QUESTIONNAIRE

Before the people at Low Impact Living perform an audit, they have the homeowner fill out a questionnaire and provide his or her utility bills. "The utility bills are really critical," says Jason. "By looking at all the bills over the course of a year, you can really understand what the drivers of energy or water use are. Is it irrigation? Is it heating? Is it cooling? Is it lighting?

"So before we even go into somebody's home, from the questionnaire we've done and looking at the utility bills, we have some sense for where we need to really focus our time. That being said, we don't ignore any part of the home, but this information gives us a way to prioritize what we're doing."

THE IN-HOME EVALUATION

After the prep work, Low Impact Living sends a team into your home to do an evaluation, which usually takes three or four hours. You should always be home while they're performing the audit, because questions about your lifestyle—which rooms you use, what temperature you set your thermostat at, even which window coverings you open and close each day—are critical to their evaluation. So they'll walk through the house and through your front and backyards with you, asking questions and gathering information.

A home auditor takes measurements, inside and out. They sketch out a floor plan, how big your rooms are, where the windows are, and how big they are. They sketch out the landscaping. How much is hardscaping (stone or concrete or even gravel areas), how much is lawn, how much is trees and shrubbery. They draw this all out on a map of your property.

The next step is to look at the *building envelope*. "We look at the windows and how they're constructed and built," says Jason. "We look at the insulation levels. And in insulation, we look at the attic. We look at the walls. We look at the subfloor, either above the basement or underneath the crawlspace. And then we look at whether the pipes and the ducts are insulated. We also try to do a sort of qualitative assessment of the ceilings, windows, doors, ducts, wiring, and plumbing fixtures and the attic itself."

After that, they go through all the different systems in your house. They look at your furnace, your air conditioner, your water heater, and all of your appliances, including the pool and spa, if you have those. They look at the lighting in your house—not only the bulbs and the type and the size, but also the controls, whether you have things on timers or dimmers, etc.

They'll ask you questions, again, about your habits and activities. How often do you use these appliances? Does your air-conditioning run all day and all night? When do you do laundry? They'll look at other electrical devices, like TVs and computers and stereos.

All of this information is gathered to evaluate the energy part of the assessment. This gives the auditor raw data needed to calculate your energy use and to do some modeling to see what changes will have the most profound effect. This information also helps to assess your overall carbon footprint, which is part of the total environmental assessment.

But the audit doesn't end there. The next step is to look at your water usage, both indoors and out. Inside your house, they're going to be looking at flow rates, and they're also looking for leaks in toilets and drips in sinks—things like that. After all, fixing a leak is some of that easy, low-hanging fruit that you want to pick first—some of the no-brainer stuff you can do to reduce your use of water.

When the auditor moves outside and looks at the type of landscaping you have, you'll find out if you have drought-tolerant plants or not and if they are native plants or not.

A respectable auditor will look at runoff on your property and sketch that out, too. In other words, when it rains, where does the water that falls on your yard and your roof go? They'll map out your downspouts and they'll try to understand, based on the elevation of your property—hills, low areas, and so on—if the water is running off into a natural area where it will sink in or it is going straight out to the street or storm drain.

If you're like most people, you have some sort of irrigation system. You've got sprinklers or you've got a drip watering system or some combination of the two. The auditor will spend some time evaluating the system and asking you, again, about your behavior. Do you take out the hose and hand water? Do you have everything set on timers? If not, how long do you run each set of sprinklers and how often?

The auditor also will look at all your household products, primarily your cleaning products and any hazardous waste storage area. They look into your recycling habits and your waste production and waste management.

Finally, before the auditor leaves, he will ask you if there are any particular interior design or remodeling tips that you're looking for or if you have any other concerns. This is the time to mention that you've been wanting to change your windows, or to ask about solar attic fans versus attic vents, and so on. It pays to put together a list of questions before the auditor comes, and you can always add to it as you walk through the property with your auditor.

THE ANALYSIS

A green consultant can visit you and give you a basic audit for maybe $100 to $175 an hour. This should include an instant evaluation of where the obvious issues are. What Low Impact Living does next is what I think makes their audits especially valuable. They use their own computer models to analyze your home, your habits, and your current spending, and then they make specific recommendations, letting you know how much the changes will cost and how much you can expect to save as a result.

For example, they will try to figure out how much energy and water your house uses, what its carbon footprint is, and so on. They plug all that information into the computer, and then they can start playing with "what if" scenarios. For instance:

- What would happen if you swapped out all of your old appliances for new Energy Star appliances?
- What would happen if you were to install new insulation?
- What would happen if you installed new windows?
- What would happen if you added solar panels to your roof?

They look at what the benefits of each change would be from an environmental perspective, and they also look at the financial implications. How much would it cost and how much would it save?

Low Impact Living has many separate computer models. They have models to consider heating and cooling and refrigerators and dishwashers. They have models for renewable energy options, like solar electricity and wind power. It's pretty amazing, sophisticated stuff.

Once they've done all of this analysis, they produce a report and they sit down with the client and explain the report. They'll even help pick specific products and services, so if, for example, new windows are called for, you know just what kind to shop for.

This home audit first shows you how to conserve energy and conserve water, then, if appropriate, it explains how you could produce power. The auditor will even do the same type of analysis that a solar installer would do to tell you exactly what size solar or wind system you would need, and how much that would cost, as well as what rebates you're entitled to.

EASY CHANGES AND BIGGER STEPS

Whether you choose a sophisticated analysis like the ones performed by Low Impact Living or you do something more basic to start with, almost every green home audit is going to turn up some of the same simple changes you can make, which are the first steps most people are going to want to attempt. We're talking about things like choosing compact fluorescent lightbulbs, changing air filters, taking shorter showers, and turning off the tap while you're brushing your teeth.

These changes are cheap and easy to make. In fact, these are the same kinds of things that I talked about in my first book, *Living Like Ed*. We'll look at many of these changes in the next couple of chapters.

Once you've taken care of the low-hanging fruit—once you've made all the really easy changes—then you can move up the ladder from there, if you will, and do some of the medium-ticket changes, then, finally, you can plan and save to make the big-ticket changes.

For instance, in the middle range, you might consider getting a new, energy-efficient dishwasher and installing an energy-saving, programmable thermostat. You could add window treatments like blinds that will help block the hot summer sun and reduce cooling needs.

Then you might start saving money for bigger-ticket changes, such as adding insulation in your attic and your walls and under your home, getting an energy-efficient refrigerator, or installing new dual- or triple-pane windows.

The goal of having a green audit performed is so you can first identify the areas where you need to conserve. Sure, your ultimate goal may be to produce all of your own power on-site. But first you need to reduce your power needs. By making all—or even most—of the changes recommended from a green home audit, you may be able to cut your electricity use by as much as 50 percent.

The great thing about an in-depth green home audit is you can use it as a road map and also as a way to measure your progress. Let's say you follow one recommendation that a company like Low Impact Living says should save you 50 kilowatt-hours of electricity each month. After some time has passed, get out your electric bill and check. Did it really save you 50 kilowatt-hours? It did! That sort of positive feedback will encourage you to take the next step and the next and the next to make your home even more energy efficient.

Sample Costs and Paybacks: Green Home Audit

The type of green home audit that I had was very thorough and it cost $1,000. That's a big chunk of money, but I guarantee you it was money well spent.

A good green home audit will help you find that low-hanging fruit: the specific things you can change in your particular home that will cost only a few dollars but that will produce real energy savings. Some of these changes will even be free, if you can adjust your lifestyle ever so slightly—say, if you can get in the habit of opening and closing your drapes or blinds each day, or if you can get in the habit of turning off unused electronic devices, or if you can stop overwatering your yard.

So, yes, you may spend a thousand dollars to get this good advice, but depending on your lifestyle and your particular home, you could save hundreds of dollars each year by making a few small changes. So your payback could be within a couple years, easily.

But even beyond that, a good green home audit will help you prioritize bigger changes so you spend your money wisely. Maybe you think your windows are allowing a lot of heat to escape in the wintertime, but a green home audit could reveal that the problem is actually a lack of insulation in your walls. Once you know that, you won't spend thousands of dollars on new windows and be disappointed in your lack of energy savings.

A good green home audit absolutely will help you identify the specific changes that will affect your home's energy efficiency *the most*. It should even show you how much those changes will cost, so you can start saving to make bigger-ticket modifications. And you can relax, knowing that the changes you make will make a real difference to the environment, to your wallet, and to your quality of life.

Ed's Green Home Energy Audit

Please don't think I'm telling you to go out and pay someone to do a green home energy audit on your house when I wouldn't do the same thing myself. I've been a believer in these audits from the first time I heard about them. But it was my first experience with one that took things to a whole other level.

As you probably already know, I've been going down this energy-saving path since 1970. I've done a lot of work to my 1936 ranch house since I bought it back in 1988. I'm very much aware of the value of things like insulation and compact fluorescent lightbulbs and programmable thermostats. But having a green home energy audit was an eye-opener, even for me. I had the folks from REAS Inc. (see Resources, page 340) perform an audit at my house. And they brought that all-important infrared gun.

Since it was wintertime, they turned the thermostat way up for thirty minutes to get the house really hot. Then they went around the house with the infrared camera. They were looking for cold spots, which showed up as dark areas on the camera.

In the summertime, they look for hot spots, which appear light on the camera. This way they can see where the heat is and where it is not.

To my surprise, there were many places around my house where we needed to fill in insulation. Even though I had recently added more insulation to my home, they found several areas—many, many areas—where heat was escaping from the house in the wintertime, and where heat could enter the house in the summertime.

So the infrared gun is a great way to start to determine where your home needs more insulation, since it will identify right away some of the most offensive spots. An infrared sensing device is essential to find where your insulation is and where it is not.

Caulking your windows is an easy first step to insulating your home.

REAS also came back another time and did a whole different test on my house. This was a blower door test. Basically, they put a large fan on my front door and blew a lot of air into the house. Then they were able to go around the house, using a pressure gauge, to identify where air was leaking out. They could identify where seals were bad, where caulking was needed, where I needed new weather stripping. They even went under the house into the crawl space.

That two-part green home energy audit added quite a few things to my to-do list. REAS helped me create a plan for additional attic and wall insulation. The people who installed the insulation for me came back and filled in all those nooks and crannies that needed yet more insulation. And I sealed up all the leaks REAS found. I also put in more window and door weather stripping. And I even sealed the crawl space under my house (for more on that see Chapter 4).

Then I had REAS come back and perform these same two tests again, to be sure I had completely solved all those problems, and found all those places where energy was leaking right out of my house and money was leaking right out of my wallet. And you know what? My energy usage and energy bills are now the lowest they've been since the late 1980s!

2

ELECTRICITY

**Making Sure Your House
Is Set Up Properly & How
to Start Conserving**

BEFORE YOU CAN CONSIDER PRODUCING YOUR OWN electricity with a solar setup or a wind turbine, the first step is to reduce your electricity needs. You don't want to produce more electricity than you actually need to, because it will require a much greater expense to set up your system and will require far, far longer for you to break even on it.

So the first step is to conserve energy. Now, there are many ways you can do this, including these:

- modify your behavior
- change your lighting (see Chapter 3)
- choose different appliances
- take more control over your home energy use
- make your home more energy efficient

Obviously, the first step is to stop wasting power, and this starts with behavior modification. It's very easy to get in the habit of turning off the lights when you leave a room or when you leave the house. Turn off the TV. Turn off the stereo, the computer, the printer. Turn off a fan or a space heater. Turn off your curling iron when you're not using it. These are simple steps that anybody can do, anywhere. There're ways to change things in a very healthy manner through behavior, and that's what we should look to first.

I find that most people don't have a healthy respect for electricity in the sense that they waste it. They squander this precious resource. I've had a respect for electricity—and, in fact, I've had a fascination with electricity—from the earliest age. I used to play with electricity. I would put wires into the wall, because I knew electricity came out of the wall. And I knew electricity also came from batteries, little Eveready batteries, and I tried to put the two together, to my detriment. I have been shocked several times, so I developed a respect for electricity from fairly early on.

Part of having a healthy respect for electricity is understanding how it works. And a key part of conserving electricity is understanding how it's measured. So I'll start here with a quick explanation of how electricity and electrical service work, then focus on ways to reduce electricity usage throughout your home.

 ## ELECTRICAL TERMS

When we're talking about electricity, it pays to know about Ohm's Law. Ohm's Law is:

volts × amps = watts

I like to compare *voltage* to water pressure. High voltage is like what you get when you have one of those nozzles that puts out a very thin, high-pressure spray for hosing off the driveway or hosing leaves off your lawn. You can simulate this yourself by putting your thumb over a garden hose and having a thin spray shoot very far. Water pressure that blows the leaves off your lawn or off your driveway is like *high voltage.*

And you can think of amperage, also referred to as *amps,* as quantity. Higher amperage equates to more electricity, or more power at one time.

So water *pressure* is like voltage, and *volume* of water is like amperage. And a *watt* is a unit of work.

If you live in the United States, the electrical outlets in the walls in your home deliver 120 volts of electricity or somewhat less, which is partly why most people refer to them as 110-volt outlets. So 110 to 120 volts is the pressure, so to speak, that your electronic items expect and demand, whether a television or a toaster or a lamp.

Some appliances do require 240-volt service, like an electric clothes dryer or an electric stove. These items will have a special outlet wired next to their intended location. But all the other outlets in your home will deliver 120 volts, roughly.

The amperage—that is, the quantity of electricity—flowing to a particular outlet will depend on the way that outlet was wired. This is determined in your home's electrical panel. Say you know that you're going to set up your entertainment center in the family room, so you want to have ample power in that area. You might choose to run a 40-amp circuit to that part of the house. For an area like a bedroom that might just have a couple of lamps and a clock radio plugged in, you might choose to run a 20-amp circuit. So you can choose the quantity of electricity being delivered through a particular circuit. That's the amount of current (like current in a river) that can go through the wall outlet or the light switch.

When you multiply volts times amps, you get watts. So if you know that a particular small television is going to draw 2 amps of electricity and you know your wall outlet provides 120 volts, then $120 \times 2 = 240$ watts. You've got a 240-watt TV.

What if you want to go the other way? Let's say you have a lamp you want to use on your nightstand. This lamp uses a 60-watt lightbulb. Since you know the outlet is delivering 120 volts of electricity, you can rearrange the equation to read:

watts / volts = amps

So 60 watts divided by 120 volts means that the lightbulb for your bedside lamp will be drawing ½ amp.

A good panel should have circuits with the proper amperage rating for all the electrical devices we have today.

MEASURING ELECTRICITY

The electricity that comes into the average American home is measured in kilowatt-hours. A kilowatt is simply 1,000 watts. So if your bill says you used 830 kilowatt-hours of electricity, you actually used 830,000 watts, or 830,000 units of work.

So, if you're using a 14-watt compact fluorescent lightbulb, it's going to draw 14 watts of power. You can look on each of your appliances, too, to see what wattage they draw. It should be listed right on your refrigerator, your washing machine, and so on.

Then, if you want to know how many kilowatt-hours of use that particular wattage translates into, the formula is easy. A kilowatt is equal to 1,000 watts. So,

watts × hours used per day ÷ 1,000 = kilowatt-hours used per day

If you want to know the annual figures, you just multiply this by the number of days you're using that lamp or appliance. Or you can change hours per day to hours per year in the formula.

Once you know that figure, it's easy to determine how much you're spending to power a particular light or appliance. You just multiply the number of kilowatt-hours by the rate you pay for electricity, which is listed on your electric bill.

HAVING THE PROPER ELECTRICAL SERVICE

Electricity is delivered from a power plant at hundreds of thousands of volts. And years ago, people in the electric business chose to transmit that power in something called *alternating current,* or A/C. It's negative and positive, cycling back and forth sixty times per second, because they learned they could transmit power over much longer distances when they used alternating current. They also learned that the higher the voltage, the less energy they're going to lose over long distances, so they transmit power at extremely high voltage.

Then the power is delivered into an area like the San Fernando Valley, where I live. That's when it is stepped down to a lower voltage. Then it comes into a neighborhood and it is further reduced, but is still at a fairly high voltage. Only when it comes to your house is it brought down to 240 volts using a step-down transformer.

You'll see three wires coming into the service at your house: two hot wires and a neutral.

Those two hot leads combined will get you 240 volts (it's actually 236, but we call it 240). The *neutral line* coming off the transformer into your street or your alley really has no current coming off it, but between either of the hot leads to that neutral, you get 120 volts. Most people say 120; it's actually usually about 117.

Most electrical devices run on 120 volts. A few things, including an electric car, an electric clothes dryer, or your heating and air-conditioning unit run on 240 volts.

Knowing that, you want to have the right amount of service coming into your house. Old houses like the one I own had 100-amp service. This is from the old days, when people did not have all the electronic devices we have today. These days, you want to have at least 200-amp service coming into your house. You also want to have a good panel with the proper amperage rating for all the different outlets in your home. And you want to have a system that has proper grounding. A ground is a safety device. With older homes, a wire often was attached to a pipe (back when pipes were made of galvanized steel, which is an excellent conductor of electricity). That pipe went deep into the ground, so the earth—literally the *ground*— became a part of your home's electrical system. Today, homes may be grounded in a somewhat different manner, but the concept remains much the same. A proper ground provides a path for the electricity to follow in case there's a problem, in case some electrical device isn't functioning properly, so the electricity doesn't run through *you.*

HEATING AND COOLING

So how do you reduce the size of your electric bill? According to the Department of Energy (see Resources, page 340), as much as half of the energy used in your home goes toward heating and cooling it. It's all about your HVAC (heating, ventilation, and air-conditioning system).

We'll go into how to choose *new* heating and cooling units in detail in Chapters 11 and 12. But first, let's talk about how you can save energy—and save money—by changing the way you use your *current* HVAC system.

One of the most obvious ways to save money is to use the system less. You can wear shorts and a T-shirt in the summertime and then set the thermostat a little warmer. Let's say you set it to 74 degrees instead of 70 or 72. You can still be comfortable if you dress for the season. The same goes for the wintertime: You can put on a sweater or a sweatshirt and turn the thermostat down to 68 degrees, instead of keeping it set at 72.

Each time you crank up your thermostat by 1 degree F, you increase your energy use by about 2 percent. So these little changes can make a measurable difference in your energy bill and your budget.

Another simple step that can make a big difference is changing the air filter for your HVAC system. Dog hair, cat hair, dander, dust, lint—all the gunk that accumulates on your countertops and under the bed and behind the refrigerator gets sucked up into that air filter, too. For your health as well as for the health of your family, you want to change the filter in your HVAC system. But you also want to change that filter for the health of your pocketbook. A clogged filter restricts airflow. And restricted airflow makes your HVAC system work harder to do its job. So changing that filter every other month—or even every month—can more than pay for itself in energy savings.

It's also important to maintain your HVAC system. You'll want to check your heating system each fall before you need to start using it. And you'll want to check your A/C in the spring. The Energy Star website (see Resources, page 340) has an excellent heating and cooling system maintenance checklist that details the things you can do and the things you might want an expert to do for you.

PROGRAMMABLE THERMOSTAT

Another way you can save a lot of energy—and money—is to run your heating and air-conditioning system only when you need it. The best way to tune your HVAC system to fit your lifestyle is to install a programmable thermostat—an energy-saving thermostat—and then use it. You can get a good thermostat for $80 or $90 nowadays. Look for a full seven-day programmable thermostat, because often folks' activities are different on the weekends than they are on the weekdays.

Here is what you can do on a seven-day schedule. Let's say it's wintertime. You wake up at 6:30 in the morning. You get ready for work. You get your children ready for school. You leave the house at 8 o'clock. You return at 5 and then you go to sleep at 11 o'clock at night.

That's a fairly common schedule. Here's how you would program it in the thermostat:

- a wake mode at 6:30 a.m.
- a leave mode at 8:00 a.m.
- a return mode at 5:00 p.m.
- a sleep mode at 11 p.m.

Those are four different stops, if you will, on this thermostat to program it for a Monday-through-Friday schedule.

And then on the weekends, let's say you sleep in. You get up at 8 or 9. And then you stay around the house and do things. Or maybe you leave to go to a ballgame. You can set the thermostat for whatever your weekend schedule is.

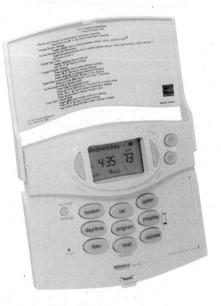

A seven-day programmable thermostat offers the most flexibility.

So in the winter, let's say you want the house to be 72 degrees. When you get up, you want it nice and warm. So you set the thermostat to turn on the heat fifteen minutes before you wake up. Then you program it to dial the heat back to 62 degrees when you leave for the day. As a general rule, most experts recommend that you dial the settings back by about 10 to 12 degrees while you're gone.

Now, let me be very clear: If you've done your work with insulation, as I advise you to do in Chapter 4, your house is not going to get that cold. Even in a very cold climate, your house may never actually get down to 62 degrees during the few hours that you're gone. But by programming your system to work less when you're not at home—and to work less at night when you're sleeping—you'll save a lot of energy.

Many people ask me if it's better to program the system to dial back the heat (or dial up the air-conditioning temperature) while you're gone, or if you're better off shutting the whole thing off. According to my friend Randy Scott, vice president of product systems management at Trane, "It's always better to program it to set up or set back versus turning it off. [Besides the large temperature swings], the other problem with turning it off is you're not getting any *conditioning*. And so in the summer, your humidity can really build up inside the home, and that can cause all types of problems."

I also get asked all the time about whether your system has to work extra hard to bring the space back to the desired temperature if you use an away mode. Here's what the

Department of Energy has to say: "A common misconception associated with thermostats is that a furnace works harder than normal to warm the space back to a comfortable temperature after the thermostat has been set back, resulting in little or no savings. This misconception has been dispelled by years of research and numerous studies."

APPLIANCES

Beyond heating and cooling, other appliances play a big role in your electricity usage, as well. In most homes, the refrigerator is the most power-hungry appliance in the kitchen. So right away, inspect your refrigerator.

Keep in mind, to make something cool, something else must get hot. With a refrigerator, the hot part is called a *coil*. The external part of the coil that's outside of the cool box—that part that's getting hot—needs to be cleaned on a regular basis. Use a vacuum cleaner and clean the coil that's on the back, the bottom, or the top of your refrigerator. Also, the coil needs good ventilation flowing to it. It needs to have enough air that can circulate around it.

You should check the seal of your refrigerator and freezer compartment, too. Make sure the seal doesn't have any gaps in it.

After all of these measures, if you have an older refrigerator, it might be worth your while to replace it. Many utility companies have programs in which they'll buy your old refrigerator just to get it out of the system.

Clean your refrigerator coils once a year.

Unfortunately, some people buy a new refrigerator and put the old one in the garage to keep soft drinks in it. Folks, please don't do this. If you want to keep soft drinks cool, keep them in your garage or buy a cooler for those few days a year when you need cool drinks for a party. Get rid of the old refrigerator. You'll save a lot of money, and you may even get a hundred dollars from the utility company.

When you're shopping for a new refrigerator, look for the Energy Star rating. Also, a little sheet on the front of each refrigerator for sale will tell you the amount of electricity, on average, that it uses each year, and also the cost at the current kilowatt-hour price to run that unit for a year. This is a very useful tool in determining which refrigerator to buy.

Of course, refrigerators aren't the only appliances in a home—and they certainly aren't the only ones that use electricity. Clothes washers, dishwashers, and freezers are among the other appliances that are available with an Energy Star rating. The older your current appliances are, the more likely you'll be able to save a lot of energy by replacing them with newer models.

With a flip of a switch, I can turn off all the phantom power devices in my home.

PHANTOM POWER

Now, obviously you know that your refrigerator and dishwasher and clothes washer are using electric power. But there's also a lot of phantom power being used in your home, power that you may not even realize you're wasting. What I'm referring to are things like cell phone chargers that do not have a cell phone attached to them, battery chargers that aren't being used to charge batteries, instant-on TVs and game players and stereos and DVD players and DVRs and cable boxes that are not on at the present moment, and printers and modems and other computer peripherals. When they aren't turned on and in use, these things are sitting around in standby mode. *Vampire power* is the term assigned to these many devices that, like a vampire, suck power from you and give you nothing in return.

My friends from a company called Green-Switch participated in a TV show called *Modern Marvels* on the History Channel. They put a meter on an older Sony Trinitron 30-inch TV, DVD player, and cable box. When they were running, those three items used 114 watts of power. When they were turned off, they used 26 watts. Almost 25 percent of their power was still being used when they were in the off mode.

Greg Hood of GreenSwitch (see Resources, page 340) says, "There's a couple of figures out there. The Department of Energy has done a study, and the California Public Utilities Commission did a study. The California study says currently that an average of thirteen percent of

Installing the Latest GreenSwitch

If I lived alone, I would never need a GreenSwitch. I don't mind having power strips sitting around. And I don't mind taking an extra minute to switch them off before I leave the house.

But I don't live alone. I have a wife, Rachelle, and a daughter, Hayden, living with me, and they aren't quite as diligent about these things as I am. So I did what any reasonable person would do: After years of trying to change them, I finally found a solution that allows me to conserve energy—and money—while keeping the peace in my household.

I had the latest version of GreenSwitch installed in my house. It's going to help with a bunch of phantom power users, including

- two instant-on TV sets
- two computers
- two printers
- various charging devices for cell phones and other gadgets

I also hope it will help my wife and daughter remember to turn off lights before they leave the house, because all they have to do is flip this one switch as they walk out the door. It couldn't be easier!

Currently the GreenSwitch is saving me from 1 to 3 kilowatt-hours of electricity every day. That's up to 91 kilowatt-hours a month and 1,095 kilowatt-hours a year. That's a substantial amount of power that I have been wasting and that I can be saving.

The GreenSwitch can be programmed to adjust thermostats and turn off every light in the house when you leave.

all electricity use in a home comes from stand-by power. And the DOE says nationally it's ten to fifteen percent, but they expect that number to rise by 2010 to about twenty percent."

So look around *your* home, and I'm sure you'll see a lot of power being used that doesn't need to be. Get rid of all that vampire power. How? Plug those devices into power strips. That way, you can go around the house and turn off nonessential items in one action. Mark the power strips in some way so you know that you're turning off only the nonessential stuff.

And you might want to put the essential stuff, such as an answering machine, on another power strip. You want that on all the time. You want your clock radio on all the time. Keep those things that you want on all the time on separate power strips. Then you can walk around your house and turn off three or four power strips and get rid of all that vampire power.

AN EASIER WAY

Some people don't like the look of power strips. Others just can't seem to get in the habit of running around and turning power strips off when they're leaving the house, then turning them back on when they come home, or when they plan to watch TV or listen to the stereo. It takes some diligence—and it takes the cooperation of everyone in the household, which as I know all too well is not always easy to obtain.

Fortunately, there's a device to handle this: the GreenSwitch. You just flip one switch as you leave your home, and the GreenSwitch does three important things all at once:

1. It turns off all the phantom power with one switch.
2. It can turn off all the lights in your house at one time, so you don't have to walk around and make sure the lights are off before you leave.
3. It can be programmed to set your thermostat to "away" mode, so you save money on heating and cooling, too.

That's a lot of benefit from flipping a single switch.

The system is totally wireless, too, so you don't have to break into your walls to install it. You simply change your power outlets over to GreenSwitch outlets, and each one has a little antenna on the back to talk to the system controller. You assign each outlet to be a Green-Switch outlet or not. You can even designate some outlets to be both.

When you leave the house, you flick one GreenSwitch. You have thirty seconds of light to see what you're doing, lock the door, then—voilà—everything nonessential goes off. And a remote control lets you flip off the vampire power when you go to sleep at night, too.

If you make a few simple changes in your behavior and then make a few simple changes around the house—installing a programmable thermostat, flipping off the phantom power devices, getting rid of that spare refrigerator in the garage, and so on—you can see some real energy savings in your electric bill, and that's good for the environment as well as for your wallet.

Sample Costs and Paybacks: GreenSwitch

The average system costs about $1,200. According to Greg at GreenSwitch, it typically will save you 10 percent to 20 percent on your electric bill. So let's use 15 percent as the average savings number. And let's say an average electric bill is $200 a month.

In that case, the GreenSwitch will save you $30 a month. That gives you a return on your investment in forty months, or a little more than three years.

But what if your electric bill is higher? What if your electric bill is $300 or $400 a month? Then you could be looking at a payback time that's much faster, in the neighborhood of two years.

If you want to put your own numbers to it, GreenSwitch has a payback calculator on its website (see Resources, page 340).

3

LIGHTING

Moving from Incandescent Bulbs to
Compact Fluorescents & Beyond

WALK INTO MOST HOMES AND YOU'LL FIND LOTS
of Thomas Edison–era filament incandescent lightbulbs.
It's technology that is a hundred and some odd years old.
Sure, there are some technologies that are that old yet are
still very attractive to us. But the inefficiencies of a Thomas
Edison–era lightbulb are easy to illustrate. Have you ever
seen an Easy Bake Oven in action? The heating device used
to bake actual baked goods in a kid's toy is an incandescent
lightbulb! That shows just how much heat these bulbs emit.

If you remember your basic science, you know heat is a form of energy.
And you don't want to waste a lot of energy creating *heat* when what you
really want is to make *light,* to make foot-candles or lumens. A typical
incandescent lightbulb converts only about 5 percent of the electricity it
consumes into light—just 5 percent!

My friend David Bergman, an eco-architect who also runs Fire & Water
Lighting (see Resources, page 341), that specializes in lighting design,
actually calls incandescent bulbs "glorified toasters." When you look inside a toaster, you see those red wires that are toasting your bread. Those
red wires are giving off light and heat. And the piece of wire inside an
incandescent lightbulb operates on the same principle, except it's giving
off a little bit more light and a little bit less heat. But it's the same idea.
In other words, you're making a lot of heat, as well as light, and all that
heat is wasted energy.

I remember a time when halogen lightbulbs were considered the latest
and greatest new technology. Really *high-tech* light fixtures used halogen
bulbs. But a halogen lightbulb is still just a type of incandescent bulb. It

has a filament; it also has a pressurized gas inside the bulb surrounding that filament. So a halogen bulb is basically a type of incandescent lightbulb; it's just a little brighter and a little more efficient. Problem is it also gives off a lot of heat. There was a big uproar a few years back when halogen bulbs turned out to pose a real fire hazard because they can get so hot.

So when people ask David about using halogen bulbs or regular incandescent lightbulbs in their homes, he literally says, "It's sort of the equivalent of lighting your home with toasters."

Now, that doesn't sound like a very energy-efficient idea. And it sounds like an even worse idea in the summertime, when the last thing you want is to be creating extra heat in your home.

Yet most homes today—by far the vast majority of houses and condos and apartments and mobile homes—use incandescent bulbs of one sort or another for *all* of their lighting needs.

So what's the alternative? You actually have several these days. Some involve changing to a different type of lightbulb. Some involve changing the way you place the lighting throughout your house. And some involve the use of more natural light, literally solar lighting.

This CFL has a ballast that separates from the bulb, so you don't need to replace the ballast each time.

Here is a CFL bulb removed from its ballast and another CFL bulb option.

COMPACT FLUORESCENT LIGHTBULBS

As the name says, a compact fluorescent lightbulb, or CFL, is a type of fluorescent. And fluorescent lightbulbs operate differently from incandescents. Instead of a filament inside, fluorescent lightbulbs have a gas that gets energized and therefore gives off light. If you remember the old fluorescent lightbulbs that flickered when you turned them on, it was because they used a magnetic type of ballast in their design. Newer designs use an electronic ballast, which eliminates the flickering, is more

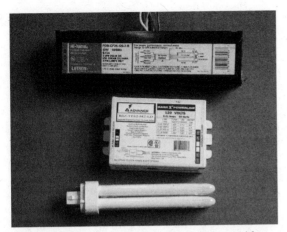

This shows a couple different ballast options with a four-pin CFL.

efficient, cuts down on weight, and makes the light come on more quickly (although some CFLs still do have a noticeable delay between the time you hit the switch and the time the light turns on).

Overall, a CFL is a much more energy-efficient type of lightbulb than an incandescent. One of the ways you can prove it to yourself is to touch a fluorescent lightbulb. It will be cool—or at least much cooler than an incandescent bulb that gives off the same amount of light. So you know right away that there's a lot less energy being transformed into heat, and that means a lot less energy is being wasted.

A CFL lasts a lot longer than an incandescent bulb, too. A *lot* longer. A typical incandescent lightbulb is good for about a thousand hours of life. A comparable CFL lasts ten times as long—or longer. I've had compact fluorescent bulbs last as long as seventeen years!

CFLs are available now at discount stores, at every hardware store, at every lighting store, and at many grocery stores. They are available just about anywhere nowadays. They're a good option for every room in your home.

LUMENS PER WATT

A *lumen* is a measure of how much light a bulb gives off. The lighting industry looks at the number of *lumens per watt* to indicate how efficient a lightbulb is—that is, how much electricity it takes to create a certain amount of light.

A typical incandescent bulb produces 12 to 15 lumens per watt. A halogen bulb is at the high end of that range, perhaps even a little higher, if you're talking about one of the new type of halogen bulbs on the market. Compact fluorescent bulbs produce at least 50 lumens per watt—even higher for commercial fluorescent bulbs, the ones used in office buildings and warehouses and other commercial applications.

So you can see that fluorescent bulbs are dramatically more efficient than incandescents. And again, being more efficient means they require less energy to create the same amount of light, plus they waste less energy producing heat.

The difference in efficiency can make it more difficult to choose the right CFL when you first go shopping for new lightbulbs. You're comparing apples and oranges. We've grown accustomed to choosing a lightbulb based on its wattage. You put a 40-watt bulb in a particular lamp in your bedroom, say, or a 150-watt bulb in the floor lamp in the den. Most people choose a lightbulb based on wattage because they're used to a 40-watt bulb putting out a certain amount of light—and many light fixtures on the market today specify a maximum wattage.

But lumens, not watts, are actually the measure of light a bulb produces. And it takes far fewer watts to produce a certain number of lumens when you switch from incandescents to CFLs. In fact, a 13-watt compact fluorescent bulb will be pretty comparable to a 60-watt incandescent one.

So does that mean you need to take your calculator to the store with you and bring along a formula so you can do the conversions in order to choose the right replacement lightbulbs? No. Lucky for us, the companies that make compact fluorescent lightbulbs understand exactly what you need to know. They realize that you've become accustomed to shopping for lightbulbs based on watts, not lumens. So they tell you right on the packaging what wattage a particular compact fluorescent bulb is equivalent to if you're comparing it with an incandescent bulb.

MERCURY IN CFLS

I should say a few words about mercury in CFLs. The CFL naysayers like to point out that these lightbulbs contain mercury. People are smart to be concerned about mercury. We should be. Mercury is a very dangerous substance. You should stay away from it. Because of the mercury, you can't just toss an old CFL into your trash can and send it to a landfill. Since mercury is a hazardous waste, you have to take CFLs to a hazardous waste drop-off site in order to dispose of them. Or you can take them to stores such as Ikea and Home Depot

(see Resources, page 341), which collect them and dispose of them properly.

So, yes, mercury is a concern. But you should know that there is only a small amount of mercury in a CFL. If you *don't* use a CFL, according to a 2002 study by the Environmental Protection Agency (EPA), you're actually putting more mercury than that out into the atmosphere. Let me explain: Most electricity in this country is generated by burning coal. When you burn coal, it is a fact—a sad fact, but a fact nonetheless—that the mercury generated goes out the power plant's smokestacks and into the air.

According to the EPA study, the amount of mercury that is pumped out of a power plant's smokestacks to power a 60-watt incandescent lightbulb is four times the amount of mercury that leaves the smokestacks to power a comparable CFL. A CFL literally uses a quarter of the energy, so it produces a quarter of the mercury emissions. It's the difference between 7 milligrams of mercury and just 1.75 milligrams of mercury.

I've also mentioned that there is a small amount of mercury contained inside that CFL. Right now, an Energy Star–qualified CFL cannot contain any more than 5 milligrams of mercury.

So when you add the two amounts of mercury together—the mercury being spewed out the power plant's smokestacks from powering a CFL and the mercury contained inside the CFL—you get 6.75 milligrams. True, that's almost the same as the 7 milligrams of mercury emitted by the power plant to power an incandescent lightbulb. If you threw that CFL in the trash when you were done with it, and it would go to a landfill, then you would be sending about the same amount of mercury out into the environment either way, by using a CFL or an incandescent lightbulb.

But here's the big difference. The mercury in a CFL is sequestered inside the lightbulb. It can be recovered. It's not out there in the air where it cannot be recovered and cannot be picked up, as is the case with a power plant's emissions. The 5 milligrams of mercury inside a CFL never has to enter the environment ever.

If you recycle your CFLs properly, the mercury can be recaptured and actually used again in the making of a new CFL.

Here's even better news: A company called TCP (see Resources, page 341), which manufactures 70 percent of the CFLs in the United States, has come out with a design that uses dramatically *less* mercury. TCP has been able to reduce the amount of mercury in its CFLs from the industry-standard 5 milligrams down to just 1.5 milligrams. That's a big reduction! These new low-mercury CFLs contain just barely enough mercury to fit on the tip of a pen.

TCP also has come out with some cool

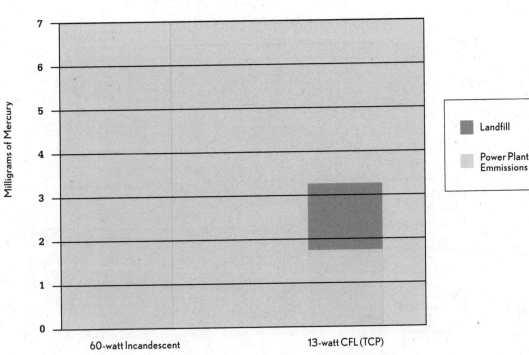

TOTAL MERCURY EMISSIONS: INCANDESCENT VS. CFLS

Milligrams of Mercury

60-watt Incandescent   13-watt CFL (TCP)

Landfill

Power Plant Emmissions

new packaging for its CFLs. When you buy a new CFL, you take it out of the box. You turn the box inside out. And then you return your old CFL to the company in that same box. TCP then recycles the old CFLs and uses the materials—not just the mercury, but the glass, the phosphor, the various components of that lightbulb—to make new CFLs. It's a great program.

Soon we may not have to worry about being exposed to mercury from a CFL at all. According to my friend Ellis Yan, the CEO of TCP, his company has found a way to neutralize that little bit of mercury found in its CFLs. If one of these new-design bulbs gets crushed, a chemical that's inside the lightbulb will literally neutralize the mercury and render it

benign. This is a great safety innovation that's still in the research and development stages, but we may see it come to market soon.

Lastly for those of you who are worried about breaking a CFL and having even that small amount of mercury on your floor, you can stop worrying. If an accident happens, all you have to do is get out the rubber gloves you use for washing dishes. With the gloves on, sweep the rubble into a dustpan. Then put all the debris into a plastic bag, zip it shut, and save it for when you're headed to a hazardous waste drop-off location. As long as you don't get the mercury wet, it's completely harmless. (Please don't grab a wet sponge and wipe up the mess. You don't want to mix mercury with water.)

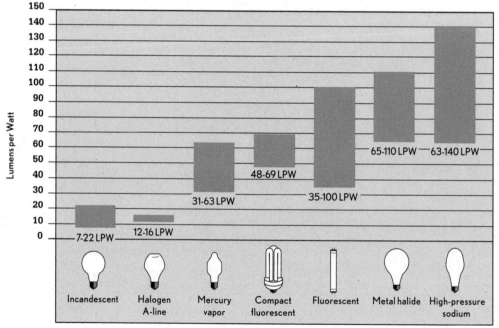

LUMINOSITY OF LIGHTBULBS

A NEW CHOICE: CCFLS

So as you can tell, I love CFLs. I'm probably their biggest fan. But now there's something even better: a CCFL, or cold cathode fluorescent lightbulb. My wife, Rachelle, tells me the name is just hideous, but this lightbulb is a beautiful thing. I absolutely adore CCFLs.

CCFLs actually have several advantages over CFLs:

1. Many experts say they last even longer, as long as 25,000 hours (compared with 10,000 for CFLs).
2. They produce even less heat.
3. They're dimmable (most CFLs are not).
4. They turn on instantly (whereas some CFLs can take as long as five minutes to reach their full brightness).
5. There's less flicker.
6. They're not affected by frequent on/off cycles, so you don't have to think about how long you're going to be out of a room and do a cost/benefit analysis to figure out if you should turn off the light or if that's going to be causing too much wear and tear on the bulb—so you'd be sacrificing longevity for a little savings in energy, which is not a great trade-off.
7. They contain far less mercury than traditional compact fluorescents.
8. They tend to be smaller and lighter than CFLs. In fact, one of their earliest common uses was in thin computers.

CCFLs work somewhat like a neon lightbulb. Interestingly, they're becoming a popular choice as a replacement for neon lighting. If you go to Las Vegas, many of those colored lights you see up and down the Strip are actually CCFLs. Hotels like The Mirage understand that operating all those lights uses a lot of energy—which costs a lot of money—so they've taken steps to reduce their energy usage by switching over to CCFLs.

I should warn you right up front that CCFLs are an emerging technology. So don't run out today and replace all of your existing lightbulbs with CCFLs, at least not yet. For starters, CCFLs are not as bright as CFLs right now, and they're also not quite as efficient. But with all of their advantages, clearly they show great promise. To find CCFLs for sale online, see Resources, page 341.

LEDS

So far the alternatives to incandescent lightbulbs have included CFLs and CCFLs. But there's another very, very attractive alternative, and that's the LED, or light-emitting diode. LEDs use even less power than a compact fluorescent. They're dramatically more efficient at producing light than incandescent bulbs—in the neighborhood of 30 to 35 lumens per watt right now, compared with 12 to 15 for an incandescent. There are some new LEDs coming to market that produce as much as 131 lumens per watt, which is just fantastic, and much better than today's CFLs. LEDs are the future of lightbulbs.

LEDs have been around for a long time. Indeed, LEDs work very well and are the best choice in many applications today. The little red lights you see on your stereo or other electronic equipment are LEDs. The numbers on your digital clock are LEDs. The taillights on some cars and trucks—particularly Cadillac and Lexus models—are LEDs.

LEDs are used in aircraft, elevators, traffic signals, Christmas lights—places where efficiency, durability, and long life are particularly attractive. You don't want to change the lightbulbs all the time with these applications, and these same features make LEDs really appealing for home use—particularly now that companies have been investing in research and development to expand the market for LEDs.

LEDs differ considerably from incandescent and fluorescent lightbulbs. Instead of a big, round bulb, a LED bulb tends to look like a cluster of small dots of light. That's because each individual LED bulb is tiny, so they wind up being clustered together to produce the desired amount of light.

They also function differently from incandescent and fluorescent bulbs. They're what's known as solid-state lighting, which means they're totally electronic. There's no filament to burn out. In fact, as LEDs wear, they simply become dimmer. They don't suddenly stop working. Switching from incandescent bulbs to LEDs is like going from a radio filled with tubes to a transistor radio. It's a big leap forward in terms of the technology.

David from Fire & Water Lighting likes to say that LEDs are today where compact fluorescents were maybe ten years ago. They're still a new and evolving technology. But they have the potential—very soon, from the look of things—to be even more energy efficient, in terms of lumens per watt, than fluorescent bulbs.

David's idea about where these lightbulbs are in the emerging technology cycle certainly is accurate from a price standpoint. LEDs are about as expensive, when compared with a regular incandescent lightbulb, as CFLs were ten years ago. Right now, you'd be paying $25 or even $50 for an LED lightbulb to replace an incandescent. But the prices will come down as demand—and therefore as mass production—picks up.

One of the many great things about LEDs is they don't contain any mercury, not a bit.

An LED lightbulb is the future of lighting.

LEDs also are great at spotlighting—producing focused, directed light—which is something fluorescent bulbs are not as good at doing as incandescents. However, LEDs are not yet good at giving off a nice even glow, though they do show great promise. (See Resources, page 341 for information on how you can purchase LEDs online.)

USES FOR THE DIFFERENT KINDS OF BULBS

If you're like most people, you've been using incandescent lightbulbs for absolutely all of your lighting needs. But when you're ready to make the switch—and reap the efficiency and the energy-savings benefits—you probably won't switch to all one type of replacement lightbulb.

I had switched absolutely all of my incandescent bulbs over to CFLs years ago. This was a bit disconcerting for my wife, since she complained about the quality (that is, the color) of the light from CFLs, and she also thought they looked ugly—you know, in those applications where the bulb actually showed. Frankly, I think the energy savings they provide renders them beautiful. But I will admit that I find beauty in places Rachelle often doesn't, and perhaps she speaks for part of the world that cares a bit more about aesthetics than I do.

In the interest of finding the best tool for the job, let's look at CFLs, CCFLs, and LEDs, and

consider when each type of bulb is the best option for your lighting needs.

CHOOSING THE RIGHT CFLS

These days, there are many choices when it comes to CFLs. There are different color options. There are different shapes and sizes. There are CFLs that produce what is considered soft white light, and there are CFLs that produce bright white light. There are some that will work with a dimmer switch and some that will work with a three-way light switch.

Most of the time in this book, we're talking about CFLs that can replace incandescent bulbs—that is, ones that screw into a socket designed for an incandescent lightbulb. In the lighting industry, they're referred to as *replacement CFLs*.

But it's important to point out that today, companies are manufacturing lamps that are designed specifically to use CFLs, and the CFLs that go in these lamps have a different kind of bottom. These nonreplacement CFLs come in two types. The older type of bulb is *pin-based*—i.e., it has two or four pins on the bottom that either plug into a ballast or directly into a socket in the light fixture. The newer type of non-replacement CFL has what's called a GU24 socket. Basically, it's a twist-and-lock kind of base. So choosing the right bulb is not simply a matter of getting the right lumens per watt of output, it's also a matter of your needs and the actual light fixture you're going to be using.

I know many people agree with Rachelle that CFLs are not the loveliest lightbulbs in

My new light fixture is designed to use CFLs.

the world, and I have to admit that they do work better in a lamp that has a shade. I've found that CFLs work very well not just behind lampshades, but in some sort of lantern, behind a screen. Any type of cover that will diffuse the light from a CFL and hide the bulb itself makes it a very attractive light. CFLs also work well in recessed fixtures, like canister lights. The fact that they are cooler in operation than incandescent bulbs is also a big benefit when you're using them in canister lighting.

Some people complain of migraines caused by the light from CFLs. I've been using CFLs since the late eighties, and it's never been a problem. For people who suffer from migraines, I want to point out that the new CFLs don't cause the same problems. Early CFLs were low-frequency designs. As it turns out, these lights actually flicker on and off many times per second. The early CFLs went on and off slowly enough that some people's brains could register the flickering, which is what triggered those headaches—much the same way that workers in buildings with old fluorescent-tube lighting would complain of headaches. Now, all of the fluorescent lightbulbs on the market are high-frequency designs. The flickering is totally imperceptible.

Speaking of long fluorescent tubes, what if you have those big, old fluorescent light fixtures in your kitchen or bathroom? Should you replace them with CFLs? You definitely can, and depending on how old your light fixture is, you could save a sizable amount of energy in the process. If your old bulbs buzz because they have a magnetic ballast, replacing them—or even replacing the entire innards of your light fixture—with a newer design is a particularly appealing option. (Some people used to have a problem with the magnets in lighting equipment, as well. As I mentioned, the new designs are no longer magnetic; they're electronic, so that's another reason to switch from old fixtures to new ones.)

There are CFLs coming on the market now that are good replacements for chandelier bulbs—even ones that use bulbs that look like a candle flame. You can find frosted replacement CFLs in those shapes and sizes. What you can't find yet are clear bulbs of this type, which are what's usually used in a crystal chandelier.

Remember, size is an important factor when it comes to replacement bulbs. Some CFLs are simply too big to fit inside a particular lampshade or wall sconce or overhead light fixture. It's always a good idea to measure your old lightbulb before you go to the store, then take a tape measure with you, so you buy a CFL that will fit. Or better yet, just carry your old bulb with you and hold it up to the CFL. That's even easier.

THE COLOR OF CFL LIGHT

Some people complain about the quality of the light from CFLs. I don't mind it myself, but I know people who object to it. It has to do with the color of the light. We've all grown up with incandescent bulbs that give off a yellowish amber or even rose-colored light.

CFLs more commonly produce what's known as a *daylight* color. While light from an incandescent bulb will feel warm to us, light from a daylight CFL will feel cold. When you walk outside in the middle of the day, what color is the sky? It's blue. What's considered *daylight light* is actually a bluish color, and it feels cold and possibly even harsh to our eyes.

Incandescent bulbs produce a light that's closer in color to natural light at sunrise or sunset, when the sky turns shades of yellow and red. It's light that feels warm. If you want to get that same character of light in a compact fluorescent bulb, then look for ones that are marked *warm white* or *soft white*.

Interestingly, Ellis Yan of TCP says CFLs can be manufactured to create pretty much any color of light in the spectrum. We aren't seeing different colors on the market just yet, but it's entirely possible.

Ellis also points out that there are regional trends, in terms of which color of lighting is more popular. It seems that people in areas that are cloudier, perhaps even gloomier— places like Seattle and parts of Canada—often really like the daylight-colored lightbulbs. They want more "daylighting" in their homes. In places like California and Florida, the soft white lightbulbs are more popular, probably because people there already get plenty of natural daylight. There's no right or wrong to color selection with CFLs. It's just a matter of choosing what works for you.

WHEN CCFLS ARE A GOOD CHOICE

Because CCFLs can be smaller than CFLs, they're a good choice for light fixtures in which a regular CFL won't fit. They're also good for fixtures from which you want instant light, with no lag time, like outside lights—or any lights, really—that are activated by a motion sensor.

As for other good CCFL applications, because most are dimmable, they're a great choice if you have a dimmer switch or you want to install one to control a particular light fixture.

CCFLs are a great choice for outdoor lighting in very cold climates. Compact fluorescents tend not to like extremes of temperature, so CCFLs are a better choice in those instances.

I've already mentioned that it's difficult to find CCFLs that are really bright—equivalent to a 100-watt incandescent bulb or brighter. That makes it tough to use them for all of your lighting needs, like a floor lamp in the family room or a lamp you use for reading. The good news is that a more diverse assortment of CCFLs is starting to come to market now. I've even seen CCFL floodlights.

WHAT ABOUT LEDS?

It's now easy to use fluorescents—either CFLs or CCFLs—to replace incandescent bulbs in many situations throughout your home and garden. LEDs can replace the other ones. Unfortunately, we're still at the point where the color of light produced by LEDs is considered very blue, very harsh—definitely a daylight type of color. But companies are working on producing LED bulbs with a warmer, friendlier quality of light, and I welcome that.

Like CFLs, you can find *replacement LEDs* that are designed to go where an incandescent bulb went before. You can also find light fixtures that are designed specifically for LEDs—especially desk lamps—which take a bulb with a different kind of base.

You'll also find LED replacement kits for incandescents used in canister lighting. And you'll find LED replacement flood lamps, even dimmable ones. Plus, you'll find LED replacements for fluorescent tubes, the kind often used in overhead kitchen and bathroom fixtures—or you can get a complete kit to change over the innards of those fixtures so they're specifically designed to use LEDs.

LED bulbs are also more attractive than fluorescent lightbulbs, so they're a good choice when the bulb is visible. For instance, if you've got track lighting, the bulbs usually show. The same goes for many types of ceiling fans that have lights built in. It may be a little tough to find LED replacements for all of these types of applications right now, but it will continue to get easier.

LEDs are also a great choice for another style of kitchen lighting. They're becoming more available for undercabinet lighting—both the kind that's hardwired into your home and the kind that is battery operated and that you can literally adhere to your kitchen cabinets for task lighting. Because LEDs have a really, really long lifetime, this is a great use for the technology.

Sample Costs and Paybacks: Switching to CFLs

If you're considering changing from regular old incandescent lightbulbs to compact fluorescents, you must be wondering what's the cost and what's the payback?

Let's say you pay $3 for a CFL.

If you consider that a compact fluorescent lightbulb uses roughly a quarter of the power of an incandescent lightbulb, it will take you just six months to recoup your investment. That's a really quick payback.

And don't forget that a CFL will last far longer. I have some CFLs in my house that are seventeen years old. Have you ever had an incandescent bulb last anywhere near that long? Not likely!

You could even make a good argument that a CFL is a lifestyle/convenience item, since you won't have to shop for lightbulbs or climb up on a ladder to change a lightbulb anywhere near as often.

LEDs have a great outdoor application, too. I've been using solar-powered walkway lights since the mid-eighties, and back then, they'd be great for a few months and then they would stop working. They had nickel-cadmium batteries that were problematic. With the newer solar outdoor lights, you can put any battery you like in them. I use nickel-metal hydride NiMH batteries.

I've had LED lights out in my walkway for a year now, and I haven't had to charge the batteries once. It's been a great timesaver to have solar walkway lights that didn't need replacing or maintenance for a full year.

 ## SOLAR LIGHTING OPTIONS

We've talked a lot about lamps and light fixtures. But one of the best things you can do to light your home and reduce your energy needs is to use the sun as your light source. It's absolutely free!

From an environmental standpoint, there's no downside to using daylight to light your home. It requires no energy. Plus, natural light doesn't have any of the side effects that you might see with man-made light sources. If the light is too bright, it's easy to adjust it—you can install sheer drapes over the windows to diffuse the light.

There is potentially one downside to using natural light to light your home, and that's

A passive solar home using natural light.

that you may wind up overheating your house if you aren't careful. Particularly in warmer climates, you don't want a lot of direct sunlight coming in through south- and west-facing windows in the summertime.

But that's the beauty of drapes and blinds and all kinds of window treatments. They allow you to control the amount of light coming into a room at any point in time—and they even help reduce heat gain in the summer and heat loss in the winter. Installing awnings over your south- and west-facing windows can help with this, too, since the sun is at a higher point in the sky in the summer, when the awning blocks the heat, then it's at a lower point in the winter, when you want that heat and light coming in through your windows. You might also consider designing a porch along the south and west sides of your house, which acts like a big awning and also gives you wonderful opportunities for outdoor living. We'll go into these ideas more fully in Chapter 5, when we talk about windows and doors.

SKYLIGHTS

How do you use natural light in a room where the light is blocked? Or what about hallways and bathrooms and north-facing rooms? How can you use natural light—true free solar energy—to light up those rooms? Easy. You have two choices: traditional skylights and a newer technology called a solar tube.

Skylights can be great. They admit lots of natural light. And when installed properly, you don't have to worry about leaks or anything of

that nature. The thing with skylights, though, is they must be installed directly over the area you want to light. Where you put the skylight is where the light comes in. You literally cut a hole in the roof of your house and install a skylight that shines right into the room below.

Obviously, this can be limiting. What if the room you want to light is on the north side of the house? Or what if there's no convenient way to install a skylight right over that room? What if there's stuff in the attic—perhaps your forced-air heating unit—that's in the way?

That's where a solar tube comes in. These tubes are like bright, shiny pipes—like small air-conditioning ducts, but they're ducts for light, for photons—and they get installed in your attic. A professional installer comes to your home and cuts a small hole in your roof (much smaller than the hole for a traditional skylight), and then the solar tube directs the light into whichever room you want. The tube doesn't have to go straight down into the house; it can turn and bend. The reflective surface inside the solar tube makes sure the light keeps getting reflected all the way down until it comes out into your room. It's quite amazing. This is the most efficient type of skylight I've seen that puts out the most lumens—again, the most foot-candles—and the brand name for it is Solatube (see Resources, page 341).

When you see the solar tube inside the house during the day, you might not even realize it's a type of skylight. It looks a lot like a recessed light, the kind people in the lighting industry sometimes call *high hats*.

Solar-LED path lighting is easy and affordable.

I had Solatube install three of their unique skylights in my house. One lights up what had been a very dark hallway. One lights up the bathroom, so we can see much better in there during the daytime. And one lights up our kitchen, making a small room seem larger. It's amazing what a difference light can make, and it's a wonderful quality of light.

The Solatube in our hallway has an interesting twist to it, too. It's not just a skylight, it's also a lighting fixture. So at night, you just flip the switch and the Solatube is a regular light, making it very clear just how much energy we were saving during the day. It's really the best of both worlds: providing free light during the daytime, then also providing the light we need at night.

The installers we used also offered a choice of covers for the Solatube. You could choose one that provided a more diffused light or one that provides a brighter light, which is what we wanted for the kitchen.

Changing your lightbulbs—and even some of your lighting fixtures—is one of the fastest and easiest steps you can take to conserve energy in your home. New, more efficient lightbulbs will use less power, and they will produce less heat, so they will reduce your home's cooling costs in the summertime.

Plus, switching lightbulbs conserves money and time, too. Because CFL, CCFL, and LED lightbulbs last longer than old-fashioned incandescents, you won't have to shop for lightbulbs as often. Changing your lighting is the perfect way to start down the conservation path.

ED'S PROJECT

New Lighting

Start switching your old bulbs to CFLs.

For years, my wife, Rachelle, had complained about the track lighting in my office. I guess it's not exactly fashionable these days. But if you've read my first book, you know I hate to get rid of anything that's working properly. Still, after years of haranguing—and after I discovered some of the wonderful new lighting options on the market these days—I decided to take on some lighting projects of my own.

The first step was getting rid of that track lighting, which I gave away, so someone else (someone who doesn't live with Rachelle) could use it, since it still works just fine.

The next step was choosing my replacement lighting for the office. I took my friend David Bergman's advice and went with a variety of light fixtures, so that I have ambient lighting and task lighting, as needed. I wound up installing two nice wall-mounted antique light fixtures and two matching hanging antique fixtures, which go beautifully with the style of my 1936 ranch house.

I should point out that even as I went with antique light fixtures for aesthetic reasons, I still was able to use new, energy-saving CFLs in them. The age of a light fixture doesn't have to serve as an excuse for you to use old, incandescent, toaster-style lightbulbs.

In fact, I've opted for compact fluorescents throughout my house. But part of my to-do list is switching these CFLs over to LEDs. As the CFLs burn out and as new, better options come on the market, I plan to upgrade all of my lightbulbs to LEDs. Although the prices are quite expensive now, I hope they'll come down as demand increases, and I intend to be out in front in using this new technology.

④

INSULATION

Keeping It Warm in the Wintertime
& Cool in the Summertime

ONE BIG WAY TO CONSERVE ENERGY—AND CONSERVE dollars—is to make sure your house is properly insulated, so the air inside stays warm in the winter and cool in the summer. Heat always flows toward cooler areas. It flows from the inside out in the wintertime. And then in the summertime, it flows from the outside in. The key is to reduce that heat flow as much as possible.

As always, you'll want to begin by evaluating your home's existing insulation. As you do this, the first place to go is up. You have to look in your attic and see what you've got up there. If you have no insulation, you'll want to install some. If you have old insulation, you'll want to make sure it's still viable—it hasn't gotten wet, it isn't losing its efficiency, and it's not there in a few spots but not in others. Then check the wall insulation. The exterior walls are obviously an important part of your home's envelope, yet they may have little or no insulation inside them.

Under the house is another good place to examine. There's real savings to be gained from sealing the area under your home, so you don't have as much heat invading your house in the summer months and as much heat escaping in the winter months.

Insulation really is a multifaceted issue. It is

- an energy issue
- a money issue
- a comfort issue
- a health issue
- an environmental issue

So let's start by looking at where you want to insulate, then talk about the kinds of insulation materials you can use.

the attic side of those doors. And you'll want to be sure there's insulation above a cathedral ceiling or an open-beam ceiling.

 ATTIC INSULATION

If you own an older home, chances are quite good that you could use more insulation in your attic. Even if you have a new home, it may not have as much insulation as you'd like. After all, the majority of home builders don't put future energy savings for the homeowner ahead of, say, their profit margin. Builders typically put in the least insulation—and the least expensive insulation—that they can.

When you have a home energy audit done, the person who performs that audit is going to go into your attic and check to determine if the insulation is there and if so, what kind and how thick it is, if there are gaps, and if it needs repair.

Most people, when they think of attic insulation, think of insulating the floor of the attic, so to speak. But that is not the only area that needs insulation. For example, you will want to make sure that there's insulation on the attic side of what are called *knee walls*—that is, walls that are attic on one side, home interior on the other. Many homes have these sorts of walls, and they often are not insulated. Attic access doors typically are not insulated, either. You'll want to make sure there's insulation on

WALL INSULATION

Homes can lose a lot of heat in the wintertime—and gain a lot of heat in the summertime—through their exterior walls.

It's worth noting here that interior walls generally are not insulated, unless you have some sort of special room, like a recording studio or a media room. But you certainly do want to reduce heat gain and heat loss through your exterior walls. If you have an older home, you may not have any insulation inside those walls. Or the insulation in the walls may be long gone—or it simply may have settled to the bottom of the walls. My walls were originally insulated with shredded newspaper, and, not surprisingly, almost all of it was gone after fifty-some years.

If you have someone perform a home energy audit, they will check for insulation. The easiest way to check the walls yourself is to turn off the power to a particular electrical outlet—just flip that circuit breaker to the *off* position— then remove the outlet's cover and peek around the side of the outlet box. You'll need a flashlight to illuminate the area, so you can see if there's any insulation in the wall around it. You can even reach in with tweezers and pull out a

Health Issues: Can You Be Too Insulated?

This quest to have a fully insulated house—which is a wonderful, wonderful goal—can have a dark side to it. An insulated environment can exacerbate problems that you might have within your home. For example, there's not as much outside air passing through your house that would allow vapors from a bunch of toxic cleaning products under your sink or around your house to clear, so they stay *inside* your house.

This can also be a problem if you have carpeting that has a toxic element to it, where there's off-gassing. Off-gassing from formaldehyde in wood products, from urethanes and other toxic coatings, and from vinyl flooring materials can cause health issues. When you have a very well-insulated home, these things become the enemy. Those gases start to really accumulate in your home, *because* you're so well insulated.

So the solution is not to be poorly insulated, of course, but to remove those toxic products from your home and to use alternatives. Great options exist. We'll go into them in much more detail in Chapter 14.

bit of insulation, so you can identify the kind. You'll want to check more than one location. It's possible that only some of your exterior walls are insulated, particularly if there's been an addition built onto your home.

If you don't have any insulation—or if you don't have sufficient insulation, which is quite likely—you usually can add it to your walls. Certainly if you have a stucco house like mine, it's fairly easy to have an installer come out and fill the walls with a loose or blow-in type of insulation.

What they did in my case was drill into the walls between the 2×4s, working on the outside of the house. They drilled above and below the

fire blocks, which are little blocks of wood in the middle of those big, long 2×4s; the fire blocks are designed to reduce the spread of fire (i.e., they have fire-prevention properties). So the installer drilled these holes every 16 inches or so, since 2×4s almost always are spaced 16 inches on center. Then they blew insulation above and below the fire blocks. It's also possible to have a contractor drill into your walls from the inside of the house and add insulation.

Either way, it's pretty easy to do this without totally disrupting your home and making a huge mess. I had the work done on my house when I was already planning to repaint the exterior. So the installers drilled the holes on the outside, blew in the insulation, then patched. Then I had a painting contractor come and repaint the whole house, so the work was invisible just as soon as that was done. If you have someone drill on the inside, again you can have a painting contractor come and patch the walls and repaint, or if you're handy, you might do it yourself.

If you happen to be building a new home or if you're adding on to your current house, it's even easier to insulate your walls properly. In this case, you can do it before the drywall goes up (or plaster, if you're going that route). Insulating exterior walls when the walls are open gives you more options in terms of the type of insulation you can choose to use. And if you happen to be building a home or adding on, you also have the option of using structural insulated panels (SIPs), where the entire wall comes preassembled and preinsulated (see Chapter 9, "Building and Remodeling").

UNDER THE HOUSE

There's also a lot of savings to be had—both in terms of energy and heating and cooling expense—by insulating under your home. If your home was built on a raised foundation and you have a crawl space, you can insulate the underside of your floor.

If you have an unfinished basement, the same goes for that space. If you plan to finish the basement and make it a more usable space, then you'll want to insulate the floor and the exterior walls. Otherwise, you want to be sure to insulate the ceiling of the basement—that is, the underside of your home's floors.

It's the same idea if you have a room over an unheated garage or porch: You'll also want to insulate the floor there.

If your home was built on a concrete slab, you still can insulate between the slab and your flooring material—particularly if you plan to install new flooring. Believe me, a concrete slab can be very cold in the wintertime. Insulating between the slab and your flooring will increase your comfort level dramatically and impact your heating costs. You can also insulate the slab's exterior edges, where they lose heat to the outside—sometimes considerable amounts of it.

CHECKING FOR WEAKNESSES

Even if your attic, your walls, and your floor are well insulated, there are certain nooks and crannies in most homes—even in brand-new homes—where heat leaks out in the winter or it sneaks in during the summer.

Canister lights—those inset ceiling lights— are gross offenders. Also check the seal around the vent over your stove in the kitchen area. My home energy audit showed a lot of loss there.

Wall outlets are another common culprit—which is why I suggest that you look around several of them to see what kind of insulation you have in the first place. Those outlets are very rarely sealed as they should be. Electricians don't always make sure the outlets are sealed properly from an insulator's point of view. So there are many outlets that are just allowing air to blow right through, coming right from outside or from under the house. Switch plates are often offenders as well.

Where else are you likely to have leaks? Attic access doors may not be sealed adequately. This is not a big deal if the attic access is in your garage. But if it's inside your house, you should know that a leak around your attic access door potentially could flow as much air as one of the regular room ducts for your heating and air-conditioning system. That's a big leak, and you definitely want to fix it. Simple tape-on weather stripping probably will be enough to do the trick, but you also might want to attach some sort of lock or clasp to make sure the access door shuts tightly.

Another place to check in your attic is around the chimney. It may need some caulking to seal it. You'll also want to check around the air return for your heating and cooling system. This intake—where your air filter is located—is a common area for leaks. If there are leaks and if there's insulation covering the box, you can wind up sucking some of that insulation material into your heating and cooling system. So you want to make sure your return box is sealed, because you certainly don't want anything to contaminate the air quality inside your home.

Are there other places where insulation may be lacking? Absolutely. My house has a curvature in the ceiling, a wonderful design element in the bedrooms. But even though we had people install new insulation in the attic—big, flat lengths of it—there wasn't any insulation blown down into many spaces in the curvatures. You could see the cold very clearly on the infrared camera when we did the energy audit. If you have sloped ceilings or gables or curved ceilings or any other architectural details like that, odds are you need some more insulation in those places, too.

During my home energy audit, we even found gaps in the wall insulation, which again had been done fairly recently by a top-notch contractor. But it turns out there are diagonal members occasionally in my walls. In a typical wood-frame house like mine, the walls have studs that are 16 inches on center. But then at certain intervals between the studs, there were diagonal pieces of wood that were put there for further support. When the contractor's crew blew in the insulation into my walls between the studs, above and below the fire blocks, they probably didn't even know the diagonal members were there. So they missed above or below the diagonals in a few spots.

As you know, a chain is only as strong as its weakest link. If you have these spots in your house where heat or cool can transfer quickly, the temperature will find a median. It will find a common ground. So be sure to fix those areas in your home as much as you can.

R-VALUE

So now you know *where* you need insulation. Next, it's time to consider *how much* insulation you need.

Obviously, it's important to know how well a certain material will insulate. The standard measurement is known as the *R-value,* which is an indication of an insulating material's *resistance to heat flow.*

The higher the number after the R, the better a particular material insulates. So a material with a value of R-45 will insulate much better than a material with a value of R-30.

Of course, certain factors do influence a material's actual, in-home R-value. The thickness of the material is a major factor. Installation can play a big role, too; when installed improperly, insulation will lose considerable R-value.

Also, if you compress some kinds of insulation, it lowers their effective R-value. And if you leave gaps between the material—or if it has to go around joists and such—that also can lower the effective R-value.

As you know, building codes in various cities and states dictate what sorts of materials must

R-VALUE CHART

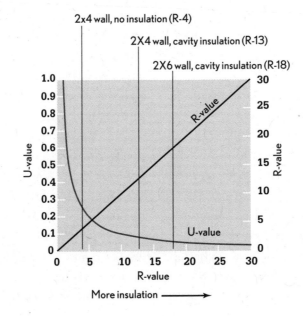

be used in a home in order to make it "up to code"—that is, to make it legal. All across the country, building codes provide minimum insulation levels for homes.

The Department of Energy has a website (see Resources, page 341) that will tell you not only what's legal, but also what is the most *economical* insulation level for your house, whether you have an existing house or are building a new home. You just go on the website and enter your ZIP code. Then you answer a few questions, and the site recommends R-values based on your climate, your home's heating and cooling system, and so on. For example, if you live in Buffalo, New York, and are building a new wood-frame home with electric baseboard heating and central air-conditioning, the site recommends an R-value of 49 for attic insulation and 30 for the floor over a crawl space. If you have an existing wood-frame home in Seattle with a gas furnace and no A/C, the site recommends an R-value of 38 for the attic and 19 for flooring over an unheated, uninsulated space. Or if you live in an existing wood-frame house in Las Vegas with a gas furnace and central air-conditioning, the site recommends an R-value of 38 for the attic and 13 for the floor over a crawl space.

It's a really good resource to use in order to make sure you get the right level of insulation to meet your needs.

INSULATION MATERIALS

So what kind of insulation should you use? Insulation can be—and has been—made from a variety of materials. Some are no longer in use today, but you may still find them in your home. And some are brand-new to market, offering us far more of a selection than was available even a handful of years ago.

The common materials that have been used to make home insulation over the years are asbestos, fiberglass, foam, cellulose, and cotton. As you might guess, some of these materials are much more environmentally friendly than others.

ASBESTOS

For years there was a material that insulated very well. They made potholders out of it. They still use it to make automobile brakes. It's asbestos—and it's something you want to steer clear of. Asbestos, of course, is very hazardous. It's very invasive to your lungs. If you breathe in asbestos fibers, you can become seriously ill.

Asbestos has been banned in most places now as insulation, but it was very common beginning in the late nineteenth century. And you can still find insulation that contains asbestos in the attics of homes built before 1950. Indeed, if you find it in an attic or in the ducts to an older home's heating or cooling system, it has to be removed by people in moon suits. Do not attempt to remove it yourself. Asbestos is very dangerous.

FIBERGLASS

While asbestos is no longer commonplace in homes, fiberglass insulation certainly is. In fact, fiberglass is the most common form of insulation used in newer homes. Fiberglass is made from glass, which is turned into long, thin fibers (hence the name). The insulation comes in thick mats, called *batts*. It must be cut to fit for installation, meaning it's not always easy to get fiberglass insulation into nooks and crannies in your attic. And it can't be added into walls in an existing home without removing the drywall first.

Most fiberglass contains formaldehyde, which is a nasty chemical compound. In high concentrations, it can trigger asthma attacks, and people sometimes become sensitive to formaldehyde even in smaller amounts. It also is considered a carcinogen. You can find fiberglass without formaldehyde in it, and that certainly is a better choice.

Even so, fiberglass can cause a problem if there's a fire. If fiberglass ignites, it can burn fast and hot and could potentially emit toxic gases. For this reason, experts recommend keeping fiberglass insulation away from light fixtures and chimneys and other heat sources.

Though I've worked with fiberglass in the past, I steer clear of it today. It is very invasive, it's bad for your lungs, it makes you itch like crazy when it touches your skin, and it's very hard to work with—the people who install fiberglass insulation have to wear special protective gear. If you want to store items in your attic—or if you have workers going up there to run wiring or check ducting or repair leaks or what-have-you—you could wind up disturbing the fiberglass and getting those fibers airborne. And once they get airborne, they can get into your house and into your lungs and into your family's lungs. It's best to avoid fiberglass; there are better options.

FOAM INSULATION

Foam insulation comes in spray-in or pour-in form, as well as in stiff sheets. Foam is generally more effective at blocking heat than fiberglass insulation, and the spray-in varieties do a great job of filling in nooks and crannies, both in attics and inside walls. There is no doubt that they are an effective form of insulation.

However, most foam insulation is petroleum-based. This includes both spray and stiff foam insulation made from polystyrene, polyisocyanurate, and polyurethane.

Clearly, petroleum-based products are not the most environmentally friendly choice available. There's a real environmental cost in drilling for oil, in transporting the oil, and then in refining it. And of course there's the issue of our country's reliance on foreign oil. There's also the toxicity factor, since there are toxic elements in these products.

There are some newer foam products that have real advantages. Some use a soybean oil instead of petroleum-based oil. However, all of the foams I've found contain volatile organic compounds (VOCs). These compounds are released into the air when the product is

Cellulose insulation, made up of recycled newspaper and paper products, is environmentally friendly and easy to install.

applied, and they can be very hazardous for your health. Even more worrisome, these products continue to *outgas* over time. That is, they release harmful fumes not just when they're first installed, but for weeks and months and years down the road.

There's just no reason to introduce these chemicals into your home environment, when you can choose a more environmentally friendly and a more health-friendly insulation option.

CELLULOSE

Cellulose insulation is much more benign; it's made from recycled newspaper and paper products. One hundred pounds of cellulose insulation actually contains 80 to 85 pounds of recycled newsprint. That's a very high use of recycled materials, and it takes a considerable amount of material out of our waste stream, which means cellulose is a good way to go.

It also takes relatively little energy to manufacture cellulose insulation, especially compared with fiberglass and foam insulation, so there's a real environmental benefit there, too. Cellulose is what is known as a *loose fill* insulation. Rather than being made into batts like most fiberglass insulation, cellulose is a loose material. It looks like shredded paper. Because it's loose, it does a terrific job of filling in nooks and crannies. Contractors can easily install cellulose under, over, and around whatever may be up in your attic or inside your walls. Installers can add a thicker layer of cellulose whenever a higher R-value is required. Since cellulose insulation's R-value is based on thickness, all you have to do is add more to achieve a higher R-value.

As it is, cellulose offers very good insulation per square inch. Plus it seals a home against what's known as *air infiltration,* which is a primary way in which heat transfers, particularly through the walls. Because of this, in tests of buildings with fiberglass vs. cellulose insulation having the exact same R-value—both in the attics and in the walls—the buildings with cellulose used 20 percent to 40 percent less energy. That's a huge benefit.

We all know that paper is quick to burn, but, fortunately, cellulose insulation is treated with additives to provide fire resistance. Studies by the National Research Council Canada showed that cellulose in a wall actually increased fire resistance by 22 percent to 55 percent compared with traditional insulation. So that's another big benefit.

Of course, paper also provides a delightful habitat for animals and other living things, like fungus. But the makers of cellulose insulation clearly do not want you to create a habitat for wildlife inside your attic or walls. So they treat the cellulose insulation to make it resistant to moisture and mold and fungus and less appealing to critters, too.

Cellulose insulation is a very good choice for homes, particularly for retrofit in existing homes. It's what I have inside my walls because it's environmentally friendly and because it's easy to apply. It can be blown into the walls through small holes, in the process I described earlier.

COTTON

Cellulose is good, but the number one best choice for insulation—what I've used in my attic and what I've used in as many places as I can—is recycled denim. It's cotton. It's wonderful insulation, it's environmentally sound, and it has a great R-value.

It's made from the scraps and clippings left over in the manufacture of blue jeans— materials that likely would wind up in landfills, if they weren't recycled in this way. Fully 85 percent of the material in cotton insulation is recycled. So this insulation takes a lot of material out of the waste stream and is not only made from recycled materials but also can be recycled.

A company called Bonded Logic (see Resources, page 341) makes UltraTouch Natural Cotton Fiber insulation. They take this post-industrial denim waste and process it into loose fibers. Then they treat those fibers with a

Recycled denim cotton insulation is made from leftover scraps from blue jeans.

borate solution that acts as a fire, mold, mildew, and pest inhibitor. Next, it's made into solid batts, much like fiberglass insulation. Then a foil material is applied to one or both sides.

Another great benefit: You don't need to wear any protective gear when you install recycled denim insulation. Unlike fiberglass, it's not an irritant to your skin or your lungs. It's cotton—the stuff you wear on your skin all the time. This insulation doesn't contain any chemical irritants. There are no VOCs. It doesn't outgas.

I have recycled denim insulation in my attic; it is doing a great job of saving a lot of heat in the winter and a lot of cool in the summer.

Recycled denim insulation has another great benefit, too: It's particularly good as a sound barrier—about 30 percent better than traditional insulation materials. Los Angeles is a noisy city, and this cotton insulation keeps the noise out of my house.

Because recycled denim comes in batts, it's easier to install it in the *attic* of an existing home than it is to install it in the *walls*. You would have to remove the drywall to add it to the walls after a home was built. That's why I'm still a big fan of cellulose when you're doing a retrofit installation. But cotton is a great choice—my number one choice—for walls in an addition to a home or in new home construction, when you can install it easily before the drywall goes up. Plus, it's by far my number one choice for an attic of any home.

RADIANT BARRIERS

If you live in a warm climate, there's another insulating option for your attic—something you may want to install *in addition* to insulation. It's called a *radiant barrier,* and it's usually a reflective material that has been designed to reduce heat gain in the summer months. Essentially, it reflects heat away from the inside of your home.

The name comes from the type of heat gain this barrier serves to reduce. Essentially, heat travels from a warmer area to a cooler area in three different ways:

- **Conduction.** When something hot touches something cool, heat is *conducted* from the hotter object to the cooler object.
- **Convection.** When air (or any other gas or liquid) is heated, it rises.
- **Radiation.** Something hot *radiates* heat in a straight line moving away from its surface, whether that something hot is your stovetop or the surface of the sun.

In the case of your home's attic, radiant heat from the sun makes your roof hot. That heat then transfers through the roof and into the attic.

So, a radiant barrier is designed to literally act as a heat barrier, reflecting heat back up through the roof in the summer instead of allowing it to transfer into your attic area. In the winter, a radiant barrier also can reflect heat back into your home, instead of allowing it to escape through the roof. For this reason, radiant barriers often are attached inside the attic to the underside of the roof.

You can also find insulation materials that include a radiant barrier, essentially a reflective facing material. These materials are what's known as *reflective insulation systems.* The UltraTouch recycled cotton insulation with foil on both sides is this type of insulation.

If you want to add a separate radiant barrier in your home, a company called Louisiana Pacific (see Resources, page 341) manufactures one called TechShield that blocks up to 97 percent of the radiant heat in the panel from entering your attic. According to LP, it can cut your energy bills by up to 17 percent a month.

 ## INSULATING DUCTING

We've talked about the major areas where you'll want to insulate your home—your attic, your walls, and under your home. There are other areas that also benefit from insulation. For instance, if you have central heat or central air-conditioning—any forced-air type of

Insulating your ductwork reduces heat transfer and prevents mold, mildew, and leakage.

heating/cooling system—you'll want to insulate the ducts that route that hot or cool air into the various rooms in your home. Those ducts may be up in your attic. They may be in your walls. They may also be under your house. You'll want to install insulation on the outside of those ducts to reduce heat transfer. This is an obvious way to save energy and save money. It can also prevent them from "sweating" in the summertime. When the attic air is hot and the air inside the ducts is cold, condensation can form on the outside of the ducts. That moisture

then can drip into your insulation, which is a potential source of mold and mildew.

Insulating your ducts helps to prevent leaks. Leakage can be a common problem wherever there are seams in your ducts, where two pieces are joined together, either to make a turn or simply to continue a long, straight run of ducting. My friend Lou Alonso of ACT Environmental (see Resources, page 341) says, "We've noticed that over the years, by testing . . . the ducts sometimes lose as much as twenty percent of their efficiency through leakage points." So blowing heated or cooled air into the attic not only wastes energy, but a duct leak could also be allowing fiberglass fibers—or even simply dust and dirt, or any mold growing up in your attic—to get into your home and into your lungs.

So what do you use to insulate that ducting? You can find fiberglass insulation for your ducting, but I would steer clear of that for obvious reasons. Instead, I would lean toward Reflectix (see Resources, page 341), a fiberglass-free insulation that you can install yourself without any special equipment. You just wrap this foil-covered material around your ducting and secure it in place. It's nontoxic and lightweight, and it is not affected by moisture or humidity. Plus, it reflects 97 percent of radiant energy, making it an extremely effective insulator.

 ## INSULATING PIPES

For much the same reasons that you'll want to insulate your heating and air-conditioning ducts, you'll also want to insulate your pipes—particularly in a very cold or a very hot climate. If your pipes run underground or if they're built into your slab foundation, they're naturally insulated. But exposed pipes are a different story.

Why insulate your pipes?

- In a very cold climate, they run the risk of freezing due to water left in them, in which case they can burst and cause tremendous damage.

- In cold weather, hot water running through the pipes can transfer its heat to the cooler outside air, which means you'll be cranking up the hot water and making your water heater work harder and longer.

- In a hot climate, you may never get cold water in your home, and you may wind up with condensation on the outside of pipes, again creating a potential for mold, mildew, and other fungi to grow.

In the past, I've used that simple foam tubing you can get at any home improvement store to insulate my pipes. It's a tube with a slit on one side, and you just slip it right over the pipe in sections. It's an easy do-it-yourself project.

But now I use Reflectix, the same product used for ducting, which is a higher-tech solution. It's also recommended for installation on pipes, making it easy to protect your home and save energy.

In the meantime, the goal is to insulate your house and its ducts and pipes as much as possible. Great insulation will help you conserve a considerable amount of energy. But of course insulation isn't just an environmental issue. It's a dollars-and-cents issue. The more energy you save, the more money you save. And there are quality-of-life benefits to a well-insulated house, as well. The more you eliminate leaks and drafts and hot and cold spots, the more comfortable your home will be.

Sample Costs and Paybacks: Insulation and Sealing

Weather stripping your door can prevent unwanted cold from entering and heat from escaping the house.

You might be surprised that the cost of all my insulation projects came to $7,000. That includes sealing up the crawl space using concrete and foam seal, which was a fairly extensive project, as well as blowing additional cellulose insulation into the walls, adding filler to the attic in areas that were not insulated well enough, and adding more weather stripping on all of my doors and windows.

Now, $7,000 is a pretty significant outlay of cash— and the total comes to $8,000 if you add in the green home audit that pointed out these specific weak spots, which obviously was a key part of the project.

I estimate my payback for this investment will be about ten years, thanks to the reduction in my need for electricity and natural gas. Now, if my house was larger, or if it had been poorly insulated to begin with, the payback period would be much shorter. That sort of house might see an energy savings (of both electricity and natural gas) in the area of $130 each month, or perhaps $1,600 per year. That's not unreasonable, and it might even be more. There are plenty of people who have $400 to $600 monthly utility bills who might be able to cut them in half with this kind of project!

Adding Insulation and Sealing the Crawl Space

As I mentioned in Chapter 1, the energy audit of my home revealed several places where I needed more insulation and better sealing. After the folks from REAS Inc. (Residential Energy Assessment Services) cranked up the heat and used the infrared gun to identify cold spots, and after they did the blower-door test to spot leaks, we came up with a five-item project list for my house.

Since then, as mentioned earlier, I've added more cotton insulation in the attic to fill in those spots that were not properly insulated during the initial installation. I've also added more blown-in cellulose insulation to the particular spots in the walls where the infrared gun showed it was lacking and I was losing heat. I've added stiff foam board insulation in spots to fill leaks and cracks between the ceilings and the attic, and I've completely sealed the crawl space under my house with a combination of concrete and spray foam insulation to prevent massive air leaks.

This last task was a real surprise for me. Here in Southern California at least, homes that are built on a raised foundation always have a crawl space underneath, and that crawl space always has vents along the perimeter of the house. Those vents usually have a sort of wire-mesh cover to keep critters from nesting under the house.

I had assumed—as most people do, I'm sure—that those vents were necessary for airflow, to keep mold and mildew and fungus and who-knows-what from growing underneath the house. But when the experts at REAS pointed out just how much heat I was losing through that crawl space, I went ahead and sealed all of those vents.

I went the extra step and sealed the exterior access to my crawl space, too. Because I have a small basement under the center of my house, I can still access the crawl space from the basement. If you have a crawl space, of course you'll

An examination of areas of your home that may not be visible to the eye can help you detect unexplained energy losses.

still need to provide some access to that area so you can get at your ducting and plumbing. But you certainly can change the covering for that access from a big-mesh screen to a solid door.

Taking all of these steps made such an improvement in my home's ability to maintain a constant temperature that I was actually able to install a smaller heating and air-conditioning unit (see Chapters 11 and 12).

5

WINDOWS & DOORS

Changing to High-Efficiency Models to Reduce Heating & Cooling Costs

INSULATION IN THE ATTIC AND WALLS IS VITAL TO making your home more energy efficient, but that's not the whole equation. The other, very important part of the equation has to do with the other major portion of your home's exterior: the windows and doors. According to the National Association of Home Builders (see Resources, page 341), the average home today has nineteen windows, three exterior doors, and one patio door—so clearly windows and doors make up a large portion of a home's envelope. Reinsulating your attic and walls without addressing the doors and windows is sort of like driving a Hummer and buying a carbon credit: It's not really addressing the whole issue.

You can lose a lot of heat in the winter and gain a lot of heat during the summer through windows and doors, not to mention the drafts and far more obvious inefficiencies caused by windows and doors with poor seals. In fact, some experts estimate that *half* of a home's heating and cooling costs are spent because of leakage—talk about a waste—and much of this leakage is caused by windows and doors. The key is to seal your existing windows and doors first, then, as you're able to, upgrade to more energy-efficient options.

LOOKING FOR LEAKS

Evaluating your current windows and doors is a key part of your green home energy audit, and there're many ways to test them. Again, the best device you can use is an infrared monitoring device, like an infrared camera, which sees heat and cold and gives you a representation of both on a screen. A blower-door test is great, too (see Chapter 1, "The Green Home Audit," for more information).

Even without high-tech equipment, you can test your own windows and doors; you can do it with incense. Light a stick of incense and bring it near your window or door to see if there's a pressure change. Move the incense close to the areas where it's supposed to be sealed. If suddenly you see the smoke from that incense moving around wildly, you know you don't have a very good seal. You have a draft.

Another simple way to check the seal on your windows and doors is to use a dollar bill. If you can take a dollar bill and fit it between the two sides of a double-hung window, for instance, or any gap around any window, then you've got a problem. If you can slide a dollar bill in and out, then you have a gap large enough for air to pass through.

You may also encounter something a little perplexing: You may find that a particular window is sealed just fine. The smoke from the incense doesn't blow around, you can't fit a dollar bill anywhere in or around the window, but you still feel a draft when you're near the window.

If the window is sealed properly, where does the draft come from? It comes from *convection*. If you put your hand on the window in the wintertime, the glass will feel cold. When the warm air from your house hits the cold glass, that air cools. As you know, heat rises and cold sinks. So the now-cold air drops toward the floor, and warmer air rushes toward the cool window glass, creating an airflow pattern that you would call a draft—and increasing your heating bills and your energy usage.

Whether we're talking about windows or any other aspect of your home, you always want to start with the cheapest and easiest fixes first. Before you start replacing your existing windows and doors—or even while you're waiting for the new ones to be manufactured and delivered—if you've found any gaps or leaks, take the time to do some caulking or install some new weather stripping; it'll pay off.

Most of the weather stripping on the market these days is of the peel-and-stick variety. You just buy a roll of the stuff, like you do tape. For windows, apply the weather stripping anywhere the window opens. Also apply it to the frame and to the window sash. For doors, you'll want to install it along the threshold and possibly even along the side of the door jamb to close up any gaps.

Caulking is easy to do yourself, too. All you need is the caulking material and an applicator gun, then you run a bead along any areas that have a leak. Most home improvement stores not only sell the supplies you need but they also sometimes provide instruction on how to apply a bead for the best sealing and best-looking results.

Weather stripping and caulking are two very cheap and easy ways to stop many of the gaps that waste energy in your home and that cause you to lose heat in the winter and cool air in the summer. These leaks might even allow dust, dirt, and insects into your home. Make sealing leaks your number-one priority.

BUYING NEW WINDOWS

Once you're ready to install new windows, you have a lot of choices to make, starting with the number of panes. Single-pane windows—what originally came with my house and most houses built before 1960—are actually difficult to find now, I'm very happy to say. Double-pane windows are the norm, more than any other window.

I call them *double-pane windows*, but my friend Pat O'Brien from Pella (see Resources, page 341), which has been manufacturing windows and doors for more than eighty years, points out that they also are called *insulated glass* or *dual-glazing windows*. All these terms refer to the same thing.

For even more insulation, you can opt for triple-pane windows, which are superefficient from an energy standpoint. I would call them supergreen—although they are more expensive, and in some climates they may be more insulation than you really need.

If sound is a real issue at your home, that's another reason to opt for triple-pane windows. Pat points out that Pella's Designer Series windows and doors with triple glazing and laminated glass can reduce exterior noise significantly over standard dual or single-glazed products. So if you live on a noisy street, these windows are a good investment.

In every case, whether you choose windows with two panes of glass or with three panes, you'll have a space between those panes. That's for insulation. That space helps to reduce heat transfer. Sometimes there's just air in that space. And sometimes, between the glass, you'll have a gas like argon or krypton that makes the window even more efficient. Those gases allow even less heat transfer than plain air.

When a window does not have any gas inside—or any coatings on the outside, which we'll talk about in just a minute—the window is sometimes referred to as being *clear*. So a double-pane window with clear glass typically will have a better insulating value than single-pane glass. But gas fills and coatings and tints further improve a window's ability to resist heat transfer.

COATINGS

When it comes to window coatings, the phrase you'll hear often is *low-e coating* or *low-e glass*. These coatings are reflective. They help to reflect heat outside in the summertime, keeping your home cooler. They help to reflect heat inside in the wintertime, keeping your home warmer. In both cases, they reduce your heating and cooling costs and your energy needs. And coatings offer another benefit, too. Low-e coatings also reflect ultraviolet light, and that means they can help reduce fading of your carpet, your drapes, and your furniture. It's an added benefit that can save you a lot of money over time.

Another innovation you'll find in coatings are tints. Coatings come in gray tints, bronze tints, and green tints. Tint can really affect the amount of light coming through a window. You'll actually find some windows on the market that transmit just 15 percent of the light, which can make for a very dark room and increase your need for artificial light. As a rule of thumb, most people seem to perceive any window that transmits about 60 percent of the light or more as clear; they don't notice that these windows are tinted or restricting light transmission.

By reducing the amount of daylight coming into your home—and by reducing the amount of ultraviolet light coming in—windows can be dramatically more energy efficient. These coatings are particularly desirable in a hot climate, whether you live in the Sun Belt or in the desert, anywhere where heat gain in the summertime is a big concern.

WINDOW MATERIALS

Of course, windows are not just made of glass. They have a frame that goes around the outside of the window. And they have a sash or a transom—the part of the window that contains the glass and fits inside the frame. (The term *sash*

refers to the movable part of a window, whereas a *transom* window is fixed, or immovable.)

Today's windows also have *warm edge spacers* that keep the multiple panes in their proper location, as well as reduce heat flow and prevent condensation. Plus they have weather stripping and closing devices that help to create a good seal.

When you're shopping for windows, you don't just choose the kind of glass you want; you also get to choose the material used for the sash and the frame. They can be made from wood, aluminum, fiberglass composite, or vinyl, which is a type of plastic.

The frame and sash material makes a big difference—not just in terms of durability and maintenance, but also in terms of the environment. From an energy-efficiency standpoint, aluminum windows usually do not perform very well. You may find wood-frame windows that have a type of aluminum cladding on the outside. That's not the same as aluminum-frame windows. In the case of wood windows that have aluminum cladding, the aluminum is there to enhance durability and reduce maintenance, to reduce the need to strip and paint the windows on a regular basis. These windows can be very efficient, but windows with frames made exclusively from aluminum typically are not the best choice.

The other options—wood, fiberglass composite, and vinyl—can all be comparable, efficiency-wise. However, they're not all comparable from an environmental standpoint. I'm not in favor of vinyl windows. A very toxic process is used to make that polyvinyl chloride (PVC). During the manufacture of PVC, a couple of kinds of particularly harmful pollution are created: vinyl chloride monomer (VCM) and hydrogen chloride (HCl). Studies have proven that VCM and HCl cause serious health issues, including liver cancer, respiratory damage, and circulatory system failure.

Vinyl windows won't get termite or water damage, but that's not outweighed, for me, by the fact that there's such a toxic process involved in making PVC. And should your house ever burn, PVC releases a highly, highly toxic gas. So I would stay away from PVC.

What about fiberglass frames and sashes? As I mentioned in Chapter 4, "Insulation," I'm not a big fan of fiberglass. It's very hard to work with and can be very bad for your lungs. The better choice is definitely wood windows. And it is, of course, best if you know those windows have been made using sustainably harvested wood. My friend Pat at Pella tells me that the industry—or at least part of the industry—is trying to move toward using Forest Stewardship Council–certified wood or wood that has been certified by another respected organization. I know Pella strives to purchase all of its lumber from certified sources, and you certainly can ask about the wood used in a particular company's manufacturing process whenever you go shopping for windows.

You also can look for windows that are made with recycled glass. As you know, I'm a huge fan of recycling, and I was delighted to learn that Pella uses about 14 percent recycled glass

in its windows. Unlike some products, where 100 percent postconsumer recycled content is the goal, windows cannot be made from 100 percent recycled glass. There are structural, strength considerations that preclude the use of 100 percent recycled content. According to Pat, when it comes to the integrity of window glass, somewhere in the neighborhood of 20 percent is the current maximum. But some recycled content certainly is better than none, so that's another area to ask about when you're shopping for windows.

INSTALLATION

Some people consider window installation a do-it-yourself job. I do not. First of all, it's not an easy task. But beyond that, proper window installation makes all the difference, particularly when it comes to air leakage. The last thing you want to do is spend all that money on new windows and then not see a difference in your heating and cooling bills because you've installed them with leaks. To my mind, money spent on a licensed installation contractor is money well spent.

If you've never shopped for windows before, you might not realize that there's a difference between windows for a new installation—whether you're building a home or doing a remodel—and windows that are being retrofitted into existing openings.

The good news is, if you're working with existing openings—if, as I did, you're changing the windows on an older home to make it more energy efficient—you don't have to rip out all the window trim that gives your home its character. If you have a Victorian home or a Craftsman home or any style of home with architectural detail, you don't have to sacrifice style—or risk ruining the paint and the wallpaper and what-have-you inside your house—when you change to new energy-efficient windows. You can get new windows that fit directly inside your old openings.

You should be able to find windows in almost any size you need. For example, Pella offers windows in a wide range of sizes. The standard offerings range from 17×17 inches up to 54 inches wide and 73 inches tall. If you have a nonstandard opening for your old windows, the company can even make windows in ¼-inch or ⅛-inch increments, so you can get precisely the right size window. And if you have a really unusual window—something particularly small or particularly large—the company has custom manufacturing capabilities, as do many of the other major window manufacturers.

WINDOW TREATMENTS

Beyond the windows themselves, there are many things you can do to conserve energy and save money. I talked quite a bit about using window treatments in my first book, *Living Like Ed,* because window treatments can really make a difference in your energy savings. You could, as I have, put plantation shutters on some of your windows. That's a window treatment that also acts as another barrier to heat or cold. Drapes work for this, too.

The idea is to open the blinds or the drapes or whatever sort of window treatments you choose during a winter day, when you want the sun and the warmth to come into your home. You close them at night to keep in the heat—and if you're away from home in the winter, you'll want to keep them closed during the daytime, too.

Some windows even have built-in window treatments. These windows have either two or three panes of glass, and then, in between the panes, they have built-in shades or blinds. These windows come in different styles, so you can choose one that will go with your decor and price range.

With these built-in treatments, the blinds can still be turned to an open or closed position. And the shades and blinds can be completely opened from the bottom up or even from the top down—say, in a bathroom or a bedroom, where you want to let in light but still have your privacy. Because the window treatment is enclosed between those panes of glass, these window treatments never gather dust, they don't have to be cleaned, and they won't gather allergens that will affect your family's health. That's a big benefit.

 # BUYING NEW DOORS

When it comes to exterior doors for your home, most of the energy loss has to do with leaks around the door. So, as with windows, you'll want to check the seal around all of your exterior doors even before you consider replacing them. Industry experts recommend checking door weather stripping at least once a year.

And then, when you are ready to replace one or more of your exterior doors, you'll surely notice that not all doors are created equal. As with windows, door materials and doors' energy efficiency can vary widely. Some doors allow a lot more heat to transfer through the door itself than others. So if you have old exterior doors on your home, you may be able to enhance your home's insulating ability dramatically by changing to new, more efficient designs.

When it comes to materials, you can get new exterior doors made from wood, doors made from steel, and doors made from fiberglass. Again, I don't recommend fiberglass. I also do not recommend hollow doors. They're very light doors, of course, easy to hang and transport, which is why many builders use them and why you'll find inexpensive prices on them in stores. But a solid door is the best choice for its insulation factor. (Hollow doors are fine for inside your home, between rooms, if you don't mind noise coming through the door.)

Steel and fiberglass doors generally have some sort of core inside that has insulating properties, and you can find wood doors that also have an insulating core. They're actually called *wood-clad* doors. Of these, the steel and fiberglass doors generally are marketed as being more durable than wood and as requiring less maintenance. They also have very good in-sulating properties, with R-values in the range of R-5 to R-6.

Unfortunately, the insulating material inside most exterior doors is a polyurethane foam. Again, polyurethane is a petroleum-based product, with all of the attendant concerns. However, some manufacturers have begun using more environmentally friendly insulation materials.

If you can't find a petroleum-free insulated door, the alternative is a solid wood door. It obviously will not contain polyurethane. Plus, solid wood is a good natural insulator, though its R-value will not be as high as one of the insulated-core doors, so there is a trade-off. Of course, as with wood window frames, when you look for wood doors, you want to seek out a company that uses Forest Stewardship Council–certified lumber as much as possible.

Most replacement doors also come with a frame, much like a window. These doors are considered *prehung*. They're already attached to the frame, so they're easier to install and they'll seal well and also swing open and shut properly.

DOORS WITH BUILT-IN WINDOWS

Some doors also have decorative inserts—perhaps a stained-glass or leaded-glass design—or they have one or more windows built into the door. Naturally, a door only insulates as well as its weakest portion, so you want to make sure any windows or other decorative inserts will not adversely affect the door's ability to keep heat outside in the summer and keep heat inside in the winter.

Most of the time, these inserts and windows will be dual-pane. You do not want a door with a single-pane insert, any more than you want single-pane windows. One way to find out quickly if a leaded-glass insert is dual-pane or not is to slide your hand over both sides. If one side (usually the outside) feels smooth, then it's dual pane. If you can feel the bumpiness from the leading on both sides, it's probably single-pane.

Interestingly, some door manufacturers have purposely installed dual- and triple-pane windows with low-e coatings in their solid wood doors specifically to increase the doors' R-value. The glass portion of these doors actually insulates better than the wood portion.

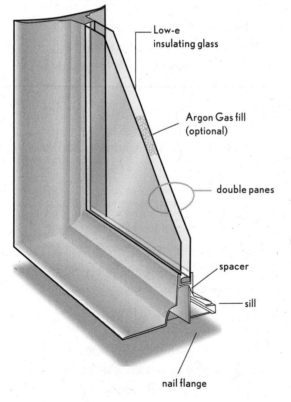

Low-e insulating glass

Argon Gas fill (optional)

double panes

spacer

sill

nail flange

Double-paned windows increase the window's ability to resist heat flow.

GETTING A GOOD SEAL

Another thing to check for when you're shopping for exterior doors is the type of weather stripping. Obviously, you want your doors to seal really well, just like your windows, to keep the heat or cold air in.

Most doors come with a compression seal. It's a soft foam–type material that gets compressed by the door when it's shut. The act of compressing this material forms a good seal—until the material gets worn out or damaged, which is why people often need to replace their doors' weather stripping. Besides durability, the other concern with this compression seal material is that it's made from PVC, which again is nasty stuff. However, for many years it was the only option for door sealing.

Now, some manufacturers have chosen another and even better approach: They're using magnets to make some of their doors seal more tightly. These magnetic seals work much like a refrigerator door, and they typically extend around the perimeter of the door and its frame to provide a very tight seal.

ENERGY-EFFICIENCY RATINGS

The sheer variety of window and door styles can be overwhelming, so I'm not going to try to influence your style. But I can help you choose more energy-efficient windows and doors—and skylights, too. It's just a matter of understanding some terms and some numbers.

Windows and doors and skylights are all rated based on their heat gain and loss, as well as their ability to transmit light. There are industry-standard ratings, created by a non-profit organization called the National Fenestration Rating Council (NFRC; see Resources, page 341). They administer the only uniform, independent grading and labeling system for energy performance of these products.

The NFRC's team of scientists has established certain protocols that the industry uses to rate a window or a door or a skylight as an entire unit. So with a window, it's not just the glass that gets rated. It's the entire unit, including the frame and sash and whatever sort of spacers are used to keep the panes of glass in place, and so on. With a door, the rating also includes the frame and any window or decorative leaded insert in the door panel.

Here's a breakdown of the various ratings that will make it easy for you to go comparison shopping:

- **U-factor:** the rate at which a window or door conducts nonsolar heat flow. The lower this number is, the better.
- **Solar heat gain coefficient (SHGC):** the fraction of solar radiation transmitted directly or absorbed through a window, then released as heat inside your home. A window with a lower rating is better at reducing cooling needs during the summer in a hot climate, while a window with a higher rating is better at collecting solar

heat gain during the winter to reduce heating costs.
- **Air leakage:** the rate at which air filters around a window when there's a specific pressure difference across it. The lower this number is, the better.
- **Visible transmittance (VT):** the amount of visible light that passes through a window's glazing. The higher this number is, the more visible light the window transmits. There's no right or wrong number with this one. You simply need to determine if glare is a concern, or if you need more or less light in a particular room.
- **Light-to-solar gain (LSG):** the ratio between the SHGC and VT. The higher this number is, the more light the window transmits *without* adding excessive amounts of heat.

Much like appliances, you can find Energy Star–certified windows and doors. According to the folks at Energy Star, a typical double-paned, clear-glass window lets about 75 percent of the sun's heat into your home. Most Energy Star–qualified windows (see Resources, page 341) transfer much less heat, usually without reducing the amount of visible light that's transmitted, so you get the light without having to crank up the air-conditioning. Local building codes also can affect your window choices. If your home is near the coast, for example, the building codes will be much more stringent about windows being able to

U-FACTOR CHART

Windows & Doors

Climate Zone	U-Factor[1]	SHGC[2]	
Northern	≤ 0.35	Any	
North/Central	≤ 0.40	≤ 0.55	
South/Central	≤ 0.40	≤ 0.40	Prescriptive
	≤ 0.41	≤ 0.36	Equivalent Performance (Excluding CA)
	≤ 0.42	≤ 0.31	
	≤ 0.43	≤ 0.24	*Products meeting these criteria also qualify in the Southern zone.*
Southern	≤ 0.65	≤ 0.40	Prescriptive
	≤ 0.66	≤ 0.39	Equivalent Performance
	≤ 0.67		
	≤ 0.68	≤ 0.38	
	≤ 0.69	≤ 0.37	
	≤ 0.70		
	≤ 0.71	≤ 0.36	
	≤ 0.72	≤ 0.35	
	≤ 0.73		
	≤ 0.74	≤ 0.34	
	≤ 0.75	≤ 0.33	

Skylights

Climate Zone	U-Factor[1]		SHGC[2]
	2001 NFRC rated at 20°[3]	RES97 rated at 90°[4]	
Northern	≤ 0.60	≤ 0.45	Any
North/Central	≤ 0.60	≤ 0.45	≤ 0.40
South/Central	≤ 0.60	≤ 0.45	≤ 0.40
Southern	≤ 0.75	≤ 0.75	≤ 0.40

[1] *Btu/h.ft². °F*

[2] *Fraction of incident solar radiation.*

[3] *U-Factor qualification criteria based on 2001 NFRC simulation and certification procedures that rate skylights at a 20-degree angle. Although reported U-Factor is higher than RES97 rated products, energy performance at the ENERGY STAR minimum qualifying level is equivalent.*

[4] *NFRC certification using the 1997 NFRC procedures for residential windows (RES 97) that rated skylights at a 90-degree angle. Skylights rated under this procedure may be present in the marketplace until March 31, 2008. NFRC labels for products using this procedure state: "RES97 rated at 90 degrees."*

withstand considerable wind and also rain, since serious storms can come in off the ocean. Your local building code will specify minimum design pressure ratings, and of course you'll need to—and certainly want to—comply.

Clearly, replacing tired, old doors and windows with new, more efficient models is a lot like adding insulation to your home. Not only will these changes conserve energy, they'll help make your home quieter and more peaceful.

And, in the long-term, they certainly will help you save money by reducing your heating and cooling costs.

But even beyond that, changing your doors and windows is, in some ways, even better than adding insulation. That's because insulation is pretty much hidden away. But new windows and doors have the added benefit of making your home more beautiful, too.

Sample Costs and Paybacks: Windows

The U.S. Department of Energy says, "About 15 percent of the average home's wall space is made up of windows. If those windows are old, loose, and leaky, they can account for 25 percent of a home's energy usage."

Changing your windows from single-pane to double-pane models is not inexpensive. You can expect to wait ten years to recoup your investment if you're switching over for cost- and energy-saving reasons. Of course, you do reap the benefits of a quieter and often cleaner, more dust-free home right away.

On the other hand, if your old windows happen to be broken or leaking, you can expect a much faster payback: in the neighborhood of just one or two years.

And the same goes for new construction. Simply opting for better, more efficient windows from the start when you're building a home has a very short, one- to two-year payback. Plus, that investment in better windows will enable you to choose a smaller, less expensive heating and cooling system.

The Energy Star folks help to put some numbers to this. According to them, for a typical home, switching to Energy Star–certified windows can help reduce your energy bill by as much as 15 percent. In dollar terms, they say the switch can save you $126 to $465 a year when replacing single-pane windows and $27 to $111 a year over double-pane, clear glass replacement windows.

Not surprisingly, your savings are going to be the most dramatic if you live somewhere with really hot summers, really cold winters, or both.

ED'S PROJECT

Replacing Old Leaking Windows

I use incense to check for window leaks.

When I first moved into my house, I realized it had some old leaking windows of the worst order. They were wonderful windows when they were purchased in 1936. But after fifty-plus years, they were very old, leaking windows that were crumbling from water damage and other problems, so they had to be replaced.

I was really lucky because T. M. Cobb (see Resources, page 341), the same company that manufactured the windows that were put in back in 1936, is still in business today. They still make the same windows, so I didn't have to sacrifice style—I didn't have to choose some other window design that might detract from the look of my house. I was able to get brand-new, energy-efficient, double-pane windows that look exactly the same as my old originals.

When I ordered new windows, I went room by room. I didn't do it all at once. You can't run up Mount Everest. You climb only as much as you can on a particular day. It's the same way you handle a project like replacing all your windows. Do as much as you can afford at one time and then tackle the others as your time and budget afford.

I changed the windows in my living room first because that room had a lot of glass space. Then I tackled the dining room windows and those in my daughter's bedroom. By 1990 almost the entire house had wonderful double-pane windows.

I should also mention that very soon after I moved in, I replaced the windows facing a major thoroughfare. I live about a block away from a very busy street, with lots of traffic noise. We also have airplanes that fly directly over the house. So I changed the windows that face that street not only for insulation but also for sound-abatement properties. You wouldn't believe the difference it made!

Since I changed to the double-pane windows, the sound from all of that is greatly reduced. It's a more serene atmosphere. With double-pane windows and insulation, I've created a more energy-efficient and peaceful home.

6

WATER USAGE

Conserving—& Even Reusing—
This Precious Resource

THERE'S AN OLD SAYING: WHISKEY IS FOR DRINKING and water is for fighting. And I think it's true. We've certainly had a lot of water wars over the years—throughout civilization, and most recently in arid states including Arizona, Nevada, and California. And we'll continue to have conflict over water as more and more development occurs and the available resources become more scarce.

Water scarcity might prove to be very challenging for places like Southern California, where nearly all of our water comes from elsewhere. In Southern California, we get our water from the Owens Valley, from the California Aqueduct, and from the Colorado River.

But there's been a lot of recent development occurring in places like Las Vegas, Phoenix, Tucson, and Scottsdale, and everybody wants their share of the water. Traditionally, they've been able to get it, but more and more development has spread those resources all the more thin. Visit Lake Shasta in California. You need only drive by it to see how low the water is. Lake Mead and Lake Powell are drawn down very, very low, too.

There are many theories from climatologists about drought cycles. What if the theories are correct about the Sierra snowpack? How much snow will there be in the future? Ski resorts are beginning to feel the pinch on this one already. What if there's less moisture coming in the form of snow and more coming in the form of rain? As weather patterns change, this could be a big problem for places like my home state of California.

Owens Valley is a source of much water used in Southern California. It has sustained significant environmental damage over the years.

But these problems are not restricted to California. Georgia has experienced a big drought. It's hit Florida and the Carolinas, too. There have been droughts in many parts of the country that traditionally haven't had a drought cycle in a very long time.

So we need to be more conscious of our water use, in both the amount of water that we waste as consumers and the amount of water that is wasted in old irrigation practices in agriculture—the biggest areas for saving water. If we can encourage our farmers to practice more water conservation measures, rather than flooding crops the way they've done with canals, they can target that water on the crops in a more efficient manner. We can save a great deal of water with these small measures.

Delivery is a big issue. The beauty of the Owens Valley project in Los Angeles that William Mulholland designed years ago was that it all ran downhill from the Owens Valley through aqueducts and through holes dug in the mountains. The water was gravity fed. Indeed not only did the designers use no electricity to get it from the Owens Valley, they generated some electricity at the bottom of the pipeline to give Los Angeles some of its first electrical power.

That's not the case anymore. It's impossible to get water from the California Aqueduct or from the Colorado River through gravity. The terrain makes it impossible. So what they do is pump the water around using lots of electricity. They reclaim a bit of it on the way downhill, but only a fraction of it.

It takes a great deal of electricity to pump water around the State of California in order to get it where it's needed. And so when you save water, you're not just saving that H_2O. You're saving a great deal of C, otherwise known as carbon, as well. You're saving a lot of fossil fuel, because at the end of the day, a small part of that electricity is produced from clean sources like hydropower and renewables, but a lot of it comes from burning coal or methane.

So if you're saving water, you're also saving electricity.

We can't just bring water to California from the Midwest, for instance. The distance is just too vast, and the resources there are stretched thin as well. You know, the Ogallala Aquifer—the vast, underground reservoir that's been available for years under a few states in the High Plains, including Texas, Wyoming, and Nebraska—is getting tapped dry, too.

The United States doesn't have the water resources that we had just a few decades ago. Changes are going to have to be made. It starts with conserving at the municipality level. Residential users can make a big difference, and so can commercial users, from hotels and hospitals to schools and offices.

WATER USE INSIDE THE HOME

From a residential standpoint, people can cut back on their water usage in a variety of ways. Some of it is behavioral, and some of it involves changing a few items around your house.

Behavioral stuff is a big part of the equation. I talked about it quite a bit in my first book, *Living Like Ed*. I think I was still a teenager when I thought, "Why am I running the water when I'm brushing my teeth? The water comes from somewhere, and it goes to somewhere. And why would I waste it?" So I started turning off the water when I brushed my teeth. I started taking navy showers to save water—turning the water off while I soaped up, then turning it back on just to rinse off—because I knew water was a resource that was scarce in many parts of the world and there was no reason to waste it. These are just a few examples, but there're many ways to modify your behavior and use a lot less water.

According to the Metropolitan Water District of Southern California, the breakdown for water usage inside a typical American home (not counting exterior usage for landscaping and such, which we'll be discussing later) is as follows:

TOILETS: 28%

LAUNDRY: 23%

SHOWER: 19%

FAUCETS: 15%

LEAKS: 12%

DISHWASHER: 3%

When trying to conserve, the first thing you want to do is fix any leaks. You can save a tremendous amount of water just by fixing things that are broken.

There are also many devices that you can install around your home to help you save water—and to help your state save energy and therefore help the environment in that way, too. Changing your toilets, changing your faucets, changing your showerheads, changing appliances, using your appliances properly, and maybe even taking the next step and using *gray water* for some of your water needs are all efforts you can make.

TOILETS

There was a move in the early 1990s in Los Angeles and in many parts of the country to switch to toilets that used a lower volume of water for each flush. In L.A., these low-flow toilets indeed were mandated for any new development or remodel.

I got my first low-flush toilet in 1990, and it was called a Porcher. It was a French toilet, it had a single button on the top, and it used a lot less water. American Standard and Moen weren't making low-flush toilets at that time. So I bought what was available and it worked well. I had it for years, until it finally started to break down. The parts were difficult to find, but by that time, American Standard and a few other major manufacturers were making a low-flow toilet that worked very well.

There's a reason manufacturers have embraced the low-flush toilet model: For quite a few years now, local governments and utilities have been offering rebates and other incentives to get homeowners and business owners to change out their old toilets for more efficient models. It's a smart plan for everybody, because we use less water and the municipalities and states spend less money—and less energy— moving water around.

In fact, low-flow toilets are now required by federal law. Toilets that are sold in this country today must not exceed 1.6 gallons per flush (gpf). Those are low-flow or low-volume toilets.

There is also the *high-efficiency toilet* (HET). It takes water efficiency to the next level and uses less than 1.3 gallons per flush. This is a new standard, and it's exciting. The Environmental Protection Agency (EPA) released its specifications for what qualifies as an HET in 2007. Best of all, the EPA has a partner program called WaterSense that's sort of the water-wise equivalent of the Energy Star program. Quite simply, in order to even be considered for a WaterSense label, a particular product must

- be about 20 percent more water-efficient than average products in that category
- provide measurable results
- be independently certified to meet the EPA's criteria for water efficiency and performance

The idea is to make it easy for people like you and me to find products that save water without sacrificing performance. Obviously, in the case of toilets, we want them to flush properly. We don't want to have to flush them a second time to get the job done, since that's not going to save water.

The EPA actually says that if all the older, less efficient toilets in American homes—just in homes, we're not talking about businesses or public places here—were replaced with high-efficiency toilets, we could save nearly 2 billion gallons of water per day in this country. *Per day!*

Obviously, I'd like to encourage everybody to make this switch. It's easy to do now, since the WaterSense section on the EPA's website includes a list of HETs, and the list is updated regularly. You can scroll down the list and see that there are twenty American Standard brand toilets, twelve different Kohler brand toilets, thirty-something Caroma brand toilets (see Resources, page 341), and so on that all meet the HET criteria. That means they've been tested and certified by independent third parties. So when you go shopping, print out this list and tell the salesperson which specific toilets you're looking for.

TOILET TECHNOLOGY

Most toilets, since the very beginning of the invention, have been of a siphon design. An Englishman by the name of Joseph Adamson invented the siphon flush toilet in 1853. Essentially, it—and the vast majority of toilet designs since—features a tank to hold water. When you flush the toilet, water rushes out of the tank and into the bowl, forcing waste out over a dam, or a trap, inside the bottom part of the toilet. When the water rushes over that bend, it literally creates a siphon—a siphonic effect—which is what pulls down waste. Then, when the bowl has emptied, the tank refills so it's ready for the next flush.

If you remember what old toilets looked like—even the ones you see now in Victorian bed-and-breakfasts and other places that strive for a period-correct look—there was a tank high above the toilet bowl. Gravity would help get the water flowing fast enough to force waste over the dam. Later toilet designs had better flow characteristics, so gravity was no longer a necessary factor and toilet tanks were moved down to the location we're used to, which is just above and behind the bowl.

Toilet technology in this country actually changed little from that point—around 1915—until 1994, when the government mandated that a flush use no more than 1.6 gallons of water.

I find it interesting, but really not surprising, that low-water-usage technology for toilets came from Europe, Australia, and Asia—it came from parts of the world that don't have the water resources that we do. Nations on these continents have been involved in this technology for years. The Japanese, for example, have become known for their efforts to create the perfect toilet.

As it happens, several different technologies are used to create today's high-efficiency toilets. You can get an HET that is siphonic, pressurized, washdown, or dual flush. I have a very efficient toilet at home that's an Australian model from a company called Caroma, and it has two buttons on top for two different flush modes. You literally choose how much water you use for a particular flush based on your, shall we say, *activities* in the bathroom. It has one button for a lesser amount of water required and a second button for a greater water requirement. So you can save a great deal of water by tailoring the flush to your actual needs every time.

My friend Derek Kirkpatrick from Caroma explains how his company's toilets work. "We've created chambers, basically they're ribs inside the vitreous china, which act as rapids. They speed the water up to create that velocity, to give a powerful push to the water that's being discharged, and as it hits the waste on a Caroma toilet—a washdown or a dual— it pushes the waste first. So it's waste first, water after. But what's very, very different in a Caroma toilet is a larger trap configuration. It's almost four inches, and it's called a Roman trap. It's very simplistic. It's just one sweeping bend down. That way, it doesn't have any places for paper to catch up or blockage to occur.

"The rapids speed the water up as it comes through in a jettison, a larger volume, at the discharge from the front of the bowl right to the waste. That's as opposed to a siphonic, which is a really slow, lazy swirl, where it takes a long time before that waste leaves the bowl and all your water is going to create that si-

phon. Whereas in a washdown, it's utilizing the most effective way to flush a toilet, and that's a large volume of water all at once, even though it's low volume in comparison to what was out there in the years past. But at 1.6 [gpf], it acts as if there's more water in the tank and into the bowl."

The other style of toilet is called *pressure-assist*. It has a button on top of the tank that you push when you want to flush. A pressurized canister actually pressurizes the water to force the waste down using less water than an old-fashioned siphon design.

UTILITY REBATES AND VOUCHERS

One of the best things about changing your toilet, in many parts of the country, is you may actually get a rebate or some other monetary incentive for doing so. Not only do you wind up with a better toilet, not only do you conserve water, but you also can get some money back in the form of a rebate, in addition to saving money on your water bill.

All you have to do is contact your local water provider and ask if they have a rebate program for replacing your older toilet with a new HET model. (Some utilities still offer rebates for installing an ultra-low-flow toilet, which adheres to the 1.6 gpf standard.)

If your utility has a rebate program, typically you simply buy whichever efficient toilet you want and then you send your receipt to the utility and the company sends you a check. For instance, recently the East Bay Municipal Utility District in Northern California was offering a $150 rebate per toilet—for up to three toilets in a single residence. The Board of Water Supply for the city and county of Honolulu was offering a $100 rebate for installing an ultra-low-flow toilet. The Water Utilities Department in Tempe, Arizona, was offering a rebate of 50 percent of the purchase price for a 1.6 gpf toilet, up to $75. The city of Austin, Texas, was offering a tiered rebate program: up to $150 per toilet for replacing pre-1996 toilets with qualifying HET models, up to $75 per toilet for replacing pre-1996 toilets with qualifying 1.6 gpf models, up to $50 per toilet for replacing 1.6 gpf toilets with qualifying HETs, and up to $50 per toilet for installing HETs in new construction.

Some municipalities even have a voucher program. In many ways, this is better than a rebate program because the toilet is free. But you do get precisely the toilet they provide—you have no choice as to the style or size or color, which obviously wouldn't fly too well in my household, where aesthetics have to be a consideration.

If your water district has a voucher program, odds are you'll get a voucher in the mail with your bill. It might instruct you to go to a particular location on a certain day with that voucher to pick up a new toilet. Then you usually have a certain amount of time to turn in your old toilet, which goes to a charitable organization to be recycled. Incentives and rebates on WaterSense-qualified toilets can be found on the WaterSense website (see Resources, page 342).

URINALS

It may seem sort of extravagant to have a urinal in your home. But you can save a considerable amount of water if the men in your household use a urinal instead of a toilet when it's appropriate. Today, there are urinals that use just a single pint of water when they flush, and there are others that are completely waterless.

Caroma has come out with a 1-pint design that actually has a motion sensor inside to detect when urine is present. After the urinal has been used, it waits a short time and then flushes automatically. It turns out that this automatic-flush design—with the motion sensor *inside* the urinal—is much more water-wise than the other sort of motion sensors you see in public restrooms, the kind that look for movement beyond the urinal (or beyond the toilet). Those sensors often "ghost flush"—that is, they often flush unnecessarily, which obviously wastes water.

While the EPA's WaterSense program has not yet issued a standard for urinals, urinals that flush with less than .05 gallon are considered high-efficiency urinals, or HEUs.

As for the waterless urinals, they typically have no moving parts whatsoever. The bowl's surface is treated to be urine-repellant, and then there's a seal that floats over the trap, so odors don't enter the bathroom. Obviously, a waterless urinal can save a considerable amount of water in a household or office, anywhere you've got some guys.

According to Falcon Waterfree Technologies (see Resources, page 341), which makes Waterfree Urinals, "Using water to dispose of water makes no economic sense, particularly in a world facing a very limited supply of readily available fresh water." The company says its Waterfree Urinals can save you money in two important ways. First Falcon systems are less expensive than flush urinals, both to buy one and to have it installed, because they have no flushing mechanism. All you need is a drainage outlet—no water pipe going in—and they typically require less than an hour to install and seconds to put the funnel-shaped, replaceable cartridge in the bottom. You'll save 100 percent of the water going through the urinal—or through your toilet—and 100 percent of the cost for that water, plus you may see lower sewer charges, both of which can be significant if you have several men in your household.

According to Falcon, in a public restroom, each waterfree urinal saves an average of 40,000 gallons of water per year—that's enough to fill nine tanker trucks. That's why the Metropolitan Water District (MWD) of Southern California (see Resources, page 342) actually has a free retrofit program; the district literally is paying to install the urinals in commercial buildings at no cost to the building owners. I'm sure you'd be entertained to know that the program is officially called Pee Green.

SHOWERHEADS

Clearly toilets and urinals are not the only places we use (and waste) water in our homes. According to the EPA, home showers use more than 1.2 trillion gallons of water each year in the United States. This is an area where we can make a real difference when it comes to the quantity of water we use.

Naturally, there are behavioral factors involved. For instance, taking shorter showers will make a difference. Perhaps you can choose to shave at the sink—by filling the basin with water (not letting the tap run)—instead of shaving in the shower. Or you can take a navy shower like I do, as mentioned earlier; it really saves water.

But even without modifying your behavior one bit, you can save a considerable amount of water simply by changing your showerhead. I've been using low-flow showerheads for a long time, and the technology has improved greatly. They used to produce this mist, which was certainly not what I would call soothing. You could stand in there a long time, and it would be difficult to get the soap off your body or the shampoo or conditioner out of your hair.

Now low-flow showerheads use very little water and they're very pleasant. They give you the illusion that you're getting more water on your body than actually is the case. They're better aerated and more comfortable.

As is the case with toilets, there are federal standards in place for showerheads. The

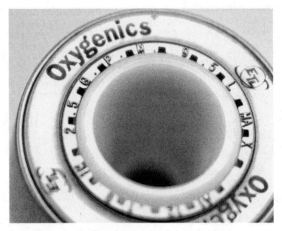

Low-flow showerheads use much less water.

water and creating less sewage, but you will also be saving energy. How so? Because you'll be using less hot water, which means your water heater won't have to work as much. So you can save money three ways—on your water bill, on your sewage bill (depending on how your utility company bills for sewage), and on your gas or electric bill—simply by adjusting your water usage in the shower.

FAUCETS AND AERATORS

current standard is 2.5 gallons per minute (gpm), which was established by the Energy Policy Act of 1992. Meanwhile, the EPA's WaterSense program is working on creating a new standard for high-efficiency showerheads, which will flow in the range of 1.5 to 2.0 gpm. Once that standard is finalized, you'll be able to find a list of these showerheads on the EPA's website (see Resources, page 341).

Not sure if you have a low-flow showerhead? If you do, the gpm rating should be marked on the side.

You currently can find showerheads on the market that flow as little as 1.2 or even 1.0 gpm. Some even have a pause button, so you can stop the flow of water without having to readjust all your settings when you start up again—this is a real boon if you decide to adopt my navy shower approach!

Here's the benefit to using less water when you shower: you will not only be using less

How else can you conserve water? From a behavior standpoint, you can stop running the tap while you brush your teeth. That alone could save 3,000 gallons a year! As I mentioned previously, you can fill the basin and turn off the faucet while you shave. You also can change to low-flow bathroom faucets or add faucet aerators.

Aerators are considered a *faucet accessory*. They cost something like five bucks, and they screw onto your faucet. An aerator will conserve water while also increasing spray velocity, so it seems as if you're getting just as much—if not more—flow. Faucet aerators also can reduce splashing. And they can provide flow rates as low as 2.2, 1.5, 1.0, or even 0.5 gpm. This is an option if you're really budget-conscious or if you really love the look of your current faucet.

As for the low-flow faucets, like low-flow showerheads, they've come a long way since I first

Sample Costs and Paybacks: Bathroom Fixtures

You can find WaterSense-qualified toilets for as little as $99. So how long will it take for that toilet to pay for itself?

Let's say your old toilet was made between 1980 and 1994. In that case, every flush uses 3.5 gallons of water. When you replace your 3.5 gpf toilet with a new WaterSense-qualified HET, you can expect to save 4,000 gallons of water a year, on average, and about $90 each year on your water bills. Clearly, it won't take much more than a year to break even on a $99 toilet purchase, if you can do the installation yourself.

If your old toilet is even older—if it's a pre-1980 model that flushes 5 gallons of water every time you use it—you can expect to save two or even three times as much money on your water bills each year. So the toilet will pay for itself in no time. Plus, your sewer bill also should drop as you send less water down the toilet, so look for savings there, too.

And if you get a substantial rebate—rebates currently range from $25 to more than $200—you could break even on a toilet swap in no time. (Note: Rebates will not exceed the actual cost of the toilet, so you can't come out ahead on the rebate alone.)

What about urinals? You can find urinals that use 1 gallon of water for each flush—the current standard—for less than $150. Even switching from an HET toilet that uses 1.3 gpf to one of these urinals when appropriate means you'll be using 25 percent less water. And if you have a higher-flow toilet, you'll save that much more.

As for bathroom faucets, aerators can be as cheap as five bucks apiece. And new faucets start at less than $20.

If you have an older faucet right now, it may flow anywhere from 3 to 7 gpm. WaterSense-qualified faucets and aerators flow 1.5 gpm or less. So you could easily be cutting your bathroom sink water use in half or more. The EPA estimates an average home will save 500 gallons of water a year by making the switch. Plus, you'll be using less hot water, so you'll be spending less on heating water at home, too.

The same is the case for showerheads. Replacement handheld showerheads start at about $12, and the wall-mount designs start at a little more than $15. So again, you don't have to save a whole lot of water—not to mention energy heating your water—to break even.

began using them. Nowadays they work just fine for getting the soap off your hands and such.

Again, there's a federal standard for faucets. New faucets cannot flow more than 2.2 gpm. But if you have older faucets in your bathroom, they can flow as much as 3 to 7 gpm. There's also a WaterSense standard for faucets and faucet aerators. These high-efficiency models flow no more than 1.5 gpm, but maintain adequate pressure and, again, they've undergone a third-party certification process. For ease in shopping, these faucets and aerators are listed on the WaterSense website (see Resources, page 342). Big-name manufacturers like Delta, Moen, and Price Pfister all make WaterSense-qualified faucets. And you can find a wide variety of WaterSense-qualified aerators from a company called Neoperl.

The EPA says, "If every household in the United States installed WaterSense-qualified bathroom sink faucets or faucet accessories, we could save approximately $600 million in energy costs and more than 60 billion gallons of water annually—enough to meet public water demand in Miami for more than 150 days!"

On a more personal level, the average homeowner can expect to save more than 500 gallons of water each year by making the switch—and again, you can expect to spend less on making hot water, too.

If you're wondering why the WaterSense program focuses on bathroom faucets and not kitchen faucets, Stephanie Thornton from WaterSense has your answer: "Bathroom faucets and kitchen faucets are used for really different purposes. Typically, in the kitchen, people want to fill things up, like fill up the sink or fill up the pot. In the bathroom, you're just running the faucet to wash your hands or wash your face, so changes in water flow don't matter, as long as pressure remains the same."

PROPER APPLIANCE USAGE

Another way you can change your behavior slightly and make a real difference has to do with the way you use your appliances. Dish washing and clothes washing can be done very efficiently.

Let me start with the clothes washing. I have a Maytag Neptune washer (see Resources, page 342). It's a major brand, clearly, and it uses a fraction of the water of a normal washer. While the EPA's WaterSense website doesn't include clothes washers, the EPA's Energy Star website does. As you would expect, of course Energy Star–qualified appliances save energy. But in the case of washing machines, they also save water. "By dramatically reducing energy and water consumption, these units cut utility bills by an average of $50 per year," according to Energy Star. "Qualified clothes washers also save 7,000 gallons of water a year."

How you use the washing machine matters, too. For starters, you always want to run a full load. Yes, you can adjust newer clothes washers according to the size of your load, and that will save some water, but the optimal way to save water *and* energy is to run only full loads.

The same goes for dishwashers. For years, I washed dishes by hand because I thought it was more energy efficient and more water efficient. But today's Energy Star–qualified dishwashers are even more efficient than I am. Now I have a Whirlpool Gold Series Quiet Partner IV (see Resources, page 342), which has made my wife a lot happier. But it's made me happier, too, because high-efficiency dishwashers like this one save a lot of energy and a lot of water over older models. In fact, Energy Star models use at least 41 percent less energy than the federal minimum standard for dishwashers, plus they save a considerable amount of water, too. And again, they even provide some savings over doing dishes by hand.

As with clothes washers, you always want to run a full load in the dishwasher. Especially since you can't adjust the amount of water used by most dishwashers, the only way to optimize water and energy usage is by running a full load every time.

GRAY WATER

Another way to use less water is to *reuse* water. This is another form of recycling, and it's not altogether uncommon in rural areas in this country, where people rely on well water and septic systems.

While you certainly wouldn't want to reuse any of the water that goes down your toilet or urinal, you can reuse what's considered *gray water*. (Waste water from a toilet or urinal is considered *black water*.)

Gray water is water that has been used *anyplace else* in your home, including in your bathroom sink, shower, clothes washer, and dishwasher. Some people consider kitchen-sink water to be gray water, as long as it does not include ground-up food waste. Other experts exclude kitchen-sink water because it can contain bacteria like E. coli and salmonella.

Altogether, gray water accounts for 50 percent to 80 percent of all waste water in a home. Reusing some of this gray water means you'll be using much less fresh water, thereby reducing your water needs dramatically. You'll also be sending less wastewater into the sewer system or into your septic system.

Now, typically, you wouldn't want to drink or cook with gray water. But believe it or not, there are purification systems that could make it potable again, though they're a rarity. Most commonly, gray water is used for landscape irrigation, which we'll go into in Chapter 10, "Garden and Compost."

Indoors, gray water is most commonly used for flushing toilets—a very logical choice. Caroma also has designed a prototype toilet that has a sink built into the tank. You wash your hands and the gray water is then stored and used for the next flush. Such toilets also are

The California Aqueduct is a system of canals, tunnels, and pipelines that conveys water collected from the Sierra Nevada Mountains and the valleys of Northern and Central California to Southern California.

in use in Japan. I think this is a brilliant idea, and I wouldn't be surprised if it were adopted by the green-building community here.

There are two big issues when it comes to using gray water in your home: plumbing and building codes. Obviously, you'll need to change an existing home's plumbing to avoid sending gray water into the sewer line. And of course you'll need a way to store the gray water until you need it.

Also, gray water is not legal in every area. It probably won't come as much of a surprise that really arid states such as Arizona and New Mexico have been faster to embrace the use, whereas the idea can be an issue when you want to get a building permit in many other states. There's a great article online that covers what is legal in various states and how to create a system that meets those requirements; you can find it on the Natural Home website (see Resources, page 342).

There are a variety of products on the market today that will treat gray water to make it safer for use both indoors and out. For example, Brac Systems (see Resources, page 341) makes a variety of home-size gray water systems, which include a storage tank, a pump, and a programmable chlorination system that uses only enough chlorine to keep the gray water sterile. The smallest system is designed for use in houses or condos that have three or fewer people living there; it holds 39 gallons of gray water. The largest system can handle up to twelve people living in a home and holds 119 gallons.

THE BOTTLED-WATER PROBLEM

I live in L.A., as you know, and I'm always amazed by how many people I see walking around with bottles of water. It's as if no one in this city even drinks tap water anymore.

States and municipalities spend incredible sums of money to bring water right to our homes. And then what do we do? We drive to the store, we burn fossil fuel, and we buy water imported from Fiji. That water was processed and put into plastic bottles—and you know how I feel about plastic, which is a petroleum product. Plus is it good for us to be drinking water that's stored in plastic bottles? I highly doubt it. I certainly don't want plastic leaching into the water I put into my body. Not to mention the fact that some of those bottles of water get shipped halfway around the world. Even the domestic bottled water gets trucked to warehouses and then trucked to retail stores. Bottled water just creates this horribly unnecessary carbon footprint.

Also, there's the issue of recycling. Industry estimates say 80 percent of the bottled water containers still wind up in landfills. This is a huge—and hugely unnecessary—problem.

Even buying water from a company like Sparkletts or Arrowhead has an obvious environmental impact. Yes, you're getting good, clean drinking water, but it's being trucked all around the country, and that's creating considerable emissions.

So what's the alternative? Water that is already delivered to our homes: tap water.

I'm not saying tap water is perfect. It has chlorine in it, and it can have some other pretty nasty substances, too. Groundwater all around the world has been shown to contain a wide

This filter treats all the water in my house, from the sink to the shower.

variety of contaminants. But I wholeheartedly believe that we're much better off *treating* the water that already comes into our homes. We're better off using some kind of water filter to get rid of the chlorine and other contaminants than we are buying bottled water that's been trucked all around the world.

Water filters certainly come in all shapes and sizes. You can buy a pitcher that has a water filter inside, so you just put the pitcher under your tap and fill it up. You can get a filter that attaches to your faucet in the kitchen or in the bathroom or wherever you choose. You can buy a whole-house water filtration system.

Frankly, I prefer to cook with filtered water and shower with filtered water and wash my hands with filtered water, too. Studies have shown that you can actually absorb more toxins from your water by *showering* in it than by *drinking* it. So I'm a big fan of whole-house water filtration systems. Some of these systems require a storage tank, since they filter water slowly, while others can filter water on-demand as it comes into your home.

 ## WAYS TO FILTER WATER

Not surprisingly, there are quite a few different ways to filter water today. For the most part, the many ways to filter water fall into two different categories: chemical and particle.

Some have a physical barrier that traps particles. And some rely on chemistry to trap contaminants.

Some of these filtration methods also are better for tap water, while others are more applicable if you're using well water or some other source for your drinking water.

Let's look at the different methods of filtration.

CHARCOAL OR CARBON

Charcoal has been used as a filter practically forever, and it's by far the most common filtration medium today. Charcoal removes contaminants from water chemically. Basically, the contaminants bind onto the charcoal in a process called *adsorption,* while the water flows right on past. There are grades of charcoal, with activated carbon at the top of the heap. One of the reasons carbon is so popular for water filtration is it's very good at removing chlorine from water. Most municipalities use chlorine to treat their water supplies. They use it to kill bacteria and to make the water safe to drink. But there's a reason chlorine kills all those organisms. It's toxic. And chlorine itself isn't the only problem. When chlorine mixes in a city's water supply with volatile organic compounds (VOCs), it can form some nasty substances, like trihalomethanes, which are known carcinogens. Also, carbon can adsorb more than just chlorine. It can adsorb a broad assortment of contaminants, VOCs, radon, pesticides, industrial solvents, benzene, some metals, and some heavy metals, like arsenic and mercury.

LifeSource Water Systems (see Resources, page 342) has developed a whole-house treatment system that filters water using medical-grade, coconut shell–based carbon. Let me be clear—this is not a water softener. A typical water softener reduces the build-up of lime scale in pipes, water heaters, toilets, sinks, tubs, and so on, which is caused by too much calcium and magnesium in the water. But a water softener causes its own problems. According to my friend Jerry Dickson of LifeSource, "What a salt-water softener does is take the calcium and magnesium out of your water through a process known as *ion exchange*. The calcium and magnesium ions are *exchanged* on a 2 for 1 basis with sodium ions. So for every one part calcium [that] is removed, it is replaced with two parts sodium in the water. Well . . . that water's not terribly pleasant to drink. And if you've got high blood pressure problems, renal problems, that kind of thing, it's really not recommended." Salt softeners waste a lot of water and cause serious problems for the environment by discharging salt-laden brine into the waste-water system. That salt brine is difficult and expensive to reclaim and can cause problems with the water table. The salt brine runoff is potentially very harmful for agriculture. That is why salt-water softeners are being banned in many parts of California. Other states are now looking into the environmental damage that salt-based water softeners may be causing.

"So when we developed our system, we wanted to address both of those problems: water waste, as well as the health implications," says Jerry. The LifeSource unit is probably bigger than you'd expect. If you're used to the carbon filters that go in a water pitcher or that screw into your refrigerator to filter your drinking water, this is much bigger. In fact, LifeSource filters are typically around 5 feet tall. So the water travels down through this granular activated carbon filter. The standard size system is certified to filter up to 1.6 million gallons of municipally treated water. That is far more than any other system is certified for at present. It works quickly, so no storage tank is required.

CERAMIC

Ceramic filters have very small openings, so they trap contaminants physically. Some ceramic filters use silver to help trap bacteria as small as .22 micron (about $\frac{1}{100,000}$ of an inch) and to prevent the growth of algae and bacteria inside the filter. Ceramic filters will trap dirt, bacteria (including E. coli and salmonella), protozoan cysts, viruses, and other debris. However, they do not trap chemicals, including chlorine, so ceramic and carbon filtration sometimes are combined in a two-stage system. These are typically not necessary with water from municipal systems, as they are required by law to remove contaminants and must test their water frequently.

Water Systems Comparison Chart

Reverse Osmosis	Bottled Water	Exchange Tank	Water Softener	LifeSource
Cost Per Gallon: $0.18 to $0.25	**Cost Per Gallon:** $0.79 to $5.00	**Cost Per Gallon:** $0.006 to $0.010	**Cost Per Gallon:** $0.12 to $0.23	**Cost Per Gallon:** $0.00202
• Expensive	• Expensive	• Expensive ($30 - $75 monthly)	• Expensive	• Inexpensive
• Yearly filter/membrane replacement and maintenance costs from $90 to $180.	• Generally good tasting water.	• Not generally used for drinking.	• Not generally used for drinking.	• Provides delicious, clean, odor-free water from every faucet in a home.
• Aggressive, low ph water.	• Quality may be no better than tap water.	• Leaves a slick feeling on skin after shower and bath.	• Leaves a slick feeling on skin after shower and bath.	• Excellent for drinking, washing, clothes, etc.
• Limited amount of water available.	• Plastic bottles should not be re-used.	• May require bi-weekly replacement and/or multiple exchange tanks.	• Requires frequent replacement of salt (sodium or potassium chloride)	• Effective service life varies from 16-25 years.
• Wastes significant amounts of water.	• Bottles may leach PCB's into the water.	• For drinking water, requires use of reverse osmosis or bottled water.	• For drinking water, requires use of reverse osmosis or bottled water.	• Various sizes available
• Not good for plants or pets.	• Plastic bottles create environmental issues.	• Deliveries may require driver access to garages.	• Good water for dishwashing.	• NO regular Maintenance or filter changes.
		• Good water for dishwashing.	• Not good for plants or pets.	• Does NOT use salt, potassium, chemicals, or magnets.
		• Not good for plants or pets.	• Banned in many communities due to salt brine backwash.	• Installations NOT restricted by any legislation
		▶ Detailed Comparison	▶ Detailed Comparison	▶ Learn More

▶ Detailed Comparison

SAND OR SILICA

Many multistage filtration systems will use sand, or silica, as the first step. Sand is good at removing physical contaminants, like dirt, rust, silt. But it's used only as the first stage in a multistage system, since it doesn't remove chemicals.

KDF

Kinetic Degradation Fluxion is another common type of filtration that's used in a multistage process. Sand might be the first stage, and then KDF is the second stage. Like carbon, KDF is very good at removing chlorine from water, and you only need half as much KDF as you do carbon. However, there's a drawback to KDF. It's an alloy of zinc and copper, and it has a tendency to leach some of that copper into the water. It is also difficult to clean and refresh because it requires hot water to backwash effectively.

DISTILLATION

Just as you can distill corn or potatoes and make alcohol, you can use electricity to boil water and create a pure vapor or steam. Distillation does an excellent job of filtration, but you could say it's too good: You distill out the things you don't want, but you also distill out all of the minerals or dissolved solids, and you need some of them that are beneficial in your drinking water. Distilled water also can become "aggressive." In other words, that water will leach impurities out of its container, so if you put distilled water in a plastic bottle, it will leach off some of that plastic into the water. For exactly that reason, drinking distilled water can be *good* when you have some sort of toxicity; if you have heavy metal poisoning or if you need to detox your body in some other way, drinking distilled water can leach the impurities out of your system. Though it can be hard on the body. Another concern with distilled water is waste. According to Jerry, when you distill water, you're wasting as much as 4 or 5 gallons for every single gallon of distilled water you produce.

REVERSE OSMOSIS

Reverse osmosis is a membrane-based filtration process. Pressure forces water through a very fine membrane that can trap particles as small as 0.00001 micron. In most cases, reverse osmosis is really a three-step filtration method. First comes a fiber prefilter to trap sediment and bigger gunk. Then comes a carbon filtration step to remove chlorine and VOCs. And then comes that membrane. Reverse osmosis multistage filters usually can remove heavy metals (including lead, mercury, copper, cadmium, chromium, and zinc), chlorine, nitrates, perchlorate, some pesticides, bacteria (including E. coli), protozoan cysts, viruses, radioactive materials, sodium, potassium, including beneficial hard-water minerals calcium and magnesium, glucose, most heavier-weight VOCs, and dissolved minerals that cause water hardness.

Jerry says reverse osmosis is most commonly used in households that have a salt water softener. Reverse osmosis was actually developed to give you drinking water if you have a water softener on the whole house, since it removes that excess sodium. However, reverse osmosis can waste as much as 5 or 6 gallons of water to produce a single gallon of filtered water, and, like distillation, it creates water that's demineralized and aggressive.

ULTRAVIOLET LIGHT

UV light is not used for water filtration, but for water sterilization. It kills bacteria and viruses—the stuff typically killed by chlorine in municipal water supplies. So if you don't get city water—if you have well water or get your water from a stream or what-have-you—then ultraviolet light can be a good alternative to using chemicals to get rid of microbes. Typically, some sort of physical filter removes particulates first, so bacteria and such don't escape UV sterilization by hiding behind chunks of other stuff.

FAR-INFRARED

This water treatment method is controversial. Proponents say far-infrared wavelengths can be used to soften water, give it a negative charge, and restructure it into smaller molecules that are easier for the body to absorb. But the bottom line, according to Jerry, is infrared works much like ultraviolet light: It's designed to kill bacteria. So if you have municipal water, again, you really don't need it.

MAGNETIC

Magnetic water treatment literally creates a magnetic field. It's primarily used for water softening, rather than filtration. According to some manufacturers, these magnetic devices can even remove existing lime scale over a period of weeks. Some of these devices require electricity to operate, while others do not need to be connected to an external power supply. However, there's some controversy concerning whether magnets really work to treat water.

CATALYTIC

Some companies say their catalytic water filtration products use technology much like that in a car's catalytic converter, which cleans up the exhaust gases. According to proponents, catalytic water filters can remove heavy metals and chlorine and viruses and pollutants chemically. They break down these unwanted substances into their basic elements, into a benign form. Some people are quite skeptical about catalytic treatment for water. But Jerry says a catalytic system can be beneficial for water softening without all that sodium. The problem with catalytic water treatment is it tends to restrict water flow into the house fairly substantially, which can become a maintenance hassle.

IONIZERS

This technology uses an electrical current to separate water into two types: alkaline and acidic. The alkaline water, which has a higher pH, ends up with negatively charged ions, and that water is used for drinking. Proponents say the ionized water is much like glacial water: It's tasty, easy for the body to absorb without bloating, and has antioxidant abilities. The other lower-pH water, the acid water, is usually discarded and therefore wasted, but some systems keep it for external use—for showers and washing hands and so on—and also for cleaning, since proponents say it's a natural germicide. It kills bacteria and fungi and viruses on contact.

There's some debate as to the health benefits of ionized water, but I think the idea is promising enough that Rachelle and I have decided to test it for ourselves. We're using a KYK ionizer (see Resources, page 342) to see if we realize health benefits from drinking it. The KYK Genesis unit includes both the ionizing feature and an activated carbon filter, so it both filters and ionizes the water. Plus, it lets you choose how acidic or how alkaline you'd like your water, with four different settings for each end of the spectrum. So far, we are very pleased with the taste and health benefits of the KYK Halen Water.

People say old habits are hard to break. But I think financial savings provide a great incentive. Maybe you've gotten into the habit of buying bottled water every day at lunch, or packing a bottle of water in your kids' lunches. Maybe you've been standing in the shower for an extra few minutes every morning trying to wake up. Maybe you've been shaving while you're in the shower instead of doing it at the sink. Maybe you run the dishwasher every day, instead of waiting until it's really full.

Over time, changing those simple habits can save a lot of water. Add in some new high-efficiency toilets and showerheads and faucets, and you're looking at major water savings. Saving water means saving money and saving energy, both on a personal level and on a municipal level. It means reducing emissions, too—particularly if you've been buying bottled water. So these little changes add up to a win-win situation, both financially and environmentally. That's what I call a serious incentive program.

Get a Water Audit

Municipalities add chlorine to water to keep pathogens at bay for our health, but it comes at a cost. Chlorine is a toxic element. Until they get some sort of a cost-effective means of using ultraviolet light or something to purify water on a large scale, we're going to continue to use chlorine.

The question is: What else is in the water, besides chlorine?

At my house the water comes from the Owens Valley. This part of our water system is very, very clean. It's really good, clean Sierra snowpack that has made its way down to L.A. in a project William Mulholland built. Added to it is some Metropolitan Water District water and some California Aqueduct water. That's pretty good water, too. They also add some local groundwater to it, which is where you get into probably the biggest problem, because there's trichloroethylene in the groundwater. There's hexavalent chromium in some of the water from plating facilities. There's perchloroethylene, which is used in dry cleaning.

Municipalities claim they're not taking any of that groundwater from places where there's contamination.

Is this true? I hope so. But I don't know. That's why I'm going to have my water tested. I've never done it before. But it's just like getting a green home energy audit. I'm going to have a water audit done. I'm going to take some of my tap water to a testing lab, one with the gas-chromatograph, mass-spectrometer kind of equipment that's going to look at it on a very accurate level and tell me how many parts per million I have of trichloroethylene or hexavalent chromium or whatever bad stuff might be in the water.

If you're at all concerned about the quality of water at your home—or if you want to make sure you choose the right kind of water filter to deal with the exact issues with your water—getting a water audit like this is a really good idea. It's a smart idea to know exactly what you're dealing with, what you're up against, so to speak. And you may find out you have excellent-quality tap water. I'd certainly want to know that, and I'm sure you would, too.

SECTION II
PRODUCE

**Thinking About Making
Your Own Power?**

You've done all the conservation work you can to lower your electric bill to a very efficient level, a smart level of power. So now that you've conserved, you might want to produce your own power. You want to make power yourself with solar or with wind.

In 1990, after twenty years of recycling, practicing water conservation, practicing energy conservation, riding my bike, and taking public transportation, I had saved enough money to start thinking about energy *production.* That year, I had my first solar electric system installed. That was a long time ago—before the days of simply hooking your residential solar system into the city power grid and before the days of really good and efficient technology—so it took a few years to get my solar system working just right. Today, it's much easier to install an efficient solar electric system.

However, I have to point out right up front that the production of power and resources can be expensive—let's make no mistake about that. But I had saved a ton of dough over those twenty years of conservation, so that's what made it possible. Again, I didn't try to run up Mount Everest. I climbed slowly and methodically to the top. You can, too.

There are many production projects—solar electric and wind energy among them—and you need to find the project that is right for you, your home, and your geography. Each project represents a different level of production and a different level of financial investment and payback.

Remember, too, that production is also the realm of the professional. My solar electric installation was designed and installed by professionals. It was not a DIY project. Working with high voltage on your roof should not be a hobby. Finding the right professional is key, so that not only is the system installed correctly but the paperwork, rebates, and tax credits are all processed correctly. I've had some of the best people in the business work on my home, and I've never regretted it. You won't either.

This section also goes beyond producing power to include building a home or remodeling—literally producing a new space in which to live a green and healthy life. Ideally, that space will take into consideration all the things we talked about in the first section of this book, as well as incorporate one or more ways to make power on-site.

What else can you produce at home? If you have room for a garden—even on a patio or a balcony or a windowsill—then you can produce both oxygen and nutritious and delicious food on-site. So this section includes a look at how to create a healthy, environmentally friendly garden.

7

SOLAR POWER

Determining if Your Home Is a
Good Candidate for a Solar Array
& How It Works

A solar tracker follows the sun's path, thereby increasing the energy output of the system.

EARLIER I MENTIONED THAT I'VE BEEN INTERESTED in electricity since I was a young child, but I've been interested in solar electricity just as long. I love the fact that you can harness the sun's energy to make power. I know firsthand that solar works—and works well—because it's been running my house and charging my electric cars with solar power since 1990. I've made some upgrades to my system over the years, but I'm not talking about major expenditures. And in all this time, the system has performed flawlessly. It's been an incredibly good investment for me.

Of course, there are costs involved in installing a solar array at your home. But once you've saved enough money on your electric bills to offset those costs, all the rest of the power you make is free. You literally get free electricity from the sun. And it gets better: I truly believe that solar is the cleanest form of energy on this planet today.

Now, not every home is a good candidate for solar. But if yours is, I highly recommend installing a solar electric setup.

So let's take a look at how solar energy works, then figure out if solar is the right choice for you.

HOW SOLAR CELLS WORK

Let's start with the smallest building block in a solar system: a solar cell, also known as a photovoltaic (PV) cell. I'll provide a quick overview here, but if you'd like more information, go to a University of California–Santa Barbara website called the Power of the Sun (see Resources, page 342) and watch a very good film called *The Science of the Silicon Solar Cell*.

To put it simply, most solar cells today are made from a material called *silicon*. I should point out that this is not the same as *silicone*. Silicone is a rubber compound. Silicon (as in Silicon Valley in Northern California, the high-tech capital of the universe) is a metal, and it just so happens to be the most abundant element on Earth. It's the most abundant mineral in the earth's crust, and it's commonly found in nature as sand or quartz, but it can be found in other forms as well. It can be mined much like gold or gravel.

But there's a *but*. Silicon may be the most abundant element on Earth, but finding very pure silicon is an issue, according to my friend Rob Wills, who has a doctor of engineering degree from Dartmouth College and who serves as a chief technical officer and an energy consultant for a number of renewable energy companies.

"Even though we say that we *can* make solar cells with beach sand, we don't make them from beach sand because it's not pure enough," says Rob. "It would cost too much to clean up the sand, which is silica or silica dioxide, and turn it into metallic silicon.

"At the moment, most of the silicon used in solar cells comes from Norway, where there are large deposits of very, very pure silica, the white rock that you see sticking out from the ground. And there's a Norwegian company that makes most of the first refined product, which is called metallurgical-grade silicon."

Yet this is still not solar-grade silicon. Solar-grade silicon has to be purified, then it gets *doped* with precise kinds of impurities—other elements, basically, such as boron and phosphorus—to create *free electrons*.

When sunlight hits the doped silicon, the *photoelectric effect* is what causes electrons to break free from the atoms to which they were attached. It helps to think of sunlight not as a wave, but rather as a beam of photon particles. This might sound a little like *Star Trek*, but let me assure you this is not science fiction. This is actual science.

When photon particles strike a solar cell, they cause free electrons to float around inside the lattice structure of that solar cell. The impurities in the silicon then cause the

Solar Power Naysayers

There are naysayers who will point out that there are environmental side effects from mining and transporting and refining silicon, and it's true. Most silicon is mined in Norway, and then it's transported somewhere—to the United States or elsewhere—to be refined. Then it gets transported to another location to be made into solar cells, which are then made into modules, and those modules must be transported to warehouses and installers and ultimately to your home. All of the steps in the process require resources. The transportation part of the process certainly involves the use of crude oil and the production of greenhouse gases.

The mining of silicon also has some environmental impact. The amounts aren't huge when you compare them with other mining operations, but there's an effect.

Also, the refining process used in creating metallurgical-grade silicon creates carbon dioxide emissions. There are amazing and probably very viable research and development plans going on to upgrade the refining process. The whole industry is sort of waiting with bated breath to see which one or ones of these will move ahead and succeed. Will they be greener? Will they be more sustainable? I hope so.

But in the meantime, is the environmental impact from manufacturing, transporting, and installing solar modules and then making power from them *comparable* to making power a different way? Is the environmental impact *comparable* to burning coal or natural gas to create power?

Of course not. There are no emissions from solar modules themselves. The only emissions created occur during the manufacturing and delivery part of the process. Once you've mined the silica and refined it into metallic silicon, you create a solar module that will last for decades, producing power with no further impact on the environment.

So comparing the environmental impact of producing solar electricity with the environmental impact of burning coal to produce electricity is like a teaspoon to a tanker truck. But yes, I have to admit, there is an impact.

I am hopeful that some of the new refining processes will prove successful and prove to be much greener and more friendly to the humans involved in the manufacturing process than the current methods are. I'm also hopeful about some of the future technologies being investigated right now that might allow us to get the silicon we need from fertilizer or from biomass—that is, from agricultural waste from things like wheat and straw and rice hulls. I'm delighted to see the solar industry making an effort to move in a greener and greener direction.

free electrons to flow in a particular direction. And that's what generates electric current. The more intense the light that hits the solar cell, the more photons you have going in. More photons going in translates directly into more electrons coming out. This is precisely why intensity of light is the key to creating more power.

CELLS GO INTO MODULES

The solar cells that make up an entire solar system have to be connected in some way. They're connected in series, just like a few batteries fit into a big flashlight. When you install batteries, you put them in so the positive end of one battery butts up against the negative end of the next battery. Solar cells are connected in exactly the same way, in series, positive to negative. The key is for solar cell manufacturers to put enough cells into a *solar module,* or *solar panel,* in series to produce a useful amount of voltage.

From a practical standpoint, the modules are designed to protect the solar cells and to be easy to install. The cells themselves are contained in plastic, then a layer of strong, transparent glass goes on the top. In addition to the glass on top, there is a backing on the underside. The backing provides protection from contact and from moisture, and the module's edges are sealed. The entire module is contained within a metal frame for strength and rigidity, so that the modules can be attached to a mounting system.

Modules also feature what's known as *bypass diodes,* so cells that are in the shade do not subtract voltage. Shaded cells actually take back, or subtract, some of the voltage produced by sunlit cells. Solar module manufacturers therefore build in bypass diodes, so the current from the sunlit cells contributes to your power supply rather than just being depleted.

GOING FROM DC TO AC WITH AN INVERTER

The electricity that's produced by solar modules is direct current, or DC. Your home runs on alternating current, or AC. So the DC has to be converted to AC in order to power your home. This conversion is done by a device called an *inverter,* which gets installed inside your garage or wherever your solar equipment connects to your home.

Some people refer to an inverter as a *power conditioner.* That's because the inverter turns the DC power created by your solar panels into sine wave AC electricity. Because the power is conditioned directly at your home, it is usually cleaner than power you get off the grid—that is, from your utility company.

I would certainly urge everybody who's going solar to make sure you install a *pure* sine wave inverter. You don't want to get a *modified* sine wave inverter. I've been down that road. It's a thorny path and I urge everybody to avoid it. Yes, there are greater efficiencies with a modified sine wave inverter, as far as the amount of current drawn on an ongoing basis, but it's not worth it. What happens is your clock will run fast. You'll have buzzing on your answering machine and buzzing on your stereo. It's not worth the trouble.

Most solar installers use just *one* pure sine wave inverter, but in some circumstances for some homes, it does make more sense to use multiple inverters—or to use an inverter that has separate inputs—one for each string in your solar array.

Rob Wills is working with a company that is experimenting with installing residential systems that have several inverters, each installed under a small group of panels directly on your roof. They do this to prevent power loss, since DC loses more power than AC as it travels through wires, and they also do this for safety reasons. "Bringing down 400-volt DC off a roof and running it into an inverter has a slightly higher fire risk," according to Rob, "not that there are any significant reported cases of fires. But one attribute of AC is that it goes to 0 volts 120 times a second." Going down to zero and then back up again is the oscillation in the current that creates the sine wave.

In contrast, Rob points out, "DC is on all the time, no matter what. So if an arc starts in the electrical wiring, with DC it's going to keep going until the wires burn through. With AC, there's a very good chance it will just go out within 120th of a second, when the voltage goes to 0."

Another benefit to installing a multiple-inverter setup is reliability. First of all, if you have a problem with one of your inverters, the entire system doesn't go down. So that modularity can be a real benefit. The system will continue working. It also will be easier to repair—in part because smaller inverters are lighter. One person can lift a smaller inverter, and it can be shipped to a repair facility. So it can be repaired and reinstalled more quickly, at least in theory, than if you had one large inverter go down and you needed someone to visit your home to fix it or haul it away.

A LITTLE HISTORY, A FEW CHANGES

The ability to transform light into electricity—the *photovoltaic effect*—was discovered by a nineteen-year-old French physicist named Alexandre-Edmond Becquerel in 1839. The first practical solar cells were invented at Bell Laboratories in New Jersey in the early 1950s, when people at the telephone company were researching silicon for applications in electronics.

The first major use of photovoltaic technology was for space. Solar cells turned out to be the best way to power a satellite in orbit. In the 1970s, the potential for earth-based solar power systems began to come into a viable range, from a price-to-performance standpoint.

Solar panels have not changed all that much since the space program in the late 1950s, but they have changed some. The most noticeable change is in their thickness. Rob points out that the first solar cells made at Bell Labs were probably a tenth of an inch thick. Now they're closer to a couple thousandths of an inch thick. They're very, very thin wafers. While they've gotten thinner, they've also gotten wider—going from just 1 square inch to 8×8 inches, or 64 square inches.

Rob also told me about an interesting change in the manufacturing process: "Until about ten or fifteen years ago, all solar cells were made by growing some sort of block of silicon and then slicing it up using a mechanical saw, which was like a spinning saw blade. . . . The downside of cutting up blocks of silicon with a saw is that the curve or the cut space was using up as much silicon as what you had left over with the cells or more.

"And so a dramatic change that happened about ten years ago was that a saw called a wire saw, which is miles and miles of thin, steel wire, [is now] drawn over the block of silicon. . . . The wire saws cut the amount of silicon needed to make solar cells by a factor of two, and so we've seen a dramatic price drop."

The fact that today's cells are thinner is especially significant, since thinner cells are more efficient. Some other innovations in design have also increased the efficiency—such as improvements in reflective coatings and other manufacturing techniques—which means it now requires fewer cells on top of a home to meet that household's electricity needs.

Ten years ago, a typical solar cell would have been 10 percent to 12 percent efficient and the module itself maybe a couple percent less. Now we're seeing many solar cells and modules up in the 20 percent efficiency range.

Of course, these days, we've gotten used to technology changing *fast*. You buy a computer and by the time you figure out how to get everything connected and working properly, it's already obsolete. So I'm not surprised that some people hesitate to install solar because they're afraid there's going to be some big breakthrough in technology that will make their system outdated in no time—or that will make systems substantially smaller and more affordable in the near future.

If that's your concern, I have to say you should not wait for some breakthrough in solar panels for the following reason: The actual panel is a relatively small part of the equation. Most of the cost and installation of solar is labor, cable, brackets, and fuses. There's so much that is *not about the panels* that's involved in this process, so whatever technological advances might or might not occur at this point are not worth waiting for. I've been waiting for a big solar breakthrough since 1990, and I'm telling you, the panels I have are virtually identical to the panels that are being put up today, nineteen years later.

The panels are not the entire equation. There's so much else that's going on. There're so many other things that are eighteenth-century technology, things like batteries and cables and brackets. Panels that are virtually identical to mine are still operating on satellites from the 1960s, so you know they're plenty durable, and they're going to be functional for a very, very long time. If your house actually is a good candidate for solar, it's time to stop waiting.

SOLAR PANEL CUTAWAY

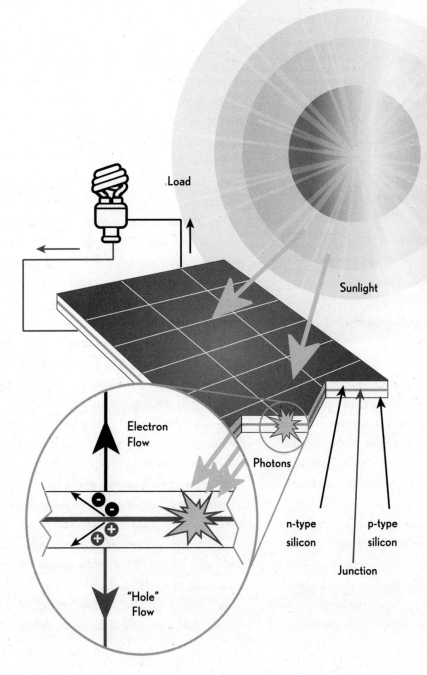

Load

Sunlight

Electron
Flow

Photons

"Hole"
Flow

n-type
silicon

p-type
silicon

Junction

IS SOLAR RIGHT FOR YOU?

Okay, so now you're convinced that solar is great and there's no reason to wait. But does it make sense to install a solar array on your particular home? There are a few things to seriously consider before you commit to installing a solar electric system:

- your rooftop's square footage (or alternate installation locations on your property)
- if you have trees or buildings that shade your roof
- the direction in which your home faces
- the pitch (or tilt) of the roof
- your geographic location, and options available from your local electric utility company

THE SIZE OF YOUR ROOF

If you're going to install solar panels, obviously they need to get mounted in a location where they can be in direct sunlight. For those of us who live in cities or suburbs, that typically means the solar panels need to be installed on top of the roof of our homes.

If you live in a more rural area or if you're blessed with a larger piece of property, then you can consider mounting solar panels on the ground—either fixed panels or even panels that move, panels that track the sun as it arcs through the sky. For most of us, a roof-mounted

system is the most feasible, so that's where we'll focus our attention first.

My friend Stephen Gates of Golden Power Capitol (stephen@simplesunpower.com), who has been in the business of designing and installing solar electric systems for nine years now, provides a good, general rule of thumb. He says the average home needs about 300 to 500 square feet of solar panels to be in the sun from 10 a.m. to 3 p.m. So, the question then is, how big is your roof?

You may have a very large roof, but much of it cannot—or, more aptly, should not—be home to solar panels. There's no point in mounting solar panels where they aren't going to produce much, if any, power. If you don't have enough roof space, or if your roof is not appropriate for solar panels for one of the other reasons we're about to cover, you might have other options. You can build a carport or a little picnic area in the backyard with an aesthetically pleasing roof over it. This way, you get a twofer: You get a carport or a shaded picnic area *and* you get an optimally designed solar structure.

A great carport can be found at the Google facility in Mountain View, California. Solar panels cover the top of carports that are used to recharge the company's fleet of converted plug-in hybrid vehicles, as well as employees' electric cars. The carport installation is actually part of the largest solar power system ever installed on a single corporate campus. It includes solar panels on the roof of several company buildings, which produce enough electricity for about a thousand homes in California or,

An aerial view of Google's Corporate Campus shows off their commitment to solar energy.

in this case, to meet 30 percent of Google's peak electricity demand on-site.

YOUR ROOF SIZE AND SHADING

Clearly, you need sunlight to create solar power. You'll never make *enough* power to break even on the cost of installing a solar electric system if your roof is shaded much of the time.

But it is important to point out that solar panels don't *just* make electricity from direct sunlight. There are actually three components to sunlight, all of which can be converted into electricity by solar panels. They are as follows:

- direct light, which obviously is light coming straight from the sun to the panel
- diffuse light, which is what you'd experience on a cloudy, foggy, hazy, or smoggy day
- reflective light, such as light coming off of snow or sand or the windows of a tall building next door

While all three types of light can be converted into electricity, there's a profound difference in the *amount* of power produced by each. Direct sunlight is by far the best, and shade is

A newer solar-electric system that offers triangular pieces.

by far the worst. As I mentioned, panels that are in the shade do not make any power; in fact, they can actually eat up some of the power produced by other panels that are in the sun.

So spend some time out in your yard at different times of the day to see how much of your roof is getting sun. Is there a tree in your yard that causes shading? Can you trim it and keep it trimmed enough to make a solar installation worthwhile? What if that tree is in your neighbor's yard? Do you have the kind of relationship with your neighbors in which you can ask about hiring an arborist to come over and trim a tree on their property?

What about tall buildings? Do you live in a single-level ranch house next door to a towering two- or three-story house or an apartment or office building? Does another structure cast a big shadow on your home? If you live in a canyon or near hills or mountains, how much shade is cast on your roof or whatever other location you might be considering for a solar installation?

Don't forget to consider the structures on your own roof that can cause shading, e.g., chimneys, vents, and gables. Quite simply, in order for solar arrays to work, you want to have very minimal shading on your roof. If you get good sun only from 10 a.m. to 1 p.m., your home is not a good candidate for solar. You want to aim to have direct sunlight from somewhere between 8 in the morning to around 4 or 5 p.m., average, year-round. These hours will extend, naturally, in the summer months—for a really good system, you've got to come online with solar power from around 7 a.m. to 6 or 7 p.m.

Simply put, there's no point in considering an installation if your roof gets too much shade—unless you have a large, sunny yard and you can build a solar-covered carport or garage or pergola or some other structure.

THE DIRECTION AND PITCH OF YOUR ROOF

Naturally, the direction of your roof affects how much direct sun it gets. If you live in the Northern Hemisphere, you want to have a good southern exposure in order to get the most from solar panels. The second best option is sun from a western exposure. If you have an eastern exposure, I would not recommend solar for you. If that's the only surface you have that's available that gets good light—if everything else is shaded or somehow obscured—you're not going to generate strong enough sun, so I'm not sure I would recommend solar power for you. If you have only a northern exposure, I would certainly never recommend solar power for you. You'd be literally throwing your money down a rat hole. It would be a complete waste.

But direction isn't the only consideration. The pitch of your roof—that is, the angle of it—also affects your home's ability to generate solar power. (If you're building a carport or a pergola, you can choose the ideal pitch, which is another benefit to going that route.)

This doesn't mean you need some crazy slant to your roof to have an optimum exposure. What we would consider a fairly normal slope actually turns out to be the best compromise for capturing the sun at different times of the year in a large part of the country.

Remember, at the summer solstice, the sun is high in the sky, nearly straight up above our homes. At the winter solstice, the sun is much lower, at a steep angle, if you will. You want to have a pitch that captures direct sunlight from the summer solstice as well as the winter solstice, so you're making good power year-round.

A very useful device called a Pathfinder, which is like an anemometer that measures wind, will give you a good idea at any time of year—from winter solstice to summer solstice, from spring equinox to fall equinox—what kind of solar power you're going to get on your rooftop. It will even tell you when you're going to get shading from a nearby mountain or the two-story house next door. You can buy a Pathfinder for approximately $250 for the handheld model or about $360 for the tripod metal case model. Or you can rent one for a week for about $25 from companies such as Real Goods (see Resources, page 342). There's now even a digital model that installers use. Although that's around $1,200, it's really powerful and can provide incredible detail as to the production potential of the site.

YOUR GEOGRAPHIC LOCATION

Another very important point to take into consideration is the power of the sun in your area. What is your latitude? Also, what are the typical weather patterns in your area? This plays a big role in determining whether solar is a worthwhile investment for your home.

There's a great resource online called PVWatts (see Resources, page 342) that can help you get a quick and easy performance estimate for a typical solar system based on your geographic location. Simply go to the website and use the PVWatts Solar Calculator, which was developed by researchers at the National Renewable Energy Laboratory (NREL; see Resources, page 342). You choose your state (or country), then select the city closest to your home in terms of location and topography. For instance, if you live midway between San Francisco and Sacramento, California, you'd choose Sacramento, since your weather patterns and topography would be more like the state capitol than foggy, chilly San Francisco.

Prompts will ask you to fill in some blanks and to make some choices regarding the type of system you plan to install, or you can use the default settings. Then the energy calculator will tell you the likelihood that a solar system will work at your home.

THE EFFECTS OF LATITUDE

I don't have to tell you that the sun feels a lot stronger as you get closer to the equator. But perhaps you might not realize that your latitude will affect the angle at which your solar panels should be installed. The proper pitch for your panels literally depends on your geographic location.

According to the experts at NREL, "The winter season has the least sun, so you want to make the most of it. The tilt should be designed so that the panel points directly at the sun at noon. To calculate, multiply your latitude by 0.9, and add 30 degrees. For example: New York is at 40 degrees. $40 \times .9 + 30 = 66$ degrees tilt from horizontal." If you go back to that PVWatts website, you'll find a list of cities and their latitudes, so you can do your own calculation.

If you install a fixed array of solar panels, you basically position them at an angle that's a good compromise between winter and summer seasons. But there's another choice: You can install an adjustable system, which enables you to tilt your solar panels to maximize their exposure based on the time of year. Solar panels make their maximum power when the sun is perpendicular to the panel—that is, when the sun hits the panel at a 90-degree angle.

That's one reason why solar panels should be installed so that they tilt. If your panels tilt in just one direction (e.g., side to side only), the system has what's called *one-axis* or *single-axis tracking*. If they tilt in two directions (e.g., both side to side and up and down), then you have *two-axis* or *dual-axis tracking*. According to PVWatts, if you live in the Northern Hemisphere, to get the maximum output from your solar installation, you should adjust the tilt of your panels around:

- March 1
- April 19
- August 23
- October 14

If you live in the Southern Hemisphere, which means you're enjoying winter when it's summer in the Northern Hemisphere, then you'll make each of those adjustments about six months later.

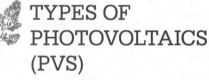 TYPES OF PHOTOVOLTAICS (PVS)

I know that I've talked as if there's really only one kind of solar panel, the kind most people picture when they think of a solar installation. But actually there are several options when it comes to photovoltaic designs nowadays, including standard frame modules and roof tiles that are the most common.

The traditional style, if you will—the style that's been around for thirty years or more—is the standard frame module. It's the kind of module that gets mounted on a rail structure. These modules sit above your roof surface, allowing airflow underneath them to aid in cooling, since heat reduces the output of solar panels. This kind of module can be installed on all types of roofs, including ceramic tile, and it also works on ground-mounted installations.

The first thing you'll notice, as you look through solar catalogs or websites, is that when it comes to solar PV modules—the basic, rectangular framed panels—some are blue and some are black.

According to engineer and energy consultant, Rob Wills, "The black ones are typically what's called a single crystal. And the blue ones are often polycrystalline and multicrystalline. The black stuff is more expensive and a couple of percent more efficient.

"The single crystal is actually grown. They start with melted silicon and draw a seed out of the melt that turns into a large, sausage-shaped thing that can be six or eight inches in diameter and three or four feet long. And then that's what's sliced up. That's the single crystal–type silicon.

"And then the multicrystalline is where the molten silicon's poured into a crucible or a mold and then it's cooled in a very special way, very carefully, and it grows large multiple crystals of silicon, which are then sawn into wafers."

So in a nutshell, it's essentially the same technology inside. But the manufacturing process is different and it can net a small difference in efficiency.

 CHOOSING SOLAR PANELS

So what are your choices right now, today? Well, if you open up a solar catalog and look at the traditional solar modules, you'll see 20-watt

Aesthetics

You certainly can choose to optimize your solar installation for performance, rather than looks. For instance, if you're not particularly concerned with aesthetics and you have a flat roof or you don't have the perfect pitch to your roof, you can install your solar panels at an angle. You can literally build a superstructure to support them and mount them at a different angle from the pitch of your roof.

Tilting the panels in a whole different direction from your roof is certainly an option, too. If you have a western exposure, you can tilt the panels to get more of a southern exposure for them.

I even built a tower on my roof and mounted solar panels on it. By installing this tower, I was able to mount more solar panels than would fit on the roof itself. You could say I increased the square footage available for solar. Plus, the tower moves; it tracks the sun as it travels through the sky throughout the day to maximize the panels' solar exposure.

Now, I find my solar array beautiful. And you might feel the same way. But it's important to bear in mind that aesthetics could be very important to other people. Before you install a really obvious solar array, ask yourself if it's going to be very difficult to sell your house someday because of what potential buyers perceive as a hideous solar installation on the roof. Are your neighbors going to be upset at the view? And, for that matter, if you live in a neighborhood with a homeowners' association, will an installation of this sort be able to gain the association's approval? Even closer to home, if someone in your household is particularly concerned with aesthetics (as someone in my household is), will you be able to maintain a harmonious home life if you install the solar panels in this way?

At the other end of the spectrum, there are solar panel—and solar installation—choices today that are more aesthetically pleasing. There are solar shingles, or solar tiles, that are very attractive and that produce a great amount of current. They are less efficient than the traditional modules. But if aesthetics matter to you, you can now get solar shingles that are invisible to passersby or neighbors. They look just like black shake shingle material on someone's roof. It's only when you climb up on the roof that you can see they are, in fact, solar panels.

panels and 50-watt panels and 100-watt panels and 200-watt panels.

Sunlight is about 1,000 watts per square meter or 100 watts per square foot. So if you have a solar panel that's 20 percent efficient, and if the solar panel is 1 square meter, then you're going to get 200 watts from the panel. That's with the typical large solar modules that I've been referencing.

You certainly could build a solar array using all 20-watt panels. But from an efficiency standpoint, you'll usually want to buy the biggest panels you can. You'll want to maximize the surface area of the panel. That way, less space is devoted to the panels' frames and more space is actually making solar energy. Also, installing fewer, larger panels is less expensive, since there is less labor involved in the installation.

In my experience, the panel's manufacturer is not all that important. Obviously it's good to choose a company that you feel comfortable with, but the bottom line is there are many reputable companies making solar panels today.

ADDING IT ALL UP

When you have a good solar installer visit your house, he or she will consider the pitch of your roof, the shading, the direction your roof faces, the square footage, your geographic location, and so on. Then he'll use all of this data to determine how much power a system can make at your home. For example, if you have enough room to install sixteen of the 200-watt panels, you'll wind up with a system that can produce 3.2 kilowatts of solar *per hour*.

Now, based on the angle of your roof and the shading and the geography of your location, your solar expert might determine that you'll get, on average, six hours of full power from your solar array each day.

So if you're getting six hours of power at 3.2 kilowatts, then you're looking at 19.2 kilowatts per day ($6 \times 3.2 = 19.2$).

The next step is to look at your electric bill and determine your current electricity usage (or your best guess of your reduced usage, if you've just recently made a bunch of the changes I talked about in Section 1 of this book). And then, based on these numbers that the solar expert has given you—how much power you can produce and how much the installation is going to cost—you can figure out two things: what percentage of your total power needs you're going to be able to meet with solar and how long it's going to take for you to recoup the cost of installing the system (see Sample Costs and Paybacks at the end of this chapter for more information along these lines).

WHAT DO YOU DO WITH THE POWER?

Once your solar system has been installed and starts making power, what do you do with it? Odds are you won't be using all of the electricity you produce at any given moment in the day. After all, with solar, you'll be making peak power in the middle of the day, when most homes are using a fairly small amount of electricity. Sure, your refrigerator could be running. You may have some electronic devices connected, like your answering machine and your fax machine. Your heater or air conditioner may come on occasionally to maintain the temperature in your home. But if you're away from home in the middle of the day—if you're at work and your kids are at school—then you're making maximum power and you're not using all of it. So in this case, you have a couple of choices. You can feed the extra power into the grid—that is, you can send that power through your neighborhood power lines to be used by your utility company—or you can store any extra power on-site in batteries. The first option is what's known as a *grid-connected system*. The latter is a *standalone*, or *off-grid*, system.

GRID-CONNECTED SYSTEMS WITH NET METERING

Most grid-connected solar installations involve something called *net metering*. A *net meter* is a special kind of electric meter that can run forward and backward. It runs forward—the normal way—when you are getting electricity from the local utility company. But when you are making more solar power than you're using at a given moment, that power gets fed into the grid and it spins your meter backward. Here's the best part: Sure, you pay for the electricity you buy from the electric company at retail prices.

But, in most areas, *they pay you* for the electricity you feed into the grid at retail prices, too. So when your meter spins backward, you are building up a credit with the utility company.

Most people who choose solar today opt to connect to the grid and use a net metering setup. There are quite a few benefits to going this route.

- You save the expense and complication of installing batteries on-site.
- You can install a smaller solar array. You don't have to install enough solar modules to meet *all* of your needs for electricity, since you can get power from the grid whenever you need it.
- You save a lot of money on your electric bill because you are literally selling power to your local utility company.

Right now, not every local utility company offers you the option of net metering, so this is something to investigate when you're considering solar. But there is the possibility that a federal law will mandate that all utilities make this option available, which would be a big boon to the renewable energy industry and to people like us who want to make our own green energy. This could happen within the next year or two.

A STANDALONE SYSTEM

Of course, if you're building a house out in the middle of nowhere and it's going to cost an arm and a leg to get the utility company to run power to your location, then it's an easy choice to go with a standalone system. It often is

This time-of-use meter allows me to purchase off-peak grid power at a very low cost.

produce anything. But by tying to the grid, it's unlimited."

In addition to the efficiency issues related to storing excess power in batteries instead of feeding it into the grid, there's one other very important downside: A standalone system usually does not qualify for rebates and tax incentives (which we'll discuss on page 137), because those incentives are designed to help utility companies reduce the need to build more power plants and to help those companies reduce their operating costs. An off-grid system is of no benefit to those utility companies.

Yet there's a big benefit to a standalone, off-grid system: If the grid goes down—if there's a brownout or a blackout in your area—a standalone system is completely unaffected. All your neighbors could be without power, but your house would be operating the same as it would on any other day.

In contrast, if you have a grid-connected solar installation and the grid goes down, your solar power also will go down. "The typical grid-tie inverter has an anti-island device," according to Stephen Gates, "which says, 'Cannot operate if there's no power coming from the grid.' If it's not picking up a signal from the grid, it shuts the whole system down or cuts the grid connection to run solely on batteries."

There's a logical reason for this. If there's a power outage in your area and the utility company sends out repairmen to work on the lines, they don't want your power to be feeding into those lines and zap the poor guys. It's a safety precaution, and a very important one.

much less expensive to install solar—or a wind turbine—in this situation, compared with connecting to the grid.

Even if you live in a major metropolis, if you do opt for a standalone system, you'll need an array of batteries on-site to store the excess power you produce. One of the downsides of using batteries, according to Stephen Gates, is power loss. With net metering, "the benefit is you store up credits with zero loss," he says. "If you try to store that extra energy in batteries, there would be [some] loss. And when those batteries filled up, even though the sun was still out, you wouldn't be able to make any power or store any power. The system wouldn't

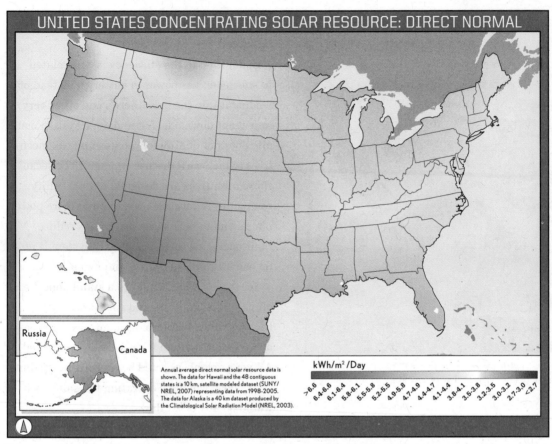

UNITED STATES CONCENTRATING SOLAR RESOURCE: DIRECT NORMAL

Russia

Canada

Annual average direct normal solar resource data is shown. The data for Hawaii and the 48 contiguous states is a 10 km, satellite modeled dataset (SUNY/ NREL, 2007) representing data from 1998-2005. The data for Alaska is a 40 km dataset produced by the Climatological Solar Radiation Model (NREL, 2003).

kWh/m² /Day

>6.6 6.4-6.6 6.1-6.4 5.8-6.1 5.5-5.8 5.2-5.5 4.9-5.8 4.7-4.9 4.4-4.7 4.1-4.4 3.8-4.1 3.5-3.8 3.2-3.5 3.0-3.2 2.7-3.0 <2.7

This map shows the best places to use solar technology across the United States.

But there is a best-of-both-worlds option that's a type of combination approach. You can tie into the grid for all the obvious benefits, but then you also install *some* batteries on-site for an emergency backup system. That way, if the grid goes down, you switch off your connection and switch over to the backup batteries, so you have power to run your refrigerator and some lights and any important electronic devices. It won't be enough power to run your whole house, but it will give you some power in case of an emergency. You'll literally wire a separate subpanel in your electrical box for this emergency circuit. As long as there's even a little sun getting through heavy cloud cover, you'll be producing power and recharging those batteries. According to Stephen, this type of setup costs an extra $5,000 or so, compared with a typical grid-connected system, since there are batteries and more complex wiring and more labor costs involved.

If you are tied into the grid and your local utility company does *not* offer net metering, you also might want to consider this same type of "partial power" setup. That way, you can have part of your house powered off the grid by your own solar array, and then you can have part of your house powered by the local utility company. In this case, you can install a smaller solar array, rather than trying to provide all of your own power on-site.

A TIME-OF-USE METER

The perfect complement to a net metering setup is a time-of-use electric meter. As you know, a *regular* electric meter keeps track of how much power you use, and it only spins forward. A *net* meter spins both backward and forward, allowing you to send power into the grid and sell that power to the electric company. A *time-of-use* meter keeps track of *when* you're using power, so that you can benefit from lower electricity prices during off-peak hours.

Now, most people pay a flat rate for electricity, regardless of what time they use it. But if you get a time-of-use meter and sign up for the accompanying billing program with your utility company, you will pay different prices for electricity depending on, obviously enough, the time of day when you use it.

Utility companies divide the day into three time periods, which usually are

- **High peak,** from 1 p.m. to 5 p.m.
- **Low peak,** from 10 a.m. to 1 p.m. and 5 p.m. to 8 p.m.
- **Off-peak,** from 8 p.m. to 10 a.m.

The price for electricity during those periods varies dramatically from state to state and even from region to region within those states. But you can always rest assured that the price is highest during the peak period and lowest during off-peak, often by a considerable amount.

If you've installed solar at your home and you're feeding power into the grid, guess what. You're making peak power during high-peak electricity hours. So you're selling that power to the utility company at the highest retail rate. And if you're able to shift your behavior slightly—so that you run the dishwasher after breakfast in the morning instead of after dinner, for example, or you throw a load of laundry in the washing machine right before you go to sleep at night—you can buy most of your power at the lowest rates, during off-peak hours.

This way, you derive the maximum financial benefits from having solar, and you can install a smaller solar setup and still enjoy dramatic benefits in terms of cost savings for a lower initial investment.

Stephen says taking this route can actually allow you to shrink the system by 20 percent: "Most of the energy that the solar array produces is going to go back onto the grid spinning your meter backwards at that higher rate. For example, if you're spinning your meter back in the daytime in the summer, let's say you get a thirty-cent-a-kilowatt-hour credit. Then you use your power at night after the sun goes down and you use those credits that you built in the daytime, but you're using them at 10 cents a kilowatt-hour.

"For every one kilowatt-hour you put onto the grid, you'll now have three kilowatt-hours of credit with the utility company."

This is the way you actually shrink the system. In this case, you can zero out your bill without covering all of your production. So if you have a smaller roof, you can take advantage of this. For electric car drivers there's an even better rate, called an EV rate, that has an even better spread between day and night.

I have a time-of-use meter at my house, too, even though I don't have a net metering setup for my solar. I have a time-of-use meter so that on the rare occasions when I do need to switch over to grid power, like when I want to charge my electric car at night without depleting my batteries substantially, I can buy electricity from my local utility company at a very low rate. I'm literally paying just pennies for each kilowatt-hour by buying my electricity off-peak.

If you do plan to have a net metering system for your solar, it's important to note that not every utility lets you sell power at a higher rate and then buy power at a lower rate. So, again, this is something to investigate before you make your final decision about a system.

"The other thing to look at is occupancy and how you use electricity," adds Stephen. "Are you using a lot of electricity in the summer, not that much in the winter, or vice versa? A lot in the winter for heating and not very much in the summer [for cooling]? These credits carry over for twelve months. So you might be running on summer surplus or winter surplus.

"So you really want to get a good idea after you've done all of your energy efficiency retrofits what your actual load is and when it is used. And how many people are there and is that going to change? Are you going to put a pool in? Are kids going to go away to college? You're looking at a twenty-five-year system, so you want to be able to design a system that will work for you as well as possible."

Stephen also brings up another great point, when you're considering whether solar will work for you. Don't forget to compute into the equation how much you pay for electricity. If you're replacing very expensive power with solar, you don't have to have a perfect setup to get a pretty good return on your investment. It turns out northern Maine is one of the best places in the country to install solar for this reason; power there is very, very expensive, so even though northern Maine doesn't get nearly the kind of solar irradiance you get in Southern California or Arizona, solar is a wise investment there.

 ## DOING IT YOURSELF

Most people will hire a solar expert to help them make this big step. But there is a segment of the population with a real do-it-yourself attitude. These are people who are handy, who have a few resources, and who can do a lot of the work themselves.

If you are one of these people and you want to do it yourself, you'll need to get prepared. There are several good books that can help you

My neighbor Bill Nye's solar setup is west-facing and flush-mounted to his carport.

put together a solar electric setup. See Resources (page 342) for a few titles.

You might go to Home Power (see Resources, page 342) to get some of these resources, or you might go to Real Goods, or you might just check out different solar possibilities on the Internet.

You could do some of the preliminary work yourself. You could climb onto your roof and see what kind of shading you have from other structures, from trees or what-have-you. Or you could buy or rent a Pathfinder and get an even better idea of how much power you can produce.

You can buy your own solar panels. These days you can go to Costco and buy a 1,000-watt inverter. And perhaps you can get some batteries from Costco or your local auto parts store.

I should caution those of you who think you're handy: You need to do this job properly. Obviously, you want to do the installation in such a way that there will be no leaks in your roof and all your work is up to code. But even beyond that, when you have electricity up on your roof where things also get wet, the work must be done correctly, with proper fusing and circuit breakers in line. It's essential that you read as much as you can and have some knowledge of electrical work if you attempt to do it yourself. As always, respect voltage. Respect

This Pathfinder helps you determine the optimal location for a solar-panel installation.

the tremendous amounts of current that are involved in batteries, and do not perform the job without proper grounding and proper fusing.

If you're going do this yourself, you must hire a licensed electrical contractor to finally hook up the system. You can do some of the wiring work yourself on the roof, but it is essential that a licensed electrical contractor ties the system into your circuit breaker box in your house. Otherwise, you're going to invite a lot of trouble from municipal authorities when you try to sell your house or if anyone learns of it.

HIRING AN INSTALLER

The vast majority of people—people who are not incredibly handy or schooled in electrical theory and residential wiring—will hire a solar consultant to do the installation.

The solar expert should arrive at your house with a Pathfinder and be armed with knowledge of the sun's arc in the various seasons. He also should have knowledge of different kinds of roofing materials and how solar panels can be mounted on different types of roofs.

Sample Costs and Paybacks: Solar Power

Environmental priorities aside, for most of us, solar has to make financial sense. Unless you're really wealthy and you'll never miss the money, you're making a sizable investment in a solar system and you need to see the payback. As a general rule, you can figure that solar costs about $10,000 per kilowatt, installed. Essentially, many entire systems can be installed for $30,000 to $40,000.

If you don't have that kind of lump sum sitting around, it may be worthwhile for you to take out a home equity loan, assuming you have that kind of equity in your home these days. If you take out a fifteen-year loan, you can make small payments over time. Obviously, you will lower your electric bill during those years, and if you save more each month on your electric bill than you pay for the loan, this would be a no-brainer. Of course, this is where it's very important to get good, reliable estimates from an expert installer, as well as to get quotes from your banker or mortgage broker.

Some municipalities also have special financing available for solar installations. For example, the city of Santa Monica, California, has a special local loan program for homeowners and business owners who want to install solar. With this program, there is a down payment, but it isn't more than $1,000. That's certainly a small out-of-pocket expense, relative to the entire price of an installed system. There are also some national lending institutions that have gotten involved in financing solar installations. You can find a list of these banks in the Resources on page 342.

Another major factor in determining whether the numbers for installing solar work for you financially is rebates and tax incentives. Any good installer should be able to tell you all about the opportunities in your area, but if you'd like another great resource, visit Green Made Simple's website (see Resources, page 342). You just enter your ZIP code and you'll find all sorts of useful information that will help make going green pay off for you financially, including through:

- ❏ Rebates
- ❏ Tax credits
- ❏ Free offers

- ❏ Loan programs
- ❏ and much more

These programs aren't just for solar, either. They include rebates and credits for changing your appliances, lighting, cars, and so on.

Now, specifically with solar, what sorts of rebates are we talking about? Here are a few recent examples:

- The Energy Trust of Oregon (see Resources, page 342) offers a rebate program with a maximum of $10,000 per residential site in that state, if you install a grid-connected PV system.
- The Florida Department of Environmental Protection Energy office (see Resources, page 342) offers a state rebate program for photovoltaic systems at $4/watt, with a maximum of $20,000 per residential solar installation.
- The New York State Energy Research and Development Authority (see Resources, page 342) offers a cash incentive program of $4 to $5/watt for a qualifying grid-connected residential solar photovoltaic system, up to 60 percent of total installed costs.

There are many technical details involved in properly setting up a solar array. The expert you choose should know everything about string sizing and wire sizing and how to hook up everything the way you want it. He should know how to size the system properly to meet your needs and get the most benefit, financially. He should know when to tie the panels in series and when to tie the panels in parallel, and he should know which panels to tie in series to work around any shading you might have on your roof so you still get the maximum power possible during those hours.

As Stephen Gates points out, "Let's say a mountain casts a shadow across your array. You want to do your series strings so that when the mountain shadow hits, it's going to hit the same string all at once and leave all the other strings alone. And then it'll get to the second string

and then the third string and the fourth string. The goal is to maintain the highest line voltage to keep inverters operating within maximum power-point tracking range. If shade is more scattered, it may be better to use microinverters, inverters that attach to each module, to isolate each module to its own converter. Such as Enphase Energy (see Resources, page 342). This strategy has a slightly higher material cost, but will yield higher output and there will be no DC run.

"That's the best way to maximize your solar exposure. If you were to twist it the other way and have that mountain shadow hit a little bit of all the strings, then that would lower the voltage on all the strings."

An expert installer will design your system with that in mind. He'll know how to get the maximum benefit from solar in your particular location. There are thousands of technical details that become second nature for someone who does this all day, every day. They'll pass this knowledge on to you.

There is another real benefit to hiring a professional installer: He will advise you on all the available rebates and tax incentives in your area and be very familiar with the process of filling out all the paperwork related to those things. He will literally handle all of the paperwork for you. Plus, in areas where there are rebates for solar (see page 342), you typically get a *higher* rebate if you work with a professional installer. Stephen says he's seen many rebates where you lose 15 percent of the money if you do it yourself.

Will that be more money than the cost of hiring an installer? Probably not. But will you wind up with a better-functioning system if you work with a professional? For the vast majority of us, the answer is absolutely, without a doubt.

The key is choosing the right installer. You don't want someone to go up on your roof and drill holes and tell you it's going be okay because they'll put silicone around the holes. You want to have solar mounted on your roof so that your roof is not going to leak. Yes, you want the installer to drill on your roof, but only to put up mounting block heads, so he can flash and then put composite roofing material or terra-cotta tile or whatever sort of material you have on your roof around that flashing. Then the solar structure gets built atop that. You want to make sure that the solar installer is a licensed electrical contractor, or that he is going to work with a licensed electrical contractor. You'll want to ask lots of questions, including these:

- How much sun will I get and when?
- What is the plan to get the electricity down into my house?
- Where will they mount the inverter or the batteries?
- How will it tie into my system? (You want to make sure that they have a good plan for this; that there aren't large distances where there's line loss, where you have a long run of wiring.)

Reputable solar installers should be able to give you references of other installs that they've done, so you can go over and see their work. You want to look at their references. You want to talk to at least one person who's been living with this company's system for two years or more, because by then the owner will know if they have a leaky roof from the installation or other problems.

You want to have at least one person on the reference list who has spent several years with their solar install; five years would be ideal to know how the system is working, i.e., how their electricity bills are. You want to make sure that whoever has done this work has done it in a way where there's a measurable, substantial impact on someone's electric bill—it should be huge if they've installed a system that's supposed to produce a kilowatt or more of output. You want to hear that the homeowners have had a substantial reduction in their energy costs so that they're getting that money back over time. You must see that.

In fact, a reputable installer should give you a plan for payback. It should be a documented estimate for how much power you will make based on your current electric bill, what the paybacks should be, and how long it will take you to get that money back.

Another great resource for this information is DSIRE (see Resources, page 342). The name is an acronym for Database of State Incentives for Renewable Energy, though this easy-to-search database contains far more than just state incentives. It also has federal and local programs, from grants and loans to rebates and tax credits.

Just as another rule of thumb, here in California, there's a 50 percent rebate program. So, based on the current rates for electricity, if you put in a system that produces somewhere between 1 and 2 kilowatts of power, your payback should be eight years, give or take. After about eight years, you should be in the profit. This, of course, varies depending upon the amount of electricity you use, what your conditions are, and so on, but if your installer has designed a good system, a system that's scaled correctly and that gets good sun, you should start seeing a profit in about eight years.

Now, if you typically move more often than every eight years, you might never actually recoup your investment in a solar installation. But there are other factors that might make a

solar installation worth considering. For example, if your home needs a new roof, that might be enough of a variable to impact whether or not solar is the way to go for your home. You could build solar into the roof itself using the new tile technology, or you could integrate solar into the design of the roof and spend less on the combined project than you would on two separate jobs. Likewise, if you're planning to do a major remodel or add onto your home, again, it might be a very good time to look at adding solar in a cost-effective way.

What if you live in an area where there are no rebates? Then you're looking at a much longer payback period. It could be twenty years before you break even on your investment. The other thing to bear in mind is if you live in a region with affordable electricity, if you're in a place like Idaho, where you're paying 10¢ per kilowatt-hour for electricity, solar may never make sense financially. Electricity is so cheap in Idaho because it's hydroelectric power made by power plants that were built in the 1930s. They're all paid off, and power there is not only very affordable, it's green. It's not made by burning coal or burning natural gas. It's not producing harmful emissions. So if your local utility is already making green power and it's very reasonably priced, you really might be better off investing your money in an electric car and using that cheap electricity to power your mode of transportation.

By and large, if you're currently paying more than 20¢ a kilowatt-hour for electricity, then solar can be a reasonable financial proposition for you. If you're paying more than 10¢, you'll have to do the math and see for yourself.

Another thing to consider is if your local utility charges for electricity on a tiered system. This is different from a time-of-use meter. When a utility company charges according to a tiered system, you pay one rate for power up to a certain amount—up to a certain number of kilowatt-hours. Then when you exceed that number of hours, you pay a much higher rate for electricity. In this case, a solar install can start to make more sense financially even if it doesn't cover all of your energy needs, even if you still have to buy some power from the utility company, because at least you'll be buying that power at a lower rate and it will keep you from winding up on a higher tier.

If this all sounds complicated, the good news is, as mentioned earlier, you can find a good financial calculator online at PVWatts (see Resources, page 342). It will help you check out rebates and costs and get a feel for the payback period for solar in your particular situation. That's a really good resource when you're trying to make the financials work.

 ## BUYING AN EXISTING SOLAR SETUP

Perhaps the most cost-effective way to get into solar, especially for middle-income people, is to buy a property where the solar was installed during the time of construction. That way, the expense is built into the home mortgage, with the increase in cost amortized over the life of the loan! Let's say you're getting a $70 reduction in your electric bill every month with a 2-kilowatt system on your roof; it's surely not $70 extra a month on a thirty-year mortgage payment.

You don't have to buy a brand-new house to take advantage of this, either. If you buy any house where solar has already been properly installed, you're going to be paying for that system as part of your home loan. So there's a lot to be said for finding a property that already has solar.

Wouldn't it be wonderful if someday, when shopping for a new home—a nice tract home—solar power was one of the options, just the way paint colors and tiles on the floors, and carpeting in the bedrooms are? I think it would be a huge selling point, and I'm clearly not the only one who thinks so. All across the country, the real estate market is down—it is suffering as I write this book. But there's one sector that's not suffering, and that is "green homes," particularly those that have solar electric on the roof. Green homes are doing well in general.

So don't forget to figure increased resale value—and having a more saleable property in general, a property that will sell faster in a slow market—into the equation when you're making your decision about solar. As long as your system isn't some horrible eyesore, I'd like to think you can more or less count on increased resale value because of it.

Tile solar panels on a newer solar electric system are seamlessly incorporated with roofing tiles.

LEASING INSTEAD OF BUYING

Pretty soon, there should be an alternative to purchasing solar for your house or purchasing a house that has solar already installed, and that's leasing. There are several companies working on a leasing program for solar, and I'm hopeful that this option will become available sometime in the near future.

Due to cost considerations, purchasing or leasing actually is a very easy decision to make for most of the population. For now, solar of any size above 500 watts is out of reach for most people, who just can't afford it.

It's the same way as in the 1980s: I had friends who had some money who bought a satellite dish to receive television signals in their own backyard. And it cost somewhere around $4,000 or $5,000 for all the equipment, the receivers, the motors, everything that was involved, to get a signal. People who had money did it. That's almost the same group of people that's switching to solar now—the demographic with some extra spending money—or the early adopters.

But the majority of people can't afford that, so they're waiting for solar to get cheaper. And, if the leasing programs in development right now come to fruition, it will, just like satellite TV nowadays. People who want satellite can turn to the DISH Network or DirecTV, where you pay for the satellite services and do not own the dish. Pretty soon, you should be able to get that same sort of setup with solar. These companies will lease you the equipment. They'll install it at your house. They'll take care of all the permits. They'll connect it to the grid with a net metering setup. They'll handle any necessary maintenance. And then you'll pay your utility bill for whatever portion you still use of that.

Just like a system that you'd purchase, the idea with these leased systems is to size each one individually for a particular home and its particular situation—based on the number of people living there, the way it's used (e.g., is there a home-based business or is the house vacant during the day while everyone's at work or school?), whether there's a swimming pool, and so on.

At the end of your lease, the company will come and take all the panels and equipment back to the factory, and the plan is that they'll refurbish things and perhaps send them to a developing country, where they can be used again. Solar City (see Resources, page 342) has already begun such a program, and it's very encouraging.

Rob Wills, my energy consultant friend, and I were talking recently, and he mentioned that we're still experiencing the first generation of photovoltaics today, even after all these decades. But there are companies developing what's considered second-generation technology, such as an extremely thin film that's applied to the back of a piece of glass to create a solar cell. These films take solar tiles to the next level. The idea is that a company could make roof shingles—or even window glass—that creates solar energy.

Some of the current thin-film technologies use amorphous silicon, and at this point they're really experimental. We don't know the longevity of those materials. And they don't put out as much current as a polycrystalline panel.

But there are other second-generation technologies being developed by such companies as Nanosolar and First Solar that don't even use silicon. Experts in the industry are predicting that these developing technologies will make it possible to produce solar power for less than a dollar per watt. Unfortunately, we're a fair ways away from seeing any kind of practical application just yet—in large part because the efficiencies just aren't there yet, but there's no harm in being optimistic.

Still, as promising as these new technologies may be, I wouldn't wait to install a solar array until they come to market. As you know, there's no guarantee that emerging technologies will ever come to market. So if your house is a good candidate for solar today, take the plunge. Find the financing. Or find a house that already has solar and benefit from somebody else's investment. After the payback period, all the electricity you make is clean, green, and free!

Perform an Audit of My Solar Setup

Recently, it was time to do an audit of my solar installation. The system was eighteen years old, and it was time to make sure everything was still working properly. Actually, I knew some aspects of the system were no longer working as they should, since the system had been losing efficiency.

So here are some of the things I needed to look at:

- The simple business of the connections. These solar panels were put up in 1990. I have four feral cats that live in the yard and, unfortunately, on the roof. Yes, I'm guilty of feeding them. So I needed to get up on the roof and figure out if they'd scuffled around there and gotten snagged on wires. Were all the wires intact? Were all the connections still good from eighteen years of weather and all sorts of other activity?

- There was some extra shading. Soon after I installed solar panels on my roof, there was a construction project next door that gave a little additional shading to my roof.

- I had prior problems with four panels that had to be replaced. So I needed to figure out if I had additional panels that needed replacing.

- The batteries for my storage system were fifteen years old. The panels were working very, very hard all the time to keep those very old batteries charged. So I needed to figure out if it was time to replace the batteries.

So what did my audit reveal? First of all, the feral cats—and most likely rodents, as well—had been chewing on the wires. So we went through and replaced all the wiring on the panels. Also, my storage batteries were no longer working as efficiently as they should. So I returned the old batteries to their manufacturer for recycling and installed all new batteries.

I use a combination of fixed arrays and a tracker for optimal output.

I've made all these improvements to my system. And I've also made other changes to reduce my electricity needs—including improving the insulation in my house and installing the new GreenSwitch, as well as a few changes I'll mention in the next chapters.

The bottom line: I've been almost completely off the grid for months. I've only had to switch over to grid power occasionally to charge my electric car at night.

Going off-grid was an elusive goal for me for many years. But now I'm there, at least most of the time. I'm sure you can appreciate how deeply gratifying this is for me. Going off-grid just might be an attainable goal for you, too, if that is indeed one of your desires.

8

WIND POWER

**Determining if Your Home Is
a Good Candidate & Choosing
a Wind Power System**

A curved-blade vertical axis wind turbine is quiet,
efficient, and well suited for residential use.

THERE'S SOMETHING ELEGANTLY SIMPLE ABOUT
harnessing the wind to create power. Wind is free and,
depending upon where you live, it can be abundant. It
certainly qualifies as a renewable resource. Wind power
creates zero emissions. Unlike a coal-fired power plant that
spews carbon dioxide and other harmful emissions, an
entire wind farm produces absolutely zero emissions.

What many people don't realize is that wind is actually a form of solar energy. The sun heats the air and the ground unevenly. Couple this with the unevenness of the earth's surface and also with the rotation of the earth, and what do you get? Wind. If you've ever heard people talk about *thermals,* then this may sound familiar. Thermals are quite simply air currents created by a difference in ground temperatures.

Not only is wind a form of solar energy but creating electricity from wind is a lot like creating electricity from solar—including the fact that some homes are good candidates for wind power and some simply are not.

So we'll take a look at how wind power works first. Then we'll consider whether your home is a good candidate and discuss the details of choosing a system.

 ## HOW DOES WIND POWER WORK?

Wind power is actually quite simple to understand. It's made using a wind turbine, which is the opposite of how a fan works. With a fan, electricity spins a motor and creates air movement—wind, if you will. With wind power, things go in just the opposite direction: Wind spins a turbine and that creates electricity.

The spinning part on a turbine is actually called a *rotor.* It's comprised of *blades*—either two or three (usually three)—and a center part, called the *hub.* The blades on a wind turbine are made of either fiberglass or wood, so they won't interfere with TV or radio reception (a common concern among neighbors of those putting up a wind turbine). Both fiberglass and wood are essentially invisible to radio waves and television waves and any other form of electromagnetic waves.

The blades are part of the rotor, and the rotor is connected to a low-speed input *shaft.* That shaft turns the gears in a *gearbox,* which is a lot like the transmission in a car. The gearbox actually multiplies the speed at which the low-speed shaft is spinning. The gearbox then spins another shaft, which is aptly called the high-speed shaft, at a faster rpm. That shaft turns a *generator,* which creates the electricity. A tail on the turbine helps keep the rotors positioned to take maximum advantage of the wind.

All of this equipment—rotors, shafts, generator, and so on—gets mounted on top of a tower. There are two kinds of towers: self-supporting towers and guyed towers. Self-supporting towers are self-explanatory. Guyed towers use guy wires, or cables, and earth anchors to hold the tower in place, which is a less expensive option than a self-supporting tower. However, a guyed tower also requires more space, since the cables usually form a radius equal to half or even three-quarters of the height of the tower. In addition to a lower cost, the other benefit to a guyed tower is that it can be hinged, so you can lower it for maintenance—assuming you have enough space to drop the tower on your property.

I invested in a wind turbine in the California desert back in 1985.

Like a solar array, a wind turbine creates DC, or direct current. As with solar, the DC electricity gets converted to AC (alternating current) via an inverter, also known as a power-processing unit or a power conditioner (see Going from DC to AC with an Inverter, page 118). In residential applications for wind power, the inverter sometimes is mounted on the wind turbine itself, in which case it may be called a *microinverter,* since it's usually a small model. Other times, the inverter gets positioned near your electrical panel.

As with solar, you can make a good case for converting the power from DC to AC as soon as possible—that is, by positioning the inverter on the tower—so there's less line loss as the power travels from the wind turbine to your home. On the other hand, if the inverter breaks, you've got to get someone to come out with a lift to fix it, since it will be too high up to access yourself. On the plus side, inverters are getting very, very reliable, so if you buy one today, it will probably be good for the life of the turbine.

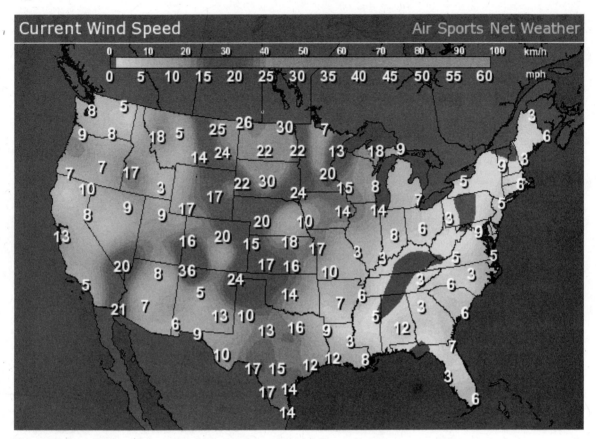

You can find wind-speed information for your area at several online resources.

WIND SPEED MATTERS

Just as you need to be sure you have sufficient sun to make a solar installation viable financially, you need to be sure you have sufficient wind to make installing a wind turbine worthwhile. Here's an interesting fact about wind: While the amount of output a solar array produces is *directly* proportional to the brightness of the sun, the amount of output a wind turbine produces is proportional to the *cube* of the wind speed.

So if the wind is blowing at 5 mph, 5 cubed is 125. According to my friend Rob Wills, the consultant for a number of renewable energy companies, depending on the turbine, you might get 12 watts of power from 5 miles an hour of wind.

What if the wind is blowing at 10 mph? Well, 10 cubed is 1,000, so according to Rob, you'd be getting more like 100 watts of power. This may sound good—and some experts say it's a sufficient amount to consider wind power—but it's probably not enough wind to make installing a wind turbine worthwhile.

If winds in your area reach 12 mph, you're starting to get into the range of really being practical for wind power production. And if you get wind at 15 mph, then you've got a really good site for wind power. As you can see, *small* differences in wind speed create *exponential* differences in power output.

Another important point: Because higher wind speeds make dramatically more power, if you live in an area where the wind pretty much blows at that same average speed all the time, you'll make moderate power. But if the average works out to be totally calm wind for three months out of the year and then for another nine months it's really raging, you actually end up making far more power over the course of a year.

This point often surprises people who consider wind power. It actually isn't important that it be windy at your house every single day of the year—as long as you aren't relying on wind as your only source of power. If you're tied into the grid and you can get electricity from your local utility company when you aren't creating your own wind power (as we discussed in the last chapter on solar, see page 130), you don't need wind every single day. Plus, there's no limit to the amount of power you can feed into the grid, so you can really benefit from those heavy-wind months. You can rack up some serious credits with your utility company by selling it all your excess wind power.

MEASURING THE WIND

So, how fast is the wind blowing at your house? It's a very important question. You have to live in a very windy area to be producing wind power cost effectively. If you don't have sufficient wind and you install a wind turbine, you're just throwing away money. You can invest that money in Energy Star appliances or a new and improved HVAC (heating, ventilation, and air-conditioning) system and be much better served than by putting money into a wind turbine that isn't going to perform on a fairly regular basis.

When my friend Robin Williams was deciding to install either a wind turbine or a solar array on his property in the Napa Valley, he took measurements. He had an anemometer (a wind meter) on the property measuring wind for a full year—since wind patterns do vary with the seasons—before making his decisions. This is quite prudent. First, get usable measurements and then decide from there.

Now, I'm sure some of you are thinking, "Wait a whole year to make a decision! You must be kidding!" Not everyone can handle that type of delayed gratification, I'll admit. But it's worth the wait to avoid making an expensive mistake.

Sometimes, in the fall here in Los Angeles, the Santa Ana winds are blowing 20, 30, or 40 miles an hour. And I think, "Boy, I need to get a wind turbine." But deciding on a project of that magnitude based on a couple of weeks of windy weather is not right. It really is best to get a year's worth of measurements before you make a decision.

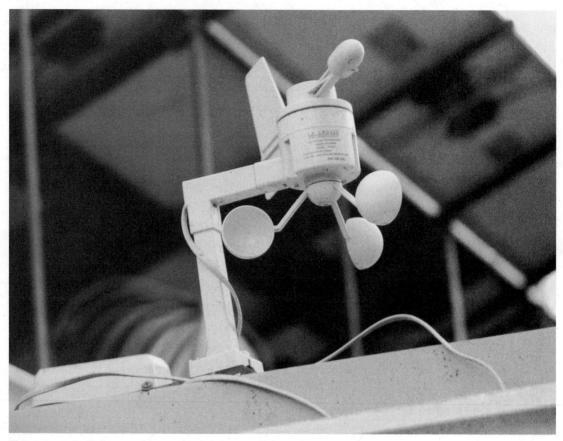

This mounted wind gauge takes quite accurate readings.

If you want to do some legwork yourself, you can get a handheld wind speed meter that's quite primitive for $20 from Real Goods (see Resources, page 343). You can do your own measurements on the cheap and find out what the wind is like at different times of the year, or you can get a more sophisticated device that will tie into your computer and record measurements over time. I bought a slightly nicer unit from La Crosse Technology (see Resources, page 343) and mounted it to my roof. It's taken quite accurate readings for months now.

Here's a great rule of thumb from Rob Wills. When you walk out the door, does your hat blow off your head? If the answer is no, then you probably don't have a good wind site. If the answer is yes, then you've got a great wind site. It can be just as simple as that. If your hat blows off your head every time you walk out the door, you probably live someplace where wind blows at 15 mph on average.

Another good approach is to look at the trees in your neighborhood. The way they grow will tell you a lot about the prevailing wind. According to the American Wind Energy Association (AWEA; see Resources, page 343),

- If you notice that the trees are *flagging,* meaning most of the branches and leaves are on one side of the tree, you know you get a lot of wind coming from one direction. If the ratio is essentially 2 to 1—if there's twice as much growth on one side of the tree as there is on the other—then you've got regular wind in the 9 to 11 mph range.
- If *all* of the growth is on one side of the tree, then you've got complete flagging, which means the wind regularly blows from 13 to 16 mph in your area.
- If the trees are literally bent in the direction that the wind blows, you've got what's known as *partial throwing,* and you've got wind blowing 15 to 18 mph.
- If the trees are just about lying flat on the ground, you've got a situation called *carpeting,* and that means you've got winds blowing at 16 to 21 mph on a regular basis.

Another great resource—and one that I'd highly recommend you go to even before you run out and buy an anemometer—is Choose Renewables (see Resources, page 343). You just go to the website and type in your ZIP code, and it will tell you if your home is a likely candidate for wind. If you're in a Class 1 zone, your spot is a poor candidate. If you're in a Class 2 or higher zone, you have better options for using wind.

You can also visit the U.S. Department of Energy's Energy Efficiency and Renewable Energy website and go to the Wind Powering America page (see Resources, page 343) for U.S. wind maps. Another great resource is Southwest Windpower (see Resources, page 343). If you choose Wind Maps in the navigation area, you can click on your state and be directed to a map online. For example, if you click on California, you'll open a new window with the California Energy Commission's California

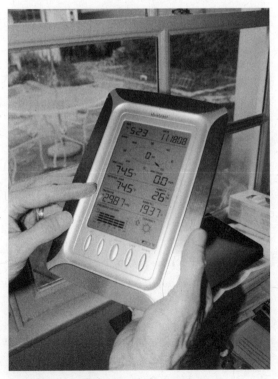

Anyone can easily use a wind gauge.

Wind Resource Maps. It provides wind-speed maps at various heights, including 30 meters, 50 meters, 70 meters, and 100 meters.

Bear in mind that these maps are generalized. So if you happen to live in the highest part of your area—on a ridgetop, perhaps—your site may be far better than the average for that locale. Conversely, if you live next door to a five-story apartment complex, your wind prospects are likely to be poorer than average.

TOWER HEIGHT AND LOCATION

Your home's location is a key factor in determining if wind power is for you, and so is your ability to mount a tall tower on the property. Because the rotors for a wind turbine get mounted on top of that tower, tower height is one of the key factors in wind turbine effectiveness.

To get real efficiency out of a wind turbine, it should be 30 feet above the ground. Otherwise you get what is called *dirty air,* air that has a lot of turbulence to it. According to the AWEA, "A rule of thumb for proper and efficient operation of a wind turbine is that the bottom of the turbine's blades should be at least 10 feet (3 meters) above the top of anything within 300 feet (about 100 meters)."

Even once you get beyond any obstructions like buildings or trees, wind speed continues to increase with height. So the taller you build the tower for a wind turbine, the more effective the turbine will be. Let's say you're considering installing a wind turbine rated at 10 kilowatts of power. If you mount it on top of a 100-foot tower, you'll make 29 percent more power than you would if you mounted it on a 60-foot tower.

On the other hand, local building codes and county ordinances in your area could seriously limit your ability to build a tall tower. Many have a maximum height restriction of 35 feet. And, of course, your neighbors may not appreciate a giant pole in your yard, either.

But if you happen to live in a rural, hilly area, you're in luck. You'd do really well to position your wind turbine up on the top of a hill, away from any buildings or obstructions. Jackson Brown has a wind turbine up on a hill on his ranch in Santa Barbara County, near the California coast. You could be standing at the base of his wind turbine and your hair would be barely blowing, but since the turbine is almost 60 feet off the ground, the wind conditions up near the blades are significantly different.

Another thing worth emphasizing, for those of you who may be on the East or West Coast: Both coasts are very reliable, consistent areas for wind. There's a prevailing wind blowing onshore most of the time on either coast, and those coastal breezes are very good for wind power.

Rob Wills points out one good reason for that, which is also why a wind turbine mounted near a lake or a pond can work really well, too. "When a stream of air goes over a rough surface, it has an exponentially increasing wind

This traditional horizontal-axis wind turbine is set up at a height to take advantage of clean wind.

speed profile," he says. "And the scaling factor for that profile depends on how rough the surface is. If you've got a sheet of water, like a pond, it's going to have higher wind speeds closer to the surface than if it's a rough surface like a forest or low bushes. And then if it's mown grass or something like that, it's going to be in between.

"Once you get up to about three hundred feet, you end up with flow that's pretty constant. But below that you end up with this exponential increase in wind speed. So the higher you can put your turbine, the higher the wind speed. . . . That is why the commercial wind turbines are three-hundred-foot towers with one-hundred-foot blades. . . . They're sitting in what's called the *geostrophic* wind.

"That doesn't help you in your residence. If you tell your neighbor you're going to put in a three-hundred-foot turbine, they're probably going to react negatively. And on top of that, you've got the problem of how do you raise and lower the thing. Maintenance becomes a huge nightmare.

"So towers in the range of thirty to ninety feet are practical for residences. And all of it depends on whether you've got support from the local town council to put in something higher. In my town, there were ordinances put in to control the spread of cell phone towers, but they also impact wind turbines. So we have a forty-foot ceiling on any structure without requiring some sort of exemption."

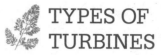 # TYPES OF TURBINES

When most people think of wind turbines, they think of modern, high-tech-looking versions of the old-fashioned windmill. They picture three blades spinning perpendicular to the ground. Those are what's considered *horizontal-axis* wind turbines. (That may seem counterintuitive, since the blades are vertical, but the piece that attaches the rotor to the generator is horizontal, so the rotor spins on a horizontal axis.)

Most municipalities will not allow you to put up a horizontal-axis wind turbine in a residential area. That's because these turbines are fairly noisy. You'll notice a sort of *fut-fut-fut* sound coming from them—at least from the straight-blade designs. The models with curved blades are much quieter. But the other problem is the blades on these horizontal-axis turbines go so fast, they're like big, nearly invisible Cuisinarts up in the sky. Birds fly into them and they're goners. Let's face it, even if *you* are willing to tolerate the noise of a wind turbine, the look of the thing, and the potential hazards to wildlife because you're getting lots of great, green power, why should your neighbors endure all that?

The good news is there is an alternative: another type of wind turbine that's much friendlier for residential neighborhoods. In fact, I have one on top of my garage. It's a *vertical-axis* wind turbine. It's a very new technology, and it's a truly exciting development in the world of wind power.

Some of these vertical-axis turbines look like one of the attachments for an old-fashioned kitchen mixer (the thing many of us used to lick the cookie dough off of when we were kids). There's a long tower, and it's got three upright blades on top that spin around in a circle. The blades are still vertical, like a horizontal-axis turbine, but instead of spinning perpendicular to the ground, these blades circle the tower.

There are a lot of benefits to this type of design:

1. **Quietness:** It's totally silent.
2. **Safety:** Of equal if not greater importance; these turbines won't harm any form of wildlife because birds and bats and all other manner of creatures can see the blades quite clearly.
3. **Aesthetics:** You can mount the mechanical components down low and put the wind collector up high, so it's less of a visual intrusion in your neighborhood.
4. **Urban orientation:** This design also can accept wind from any direction. So if you have a lot of changeability in wind direction—if you have more turbulence, as you typically do in residential and urban environments—the vertical axis can actually work quite a lot better than a horizontal-axis turbine.

When you're ready to comparison shop for wind turbines, you can find a good list of horizontal-axis turbine suppliers on the AWEA's website (see Resources, page 343). The two biggest suppliers in the United States are Southwest Windpower and Bergey WindPower (see Resources, page 343). Both are reputable companies that I would recommend.

As for the vertical-axis wind turbines, you'll find a good list of these suppliers at EcoBusinessLinks (see Resources, page 343). I'm currently working with a company called Enviro Energies (see Resources, page 343) that makes a turbine called the MagWind. It has a sail-like blade design and a magnetically levitated generator, just like the way the bullet trains work in Japan. With this mag lev design, the generator doesn't have any friction or gears to wear out or reduce performance. Through this new design, I'm hopeful that it will produce power at even low to marginal wind speeds.

 ## HOW MUCH POWER CAN YOU MAKE?

Before you shop for a wind turbine, the big question is: How much power do you need?

The "average" American household uses about 25 kilowatt-hours of electricity each day. Since by now I imagine that you've taken many of the steps we covered in the first section of this book, you're using less power than you were before. Perhaps you're using less power than that average American household.

The key is to figure out how much power you actually are using. Take a look at your electric bills for the last year and see just how many kilowatt-hours of electricity you've been buying. (If you've implemented conservation changes within the last year, I commend you, but I'm afraid you'll have to go ahead and make your best guesstimate in terms of your new and reduced power needs.)

Once you have a feel for how much power you need, then you can start looking at different wind power systems on the market. You'll find that small turbines range from 20 watts to 100 kilowatts. This means the manufacturer has rated them for that number as a *maximum* power output per hour. You're not going to make more than the maximum power rating— and you'll often make less. Most turbine maximum power ratings are at 25 to 30 mph wind speeds.

Also, when you're comparison shopping, pay close attention to the wind speed required for a particular power output. The idea is to match the wind turbine to your wind speeds.

Rob Wills points out that many reputable wind turbine manufacturers will have the power curve for each turbine posted on their websites, which shows the amount of power being produced at different wind speeds and also the maximum wind speed that the turbine can handle. "[That power output] is very close, typically, to the cubic curve of energy in the wind stream versus wind speed," according to Rob. "However, it's also a function of how big the capture area is, how big the blades are, how long the blades are, how big the vertical-axis collection system is."

Some experts, including the AWEA, say a 4- to 10-kilowatt system can meet the needs of a typical home. According to the Department of Energy, a 1.5-kilowatt (kW) wind turbine will meet the needs of a home requiring 300 kilowatt-hours (kWh) per month, for a location with a 6.26-meters-per-second (14-miles-per-hour) annual average wind speed.

I should also point out that all wind turbines have a storm-mode setting, a self-protective mode that provides overspeed protection. In extreme wind conditions, the turbine's design will allow it to become less efficient, so it doesn't capture all of the power of hurricane- or gale-force winds. Typically, the rotors will do something called *side furling* to get out of the direct line of the wind. Now, some models of wind turbines will make more power in storm mode than others. If you live in an area that gets these kinds of gale-force winds on a fairly regular basis, you'll want to check out the storm-mode power output capacities for different turbines, which vary by design. Choose one that produces the most power in these situations, so you get the maximum benefit.

INSTALLATION CONSIDERATIONS

As with solar, the vast majority of people will hire a professional to install a wind power system. You get not only the experience and expertise when it comes to the physical installation but also your installer's knowledge regarding the zoning and building codes in your area.

Plus, the installer will visit your home, take wind measurements, and then have the proper software to compute the output of a wind turbine if installed there, so you can get considerable help in choosing the right equipment for your location.

A professional installer also will help you determine whether it's best in your particular situation to go with an off-grid system or a grid-connected setup.

OFF-GRID SYSTEMS WITH BATTERIES

Like solar power, you can do a wind power installation that is connected to the grid, or you can do a standalone system. In most cases, it's easy to decide which way to go.

Obviously, it makes sense to consider a standalone system only if you live in an area with regular, fairly serious wind conditions.

Other important considerations include the following:

- Are you far enough off the grid where you would have to pay an exorbitant amount of money to get connected? It can cost from $15,000 to $50,000 *per mile* to run a power line these days.
- Do you live in an area with spotty electricity service, where you experience regular brownouts or blackouts?

- Do you have philosophical reasons for becoming self-sufficient?
- Do you have a backup power source—such as solar or a diesel generator—in case there is no wind for a period of time?

If you decide to do an off-grid, standalone installation, you'll need a substantial array of batteries on-site, so you can store power when you're making more than you're using. This stored power will tide you over when the wind isn't blowing, or it isn't blowing hard enough to meet your demands for electricity. A typical battery array will store three days' worth of power, and if you really cut back—if you use only a couple of lights and keep the refrigerator going but don't use, say, your computers or your 52-inch television—then you may be able to stretch that a bit.

Battery technology has improved over the decades, but we're still using lead-acid batteries for this type of storage system. You won't want to use regular car batteries, because they don't like to be charged and fully discharged. Deep-cycle batteries—like those in golf carts and wheelchairs—are a better choice, since they can handle regular charging and discharging. They're designed to go through this cycle, down to an 80 percent discharge, literally hundreds of times.

Another important point: You're not going to want to put the batteries for your wind system in your house. They need to be away from your living space (for example, mine are in my

This hybrid system is benefitting from both solar and wind technology.

detached garage), since batteries contain not only corrosive substances but also explosive substances. If you live in an area with extremely hot summers or extremely cold winters (or both), you also will need to put the batteries in an insulated location. Lead-acid batteries do not like temperature extremes.

GRID-CONNECTED SYSTEMS

The vast majority of people won't try to do a standalone wind turbine installation. When it comes to wind power, most people will choose to install a grid-connected system.

As we discussed in the solar power chapter, there are some inherent inefficiencies with a battery storage system. There's loss of power

through the batteries, since they don't hold every bit of energy that you attempt to store in them. And then there's loss of power when the wind is blowing but the batteries are full and you simply can't store any more energy.

You don't have these problems with a grid-connected system, because any power that you are not using in your home goes straight into the grid. And for those times when you need more power than your wind system is making, you just pull it off the grid. So the grid acts like a gigantic battery storage system.

Now, if you're worried about power outages, then you might want to do a combination system, like we discussed with solar. In this case, you'd be connected to the grid most of the time, but you'd have the option of disconnecting and running off a smaller array of batteries in case of an emergency.

It makes sense to consider a grid-connected wind power system if:

- you have sufficient wind
- your local utility charges a fairly high rate for electricity, say 10¢ per kilowatt-hour or even more
- your utility will allow you to connect to its grid for a reasonable rate
- your local building codes allow you to erect a wind turbine

Ideally, you'll want to switch over to net metering with a time-of-use meter, as we discussed in Chapter 7, "Solar Power" (see page 130). This way, you can sell power to the utility company whenever you're making wind power, day or night. If you happen to get most of your wind during the middle of the day, all the better, since you'll be selling all of your excess power to the utility company at its top retail price.

Even if your wind speed is fairly uniform throughout the day and night, if you have a fairly normal schedule, you won't be using much power during peak hours, so you can sell most of your power production to the utility company. If you can make some adjustments to use most of your power at home during off-peak or low-peak periods, then you can buy that power at a substantially lower rate, which will lower your electricity bill dramatically.

Being connected to the grid has another huge benefit: You can install a smaller wind system, since you don't have to generate 100 percent of your power on-site. This will save you money, making wind a much more budget-friendly option.

WIND AND SOLAR HYBRID SYSTEMS

Another option, both for those of you who want to go off-grid and for those who want to be grid-connected, is to install a system that uses wind and solar to generate electricity.

For much of the United States, the sun is strongest in the summertime, and the wind is strongest in the wintertime. So then a hybrid system makes a lot of sense—assuming you can afford the dual investment. You also can install a smaller wind or a smaller wind-and-solar system if you add a diesel-powered generator to the mix. That way, if it's not windy and it's cloudy or dark out, you can charge the batteries for a standalone system using the generator. Naturally, you'll need a controller to manage what's making power and when, but today's electronics make that a lot easier than you'd imagine.

If you're living off-grid, the ideal situation for a solar/wind hybrid setup would be to live in a place where the wind really picks up at night. That way, you'd be producing solar power during the day and wind power once the sun was not so strong. (If you're connected to the grid, this is not such a big deal. In fact, if you've got net metering with a time-of-use meter, you again want to make most of your power during peak hours, since that's when the utility pays you the most for the power you sell it.)

If your home is a good candidate for wind

power, I highly encourage you to go down this path. I'm even a little jealous. I've often spoken of the elegance of wind power. In fact, I believe sailboats are the most efficient form of transportation specifically because they're wind powered.

I realize installing a wind turbine is not always an economical proposition, or even a feasible proposition in some locales; but where it works—financially, in terms of zoning, and as far as potential to produce sufficient electricity—wind is one of the cleanest, greenest sources of power possible. And as with solar, once you've recouped your initial investment in a wind turbine, you not only get green power, you get free power. That's tough to beat!

Once you consider all the factors that affect your installation, odds are your payback period will fall into the very broad range of some time between six and thirty years. Now, if you're looking at a system with a twenty-year life expectancy and a thirty-year payback, clearly that's not a very wise investment.

A system with a six-year payback is a no-brainer—especially when you consider that it will increase the value of your home, so even if you sell before the six years are up, you should recoup the balance of your investment through your home's increased resale price.

However, a typical installation still has a payback period of about fifteen years. That's a serious commitment of funds to get a fairly long-term payoff, but again, a good-performing, reasonably attractive system can increase your property value.

Sample Costs and Paybacks: Wind Power

Most wind turbines can be expected to last twenty to forty years. So if you expect to live in your home for that sort of long-term timeframe, then you can absolutely expect to make money on a wind power installation.

Of course, most of us don't want to wait anywhere near that long to get our money back out of an investment—and a wind power system is definitely a substantial investment.

As a general rule of thumb, you'll need to budget $3,000 to $5,000 for every kilowatt of power a system produces. So it would cost approximately $40,000 for a 10-kilowatt system, installed.

How long, then, will it take for you to recoup your investment? That depends on a few variables:

- **What do you pay for power?** The AWEA figures that installing a

5-kilowatt system can make financial sense if you pay more than $50 a month for electricity, and installing a 10-kilowatt system can make sense if you pay more than $100 a month. As with solar, the more expensive electricity is in your area, the better off you are to investigate alternatives.

- **How much wind do you have?** The higher the wind speeds at your home, the more power you can produce, which of course affects payback periods considerably. If you must supplement your power production via a solar array or a diesel generator or a connection to the grid, that will obviously affect costs and paybacks.

- **Are you looking at a net metering setup?** If you're selling electricity to your local utility, this can make a wind power system much more cost effective. First, if you have a time-of-use meter, you can get credits for producing power during peak hours, then buy your electricity at a lower rate, so you don't need to produce as much power to break even, cost-wise.

- **Will you be connected to the grid?** Simply being connected to the grid gives you the option of installing a smaller system, since you don't have to produce all of your power on-site.

- **Are there rebates or tax credits available in your area?** As with solar, there may be federal, state, and local rebates and tax credits for installing wind. These can dramatically offset the cost of a system and shorten the payback period considerably. As with solar, a good wind installer will have considerable knowledge about the rebates and credits available, and should do all the paperwork for you. For a list of current rebates and tax credits available, see Green Made Simple's website (Resources, page 343).

- **Are there any special loan programs available for a wind power system?** If you save more money each month on your electric bill than you pay on your loan, you can be cash-flow positive on a wind system right away. For a list of loan programs in your area, see Resources on page 343. Or, as with solar, you may be able to get a home equity loan that makes a wind installation financially doable.

Installing a Wind Turbine

Yes, I know, I'm supposed to be the expert here, but even I can make a mistake. As I mentioned, I had a vertical-axis wind turbine installed on top of my garage.

Now, I love the idea of wind power. In fact, back in 1985 I invested in a wind farm. I bought half of a wind turbine on a commercial wind farm, and through that investment, I've been putting enough electricity onto the grid to power ten homes. I'm a huge proponent of wind power.

But I've also learned a valuable lesson. It *seems* plenty windy here where I live. Santa Ana winds blow sometimes 20, 30, or even 40 miles an hour. Even when it's not blustering like that, it seems windy enough to make some real power. My problem is that I didn't do what I'm telling you to do. I didn't take measurements of the wind at my house at different times of year.

My wind turbine is on top of my garage, but technically it's mounted on a 20-foot pole attached to the side of the garage so it can be lowered, if need be. I chose this height to match the height of the solar tracker on my garage. Well, guess what? Not only do I not get *enough* wind at my site to make the installation worthwhile, what wind I do get is dirty. It's turbulent. It's disrupted. It's lousy for producing wind power.

When you're looking at wind, you must first measure the wind over a long period of time. If you can't wait a year, at least measure it for three months using an anemometer. Take measurements and track the amount of wind you're getting.

Also make sure you're getting clean wind. Make sure you don't have dirty air caused by too much blockage, by trees and buildings and other obstructions.

The moral of the story is this: If you don't have 10—or, better yet, 15—miles per hour of clean, free-flowing wind on average at your house, don't install a wind turbine. Do not go any further. Do not pursue wind power if you don't have sufficient wind speeds. Learn from my mistake. I've got a lovely piece of art on a stick

Vertical-axis wind turbines can be mounted directly to the roof.

in my yard. Trust me: There are better ways to spend your money. Still, I remain optimistic. I'll continue to research new wind technologies like the Enviro Energies Mag Wind that can operate in lower wind speeds in the hopes that someday I can make some additional power from clean, green wind.

9

BUILDING & REMODELING

Building a Home from the Ground up
or Doing a Little Home Improvement

THE THEME OF THIS BOOK IS CONSERVE, THEN
produce, then manage—and that's particularly true when
it comes to building a home or remodeling an existing home.
In order to conserve when building or remodeling, you
want to use the most energy-efficient materials possible.
You want to use as much recycled content as you can, so
you're conserving new resources. You want to really be
smart about choosing the right doors, windows, insulation,
and lighting.

You also want to conserve space. The larger the home you build, the
more materials, the more heating, the more cooling, the more everything
that's required.

The idea is to build everything as smart as possible. Choose the best
building materials. Choose the highest recycled content. By building with
an eye toward energy efficiency, you're going to get your money back in
fairly short order (especially considering the way energy prices are rising).

Every dollar that you spend on conserving energy—on reducing the
amount of electricity that you use in your home—will net you a $5 reduc-
tion on what you would otherwise spend to install a system to produce
solar electricity. That's the scale that people in the solar world use.
The experts say, "Spend your money on conservation first." The idea is
to reduce your need for electricity as much as you can before you even
consider installing some sort of power-producing system, because every
dollar that you spend saves you five in solar or wind or whatever sort of
energy-production method you choose.

Of course, I realize not everybody has the money to build the absolute greenest home possible. The key is to make wise choices that will give you a good return on your upfront investment. The things I would absolutely include in new home construction—or in an addition or a remodel—would be the thickest walls possible, great insulation, energy-efficient windows, Energy Star appliances, Energy Star heating and air-conditioning, and passive solar and Sola-tube skylights for free, healthy lighting during the day. If there's a little bit of wiggle room, financially, I'd go the extra mile and install solar hot water (see Chapter 13, "Heating Water"). If there's yet even a little more wiggle room, I would install a kilowatt of solar power, some small amount of solar that you could later add to in a modular sense as the resources became more available to you.

THE U.S. GREEN BUILDING COUNCIL

It can sometimes be a little tricky to discern which home builders are truly green and which ones practice a sort of *greenwash,* which is like whitewash. Sometimes it can be tricky to identify which products and practices are best— or which are best in your area, since there's certainly a regional aspect to green building. Practices that work best in a desert environment don't necessarily work best in a snowbelt environment or a hot, humid environment. As

is the case with so many things, it makes sense to buy local. So different choices are greener in different areas.

Fortunately, the U.S. Green Building Council (USGBC; see Resources, page 344) has made huge strides in creating a national standard for green building. Actually, there have been local and regional groups in some parts of the country over the years that have set up green standards and established green best practices. But the USGBC has made a unified, concerted national effort to standardize—or at least clarify and categorize—what constitutes green building, to create a consistent standard that can be applied throughout the United States and beyond.

I'll go over these standards in some detail because they make a great guideline for green building, whether you decide to pursue certification or buy a house that is certified or not. The USGBC has done a really good job of hitting the important points with regard to building green.

The council actually started out by creating standards for commercial buildings. But in 2008, it released its first residential guidelines. These guidelines were in the beta-test stage for several years, in an effort to again take into consideration regional variations and what works best with contractors, subcontractors, and other people in the trades. According to the USGBC, the goal is to identify good practices, better practices, and best practices, and set the industry standards.

What the council came up with was a very collaborative effort. A volunteer committee made up of experts and people actively working in the building and construction industry in all capacities came together to create the LEED (Leadership in Energy and Environmental Design) for Homes Rating System, which I highly recommend that you download from the USGBC website. The USGBC states

> LEED for homes is a rating system that promotes the design and construction of high-performance green homes. A green home uses less energy, water and natural resources; creates less waste; and is healthier and more comfortable for the occupants. Benefits of a LEED home include lower energy and water bills; reduced greenhouse gas emissions; and less exposure to mold, mildew and other indoor toxins.

So over time, it *costs* less—sometimes dramatically less—to live in a LEED-certified home. It's *healthier* to live in a LEED-certified home. Plus, in hundreds of cities across the United States, LEED-certified homes qualify for tax rebates, special zoning allowances, and other incentives.

One of the great things about the LEED for Homes Rating System is it allows for flexibility. It functions as a checklist so a home builder may choose to do some things and not others. It's not a rigid set of guidelines. It provides options, in terms of how much money you want to spend, in terms of the way you accomplish various goals and in terms of how far down the green path you want to go, which often again is tied to financial considerations.

And so while the rating system is new, because of the built-in flexibility, many builders have found that they were already doing what it takes to build a LEED-certified home. Although it's a new standard, it's not news to many builders.

It's also important to point out that the LEED rating system is designed to rate—and certify—a house, not a builder. When you're looking for people to work with in building a home or remodeling, you don't have to find a LEED-certified builder. You just need to find a builder who builds LEED-certified homes. (It is possible for builders to become LEED certified, but it's cost prohibitive, so even builders who intend to exclusively build LEED-certified homes rarely take this extra step.)

 ## LEED CERTIFICATION

So what exactly is LEED certification? Well, obviously, it's not some loose, "because I said so" kind of green thing. A builder can't just call a house LEED certified, even if he followed the LEED criteria. He has to have an independent third party visit the house and evaluate it. There are LEED Green Raters who perform field inspections and do performance testing. They work through the checklist for the LEED for Homes Rating System and assign a point score to the home.

What are they looking for? The LEED for Homes Rating System measures the overall performance of a home in eight categories:

1. Innovation and design process
2. Location and linkages (includes the placement of homes in socially and environmentally responsible ways in relation to the larger community)
3. Sustainable site
4. Water efficiency
5. Energy and atmosphere
6. Materials and resources
7. Indoor environmental quality
8. Awareness and education (that is, education of the homeowner, tenant, or building manager about the operation and maintenance of green features)

It's also important to mention that LEED certification doesn't happen *after* a home is completed. It's a process that starts before anyone breaks ground. Once a builder puts together a team (architects, contractors, and so on) that will be working on a particular house—or housing development—the team develops a plan and a strategy for achieving sustainability. Then the project receives a preliminary LEED rating. This gives the team a chance to do some tweaking to the design, to make some adjustment to the materials choices, and more, so the home can meet the certification standards.

The house also gets inspected in the middle of the construction process, usually right before the drywall goes up. This is, in large part, to ensure that the materials, equipment, and systems have been *installed* properly. The greenest materials are only really green when they're installed properly.

After construction is finished, there's another field inspection with a considerable amount of performance testing, including testing for duct leakage in the heating and cooling system, testing for home envelope leakage (walls, doors, windows), and testing airflow into and out of the house. It's only then that the house either achieves certification or it doesn't.

LEVELS OF LEED CERTIFICATION

To become LEED certified, a home has to meet certain prerequisites. These are minimum standards for green building, and indeed for smart building. The home usually doesn't score any points for meeting these prerequisites, but they are absolutely required. These are what the LEED documents refer to as "good practices" and they include:

- erosion control during the building process
- no use of invasive plants in the landscaping
- the use of Energy Star–qualified lighting
- construction waste management planning
- good air filters

There are good practices. If a builder goes to the next level in a particular area, if he chooses to employ what LEED has identified as a "better practice," then the home usually gets 1 point for that. And if the builder goes even beyond that, if the home features a "best practice," that is usually worth 2 points.

Here's another important consideration: Some people assume that a home is either LEED certified or it's not. But there are actually *levels* of certification, which is part of the flexibility of the overall rating system. These levels of certification are based on the number of points that the house receives. So a house can be:

- LEED Certified if it receives 45–59 points
- LEED Silver if it receives 60–74 points
- LEED Gold if it receives 75–89 points
- LEED Platinum if it receives 90–136 points

The points total alone doesn't guarantee certification. A home also must meet certain minimum point requirements in several of the eight overall categories. In other words, it can't be energy efficient overall, but wasteful when it comes to water. It can't reduce waste on the jobsite but use materials that are not durable in the actual construction. It has to achieve a certain balance, as well as a certain overall point score.

SIZE MATTERS

I mentioned the importance of conserving space—of building smaller—and LEED puts a lot of emphasis on this as well. In fact, the LEED point system is actually a bit more of a sliding scale than the previous point break-down implies. That's because the rating system takes into account the size of a home and the number of bedrooms it has. Then it adjusts the point scale accordingly.

So, for instance, if a home has three bed-rooms and it's 1,900 square feet, that's considered average. If it has three bedrooms and it's just 1,500 square feet, the threshold for each level of certification is reduced by 6 points—so, for example, the house needs to get just 39 points to be LEED Certified. By the same token, going larger than average raises the certification thresholds, so a 2,300-square-foot, three-bedroom house has to get 5 more points to reach each certification level's threshold.

The LEED materials explain: "All things be-ing equal, a large home consumes more materi-als and energy than a small home over its life cycle (including pre-construction, construction, use and demolition or deconstruction). The adjustment compensates for these impacts by making it easier or harder to reach each LEED for Homes certification."

According to the USGBC:

- A 100 percent increase in home size yields an increase in annual energy usage of 15 percent to 50 percent, depending on the design, location, and occupants of the home.
- A 100 percent increase in home size yields an increase in materials usage of 40 percent to 90 percent, depending on the design and location of the home.

I would certainly encourage people to build a smaller rather than a larger home. But I understand that different people have different needs and different standards for what is comfortable and for what is necessary and so on.

My friend Susan Colwell, president and CEO of My Green Cottage (see Resources, page 344), a national builder of green and LEED-certified homes, says, "You're kind of looking at two different animals there, when you look at size and energy efficiency—and green, almost three different things. With size, you really want to keep things scaled down as much as possible to be responsible. We can, however, make any size home as energy efficient as possible. I can get a six-thousand-square-foot home to be seventy-five percent more energy efficient than a typical home that size. However, you're going to be greener and more responsible if you're doing a two-thousand-square-foot home and getting that to be seventy-five percent more energy efficient. Because we're going back to that conservation aspect."

EARNING POINTS

When it comes to LEED standards, a home's size determines the number of points needed to achieve certification. But how does a house actually earn points? Well, all kinds of green choices can earn the points needed for certification. In LEED parlance, this includes such things as:

- using better-than-basic insulation
- using exceptional windows
- getting down to a level of minimal leakage through the home's envelope (walls, windows, doors, etc.)
- installing a very high-efficiency heating, ventilation, and air-conditioning (HVAC) system
- greatly reducing distribution losses through the HVAC system
- installing high-energy-efficiency appliances
- installing a water-efficient clothes washer
- installing a renewable energy system, such as solar or wind power

As you've probably noticed, most—if not all—of these are steps you would take anyway when building a home. So while going for LEED certification certainly does add some complexity to the building process, it's not going to make you do anything outside the ordinary.

Let's look at some of the things the LEED guidelines focus on, as well as the things you'll want to focus on regardless of whether you actually decide to pursue LEED certification.

CHOOSING A SITE

Where you build your home obviously makes a big difference. I picked the area where I live quite specifically—not just Studio City, but the specific part of Studio City—because of the low energy usage that was possible. I can ride my bike from my house to all the studios in the San Fernando Valley. I can ride my bike with relative ease to the other side of the hill, into the city proper. And I'm right near a transportation hub at Laurel Canyon and Ventura Boulevard that I can walk to. Part of my energy-conservation strategy with siting was to live near a transportation hub and to live in a place where I could walk to lots of restaurants and shops and the post office and the market.

The LEED for Homes Rating System goes so far as to give a house 1 to 3 points of extra credit for being within a quarter-mile or a half-mile of what are considered *basic community resources,* places like an arts and entertainment center, a bank, a community or civic center, a convenience store, a day-care center, a fire station, a fitness center or gym, a laundry or dry cleaner, a library, a medical or dental office, a pharmacy, a police station, a post office, a place of worship, a restaurant, a school, and a supermarket.

The more services you have nearby, and the closer they are, the more LEED points are awarded to the house. Access to a nearby open space, like a park or a pond with a walking or bike path, is also good for a point.

HIGH-DENSITY INFILL

Beyond proximity to public transportation, shops, restaurants, and public services, what else makes for a good building site? The LEED for Homes Rating System gives extra credit for building in existing neighborhoods, rather than having to build roads and run utility lines, sewer lines, and water lines and possibly even install sidewalks and streetlights in a new area. (For developers of housing tracts, this is a major consideration.) If you choose (or if a developer chooses) a lot that's considered *infill,* you get 2 points toward certification. By LEED standards, that means 75 percent of the lot's perimeter is adjacent to previously developed land. You can get 1 point for either building on the edge of a developed area (where at least 25 percent of your lot's perimeter is adjacent to already developed property) or building on land that had been previously developed. You also can get 1 point for choosing a lot that's within a half-mile of existing water and sewer lines.

"Infill lots are really, really green," says Susan. "Let's say you have a community inside a city, and in between some houses you have a vacant lot. And it's never been built on for whatever reason, or it has a derelict house or a dilapidated house. The most responsible use of that particular land in that particular area is to rebuild on that space."

The opposite approach would be to take a beautiful, pristine piece of land and grade it or otherwise completely transform it so that you can build on it. Susan refers to that as *visual pollution.*

Density is considered a big plus, too, when it comes to building green. "Believe it or not, and this might shock you, New York City is considered a green city," says Susan, "because there's so many people occupying such a small land mass. That's one of the biggies for green. You don't want to take up a lot of space to house the people. And then once you've got the people there, you don't want them to jump in their cars and start driving everywhere. So Manhattan—for their mass transit and for the amount of structures and people per square mile—is really considered a green area."

The LEED rating system definitely rewards high-density building. If you build a home on $\frac{1}{7}$ of an acre of land, it will get you 2 LEED points. Build on $\frac{1}{10}$ of an acre and get 3 points. Or build on $\frac{1}{20}$ of an acre and get 4 points. This program not only encourages individual home building on small properties, it also encourages high-density housing developments.

POSITIONING THE HOUSE ON THE SITE

Once you've chosen a site for your house, the next question is, how will you position your home on the site?

If I were building a house on my current site, I would redesign the house so the solar panels got better exposure year-round. I would either go up to a second story or adjust the house to maximize the southern exposure and avoid shading from trees and neighbors to get better exposure on my solar panels.

I also would build a passive solar house. That is, I would position the house to have just the right southern exposure. My ideal house would have an overhang—a porch or an extended roofline or awning—that was designed so that sunlight was allowed in through the windows as we drew near the winter solstice. That sun would come in and light my rooms and provide warmth during the wintertime, when I want that free heat for my home. And then when it got into the fall and spring equinox, the overhang would be designed to allow only minimal exposure during those periods. And as you approached the summer solstice, the overhang would provide maximum 100 percent exclusion of sunlight on glass surfaces.

That southern exposure and extended roofline would bring more light from the sun in the winter, so I'd need less energy to light the house. It would bring more heat in the wintertime, so I'd use less energy to heat the house. It would help keep the house cooler in the summer by preventing sunlight from entering and heating the rooms, so I'd use less energy to cool the house. And it also would allow me to produce more solar power than I currently am. It would be a grand slam.

Now Susan does bring up an important point about passive solar: "Some lots, you would have to remove so many trees in order to get passive solar gain that that would not be very responsible. So you wouldn't want to do that. But if you have a location where you

LEED-certified homes and green construction can be applied to many different styles of homes.

don't have to remove a lot of trees to have the passive solar design, then you need to take a look at things like overhang. And placing the ridgeline of that home from east to west. And placing most of your windows on that south-facing side."

Another important factor when it comes to positioning a house on a site, which Susan touched on, is the existing landscape. You certainly don't want to be cutting down hundred-year-old trees to build your home—or at least not any more than you absolutely have to. The LEED rating system gives a point for minimizing the disturbance to a site both during construction and for the long-term.

The LEED system also rewards you for installing permanent erosion controls, especially if part of the lot is steeply sloped. Retaining walls and terracing not only make the property safer and more usable, they also get you another LEED point.

 FRAMING THE STRUCTURE

Now that we've covered where to build, the next question is how. This brings us to far more choices:

- You can build a traditional wood-frame house (also known as a *stick-built* house in industry jargon).
- You can use steel for the frame instead of wood.
- You can use newer materials, such as structural insulated panels (SIPs) or insulating concrete forms (ICFs), among many other options today.

Susan says, "The eco-friendly method of framing a structure really has to do with the area itself. So, for example, if we're building a home in the Southeast, we're going to use some different materials than we would use in the Northeast. If we're building a log home, we're going to be looking at a responsible use of lumber.

"For any of these homes that we're building, we're going to [try] not to ship loads over five hundred miles. And we also take it a step further in saying, 'Not only are we not going to ship over five hundred miles, but we're not going to send less-than-full truckloads.'

"We practice something called *lean construction practice* and *lean construction management*. And what that means is basically we're taking every single aspect of this construction process and we're leaning it up so that: (a) it doesn't cost any more, and (b) it's also better for the environment, because we're not running a bunch of trucks up and down the highway fifty times to deliver one two-by-four."

When it comes to framing, you have a lot of choices these days. Susan's company doesn't sell stick-frame houses, but if you're considering going that route, she suggests one way to conserve resources: Instead of framing the walls with the 2×4s spaced 16 inches on center, you can space them 24 inches on center. Of course, you'll need to check the local code books and engineer the home properly for strength, but this move certainly will conserve lumber.

"We don't sell traditional, site-built structures because they are so wasteful," says Susan. "We will use whatever substitute building method is right for that environment. For example, in many parts of the country we'll use a timber-frame structure with SIPs (structural insulated panels) because the total embodied energy to produce a timber frame structure is very low. The wood used for the frame is always sustainably harvested (FSC certified, whenever possible) and the panels are made with OSB (Oriented Strand Board), which preserves hardwood. When you enclose the frame with SIPs, you get a superefficient building envelope and the frame itself is visually stunning. Many clients say it's like living inside a gorgeous Thermos bottle."

So that style of building makes a lot of sense in some parts of the country. In other parts of the country, Susan's firm will use modular construction to control waste. And in other areas, they'll pour concrete walls on-site. It just depends on the area and what's best for that environment. Whenever possible, My Green Cottage and other companies like it make it a point to use local materials—both to reduce shipping costs and emissions from the shipping process and to stimulate the local economy. It's important to figure out the best building style for your particular location.

INSULATING CONCRETE FORMS (ICFS)

When it comes to framing your house, one good LEED-approved option is insulating concrete forms (ICFs), a relatively new building technology. Quite a few different manufacturers make ICFs, and each company's design is different. (You can find a list of manufacturers on the Insulating Concrete Form Association, or ICFA, website; see Resources, page 343). In spite of the wide variety of designs on the market, there are some similarities across the board.

At the most basic level, when you pour concrete, whether you're making a driveway or a retaining wall or a foundation for a house, you need to use forms. The forms literally form the outline into which the concrete will be poured. Most of the time, concrete contractors build wood forms on-site, and once the concrete has set, they remove the wood and leave the concrete.

ICFs are different. For starters, these forms are left in place after the concrete has been poured. What's more, these forms are used for pouring concrete *walls*. (Contractors also can pour concrete walls without using ICFs, but ICFs do offer some substantial benefits. Both methods are generally considered green, which is why Susan's company, My Green Cottage, uses both approaches.)

Now, the forms themselves, the ICFs, are made of foam insulation. So you wind up with a kind of a sandwich wall: you have two layers of polystyrene insulation on the *outside* with concrete in the middle. And like any concrete wall, rebar is used to reinforce that concrete within the ICFs. Again, out-gassing is not a problem with this material.

Because the ICFs are left in place, they've also been designed to act as a backing material. Inside the house, a builder can attach drywall to the ICFs. Outside, a builder can attach stucco or siding or brick.

There are essentially three kinds of ICF building materials:

- **Blocks,** which interlock like children's toys. These are the smallest kind of ICF. They're typically 10 inches wide, with a 6-inch cavity in the middle into which the concrete is poured.
- **Panels,** which are attached using connectors, or ties. These are the largest type of ICF; they range in size from 1×8-foot to 4×12-foot panels. They can be assembled into units using those connectors at the job site or prior to delivery.
- **Planks,** which are similar to panels but get connected with ties during the setting process, so they can't be pre-assembled before delivery. They also come in smaller sizes than panels, usually 8 to 12 inches tall and 4 to 8 feet wide.

Even within these three categories, there are at least three other options:

- **Flat wall systems,** which have two layers of foam on the outside, and into

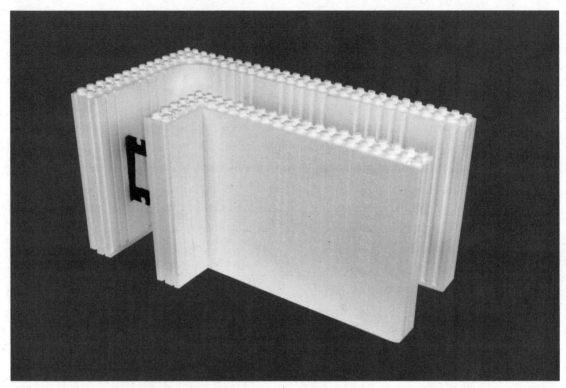

Insulated Concrete Forms like this one help accumulate LEED points as well as save you energy.

which a contractor will pour concrete. The end result is much like a more traditional poured-concrete wall, with a uniform thickness of concrete throughout, but you wind up with the two layers of insulation left in place.

- **Waffle grid wall systems,** which have a waffle pattern within the forms. The concrete winds up thicker in some areas and thinner in others, with foam filling in the blanks.

- **Screen grid wall systems,** which create horizontal rows and vertical columns of concrete with foam remaining inside the grid

ICF makers also offer different size cavities for the concrete. You can find standard sizes with 4-, 6-, 8-, or 10-inch cavities. But some systems can be put together to create cavities ranging all the way up to 24 inches, usually going up in 2-inch increments.

So, what are the benefits of this construction technique?

- ICFs can be used to build a house that requires about 44 percent less energy to heat and 32 percent less energy to cool than a comparable wood-frame house, according to research by Building Works, Inc. (see Resources, page 343).

- They have R-values ranging from R-17 to R-26.
- ICFs provide a sound barrier, creating a house that lets in just ⅙ of the noise of a comparable wood-frame building.
- They act as a natural barrier against air, providing a very tight envelope, often 50 percent tighter than a comparable wood-frame home.
- They act as a natural barrier against moisture, helping to prevent problems with mold, mildew, and rot.
- ICFs create a building that is up to 8½ times stronger than a wood-frame building, so they're better able to withstand hurricanes, tornadoes, earthquakes, and more common occurrences, like teenagers slamming doors.
- They typically have a two-hour fire rating (compared with fifteen minutes for a comparable wood-frame wall).

Currently, houses built with ICF exterior walls cost slightly more to build than wood-frame construction. However, the higher cost of materials is almost completely offset by much lower labor requirements. Also, the increased up-front cost can soon be offset by energy savings. And it's tough to put a dollar figure on the increased quality of life you can enjoy from the quieter, more airtight and mildew-resistant home.

Again, you can accumulate LEED points for using ICFs when building your home. According to the ICFA, those points can add up in several categories, including energy optimization, using recycled materials, using regional materials, creating a durable structure, and creating a sustainable site.

STRUCTURAL INSULATED PANELS (SIPS)

Another new material that's really worth considering is structural insulated panels (SIPs). If you live in an area where SIPs make sense, as I do, they're a really good choice. As the name implies, they're designed specifically to insulate a structure, and they do that job really well.

Indeed when I spoke to my contractor about getting a new air conditioner for my home, he wanted to scale it very close. In the old days, you'd install a much bigger A/C unit than you thought you were going to need, because you *might* need it one day. But today, the energy efficiency experts recommend that you scale an A/C unit very close to your actual square footage.

So since the contractor was scaling his recommendation of a new A/C unit to the current size of this 1,585-square-foot structure, I said, "Look, Rick, it's probably going to be eighteen hundred, nineteen hundred square feet when I'm done. We're talking about adding on, making a full bathroom when there's now half a bath. Making another guest bedroom here on-site. Going further out in the yard. So I know you talk about getting really tight on that A/C unit, but add on another four to five hundred square feet just to be safe."

And he said no. I said, "Why? I'm going to need it. We're going to do a construction project."

And he said, "You don't need it, and here's why. Because even though you're adding more square footage, if you are who I think you are, when you do your addition, you're going to get rid of these old thin walls from the 1936 house—even with the good insulation, even with the double-pane windows—and you're going to use SIP material for the new walls in your house. You won't need an extra BTU of air conditioning for what you're doing. You can add five hundred, eight hundred square feet on, and you won't need a bigger A/C unit. I promise you, you won't need it."

So what exactly are SIPs? My friend Barry Rosengrant, CEO of E-Space Systems (see Resources, page 343), works directly with the makers of SIPs and keeps close tabs on what's happening in the industry. He explains that an SIP is a sandwich type of product. On the outside, you have particleboard. It's called oriented strand board (OSB). "It's like a plywood," he says. "And it's typically a quarter-inch thick."

In between those two outer layers of OSB, you have an expanded foam filling in the gap. That foam layer can be 3, 4, 5, or even 6 inches thick, and it provides insulation. The thicker the foam, the more insulation it provides. Right now, that foam is either a polystyrene or a polyurethane. "The urethane people will say their foam is better," says Barry, "and the styrene people will say their foam is better, and the truth is there's not a lot of difference. The urethane, I think, is a little more expensive and is only used maybe by five percent of the SIP makers. The rest of the SIP makers use expanded polystyrene. And that material has now been deemed to be green. It took a number of years for whatever components are in the styrene . . . to meet the green

This structural insulated panel (SIP) is a great choice for energy-efficient building.

certification level." Now that they have, the material doesn't outgas. So it's good for your indoor air quality.

SIPs usually come in the same size that's standard for plywood, which is 4×8 feet, although you can order larger SIPs from most manufacturers. They're actually available in sections as large as 8×24 feet. They also come from the factory with openings already cut for windows and doors, which makes installation really fast. Your home can get enclosed in a matter of days—or less.

There're a couple-dozen companies making SIPs now (see Resources, page 344). When it comes time to choose one, it's wise to go with a reputable company. Insulspan and Premier are major suppliers. You also may want to check references, or use a company your contractor has had good experience with in the past. Besides price, the big concern is that the window and door openings are in the right place when the panel gets to your job site. If they're not, the panel can be recut, but that's labor intensive and you want to avoid it.

A FRAME FOR THE SIPS

The SIPs do have to be attached to some sort of frame, whether it's wood or steel. Barry's company, E-Space Systems, has developed a unique space frame system for hanging SIPs that makes it possible to build a super-energy-efficient house very quickly. The company has a patented connector system that allows engineered wood crossbeams to be bolted to vertical columns.

The company's space frame design also helps to reduce disruption of the site when you're building, which is a key LEED concern. You don't need to grade, for example, which can cause problems with erosion. Instead, Barry says, "E-Space can step down a hill without grading, as Sonatube-formed concrete piers support the space frame from which SIPs are hung. No conventional foundation is needed. Floors can be suspended at any level on the vertical frame—above the flood plain in the Gulf States, for instance."

Barry points out that his company uses only materials from ecologically sound sources. The company uses recycled wood chips, fast-growing "junk trees," and bamboo. All of the components are made from sustainable materials, and they all come cut to size, so there's no waste at the construction site.

BENEFITS OF SIPS

Structural insulated panels have some real advantages:

- They are incredibly energy efficient. According to the Structural Insulated Panel Association (SIPA), "SIP homes have repeatedly demonstrated annual energy savings of 50 to 60 percent when combined with other high-performance systems."
- SIP walls have a much higher real-world R-value than stick-built walls, because SIP walls can be built with long, continuous spans of this

material—instead of gaps where there are wood 2×4s or voids where insulation has to go around wiring or simply comes to the end before the beginning of another batt. An SIP wall with an insulation value of R-25 will have an actual installed, effective R-value of R-21.6. By comparison, a similar stick-built wall with fiberglass insulation that has an R-value of R-19 will more likely have an effective, installed R-value of R-11.

- SIPs are recyclable and reusable. If you want to remodel, you can literally take down an old wall and reuse it in a new location.
- SIPs produce a very strong structure that's exceptionally resistant to wind and storms and earthquakes.
- They're fire retardant.
- SIPs come cut to size, so building an SIP home can produce little or no waste on the jobsite. Building a typical wood-frame home creates dumpsters full of waste that has to be hauled away.
- When used with a space frame, SIPs allow for a very flexible design. You can have long open spans, rather than needing structural supports in the middle of rooms. You can have very high ceilings. You can build balconies easily. In terms of design, you can do some creative things.
- The house can be assembled very quickly. "The major quantifiable

feature is that a space frame goes up in a couple of days and can be enclosed with SIPs in a couple more days. No skilled labor is required to enclose a space that is roofed and out of the weather within two weeks for plumbers, electricians, etc., to work within," says Barry.

From a LEED perspective, off-site fabrication is a big deal. It can net you 4 points for materials efficiency.

FSC LUMBER

If you decide to go with a wood-frame house, or if you decide to use wood as a framing material for SIPs, the question is, what's the greenest wood you can use?

There's actually a nonprofit group called the Forest Stewardship Council (FSC, see Resources, page 343) that certifies wood as having been harvested in a green, sustainable way. The FSC was formed in 1993 by a diverse group of all of the experts and interested parties in the lumber business—loggers, foresters, environmentalists, and sociologists—not unlike the group that formed the committee to come up with LEED home-building standards.

So if you look for wood with the FSC logo on it, you know that wood came from a forest that has been certified as being well managed. This wood is widely available, even in the big home-improvement chain stores.

Sample Cost and Payback Analysis: SIPs

Let's say you're considering using SIPs for the exterior walls of a 2,000-square-foot home that will have three bedrooms and two bathrooms. How would using SIPs compare, cost-wise, with traditional wood-frame construction? Obviously there's going to be serious long-term energy savings from choosing SIPs. But in the short term, will it be more expensive to build this structure? Or will I actually be saving money?

E-Space Systems' Barry Rosengrant says the advantage of using an E-Space space frame and SIPs is you can build the house in far less time—$\frac{1}{10}$ or even $\frac{1}{100}$ of the time. So obviously there's a huge cost savings from a labor standpoint.

Also, he says, "We eliminate many of the trades. Carpenters aren't required. You simply bolt this together and run a screwdriver and that's it. So there's less mistakes." And you can use less expensive labor. As Susan mentioned, you won't need a crane, either.

When you figure in the materials costs, Barry says that it should work out to be about the same as more traditional construction methods. And then when you figure in the monthly savings on energy bills, you come out ahead in no time.

Another benefit to doing fast space-frame construction with SIPs that come cut to order just might be one you hadn't thought about: Using this approach to building can make financing easier. As Barry says, "You don't need a construction loan if you get [the house] up in a week or two."

You also save the costs of renting dumpsters and paying for waste to be hauled off to a landfill. Plus, you keep a tremendous amount of waste out of landfills, which has obvious environmental benefits.

Besides being sustainable, the other factor to consider is the distance the wood has to travel to get to your site. There's obviously a substantial environmental impact in transporting wood halfway around the world. When wood is logged and milled locally, considerably less petroleum is used and considerably fewer harmful emissions are created.

Another great option is using reclaimed wood. Recycling wood can be a far greener choice than using new wood. Using reclaimed wood for framing also can get you extra credit on the LEED for Homes Rating System.

ROOFING MATERIALS

I've talked about walls and framing. The other key component of a home's exterior is the roof.

The many choices when it comes to roofing materials today include asphalt shingles, wood shingles, clay tile, slate, recycled materials that look like slate, recycled materials that look like wood shingles, metal, or living things (also known as a green roof).

My first choice will always be to use recycled materials, particularly materials that are also recyclable themselves. But let's look at each of these choices and see how they fit into a green home-building plan.

ASPHALT SHINGLES

Now, most people in the United States have asphalt shingles on their roof. About three out of every four houses has this kind of roofing material. Why? Because it's the most economical option, both in terms of materials cost and installation cost, but there are obvious trade-offs. Asphalt shingles are a petroleum-based product. They don't last as long as the other roofing options. And in many cases, they cannot be recycled because they contain fiberglass. When selecting composite

or asphalt shingles, try to find ones that are recyclable or, even better, ones that are made from recycled materials. Then they become a much better choice.

WOOD SHINGLES

What about wood shingles? Well, in my area and in many parts of the country, the only way to make wood shingles acceptable under the fire code is to treat them with toxic chemicals. So while wood is natural, the toxic treatment certainly is nothing I want to endorse. If you don't have serious fire concerns in your area, you *can* find FSC-certified wood shingles, which is certainly better than using old-growth cedar forests for your roofing material. Wood shingles also offer twice the insulation value of asphalt, but as you know, wood can shrink and swell, which leads to cracking and other moisture-related damage. This means they're not the most durable option available.

CLAY TILE

Clay tile is another popular choice in Southern California and of course in many other parts of the country. The Spanish or Mediterranean look has been popular with builders and home-buyers for decades. Clay tile can be very durable. You can expect a well-made clay-tile roof to last fifty, sixty, possibly even eighty years. These tiles are also effective for insulating and quite good in terms of fire resistance.

On the other hand, clay tiles can be much heavier than wood and asphalt shingles, so the roof needs to be built properly to support them.

Also, these tiles are more expensive than wood. The good news is you can recycle clay roof tiles. You can also purchase tiles that are reclaimed and reuse them, so that's a big plus.

SLATE

Another heavy and expensive but recyclable and long-lasting option is slate, a natural stone, which has long been the popular choice for high-end homes in the Northeast. One reason for this regional emphasis is slate's ability to shed ice and snow.

SLATELIKE MATERIALS

While slate is obviously a finite resource, there's another option these days: roof tiles made from recycled rubber and plastic that look like slate. They're not only much lighter, they're much less expensive. And with as much as 80 percent postindustrial recycled content, they help to remove a considerable amount of material from the waste stream—and they're recyclable—so they can be a good green choice.

WOODLIKE MATERIALS

Companies also have begun manufacturing roofing materials that look like wood shake but that are made from recycled materials—sometimes plastic and rubber, sometimes vinyl and cellulose fiber—with as much as 100 percent recycled content, so there's another cool new option. These fake shakes are quite durable and fire resistant, and, again, they are recyclable.

Roofs and Heat

There's one very important thing to think about when it comes to reducing your cooling costs in the summertime, and that's the color of your roof. As I'm sure you know, darker colors absorb heat and lighter colors reflect heat. So the lighter your roofing material, the more it will help to keep your home cool.

Of course, color is not the only factor that affects how much heat your roofing material will reflect back off of it rather than transfer down into your home. You can find out which roofing materials do a good job of reducing heat gain on the Cool Roof Rating Council's website (see Resources, page 343).

The LEED for Homes Rating System rewards home builders for using FSC-certified lumber in the framing of a roof, as well as for using roofing materials with recycled content. Using local materials can earn points, too.

METAL

Another option that can have considerable recycled content is a metal roof. Metal roofs can be made from steel, copper, or aluminum. Galvanized steel gives a kind of a vernacular look in some regions, conjuring images of farm buildings and the like. At the other end of the spectrum is copper, which is quite high-end looking.

And while some people do assume that metal roofs are hot, the truth is just the opposite: They can have a real cooling effect on a home. Metal reflects heat, and it provides a good level of insulation, as well. It's also a good choice in snowy areas. And it's obviously quite durable, not to mention fire resistant.

The important point here is to seek out roofs that have a high percentage of recycled content, since manufacturing a new metal roof requires a considerable amount of resources, both in terms of materials and energy.

your roof and runs off—and then using it to water your garden. If you plan to do this, you'll want to carefully consider roofing materials, since some materials can leach hazardous substances into the water. According to the National Sanitation Foundation (NSF; see Resources, page 344), "Roofing materials can introduce metals, asbestos or particulate matter, depending on their material makeup." Asphalt shingles have been known to leach petroleum into rainwater. And the longer the water stays on the roof—whatever kind of roofing material is up there—the more potential there is for undesirable substances to leach into it.

A LIVING ROOF

You also can earn a point toward water management—and possibly earn points for reduced heating and cooling costs (i.e., energy efficiency)—by installing a vegetated roof, or a living roof, on top of your home. This type of roof features live plants and can provide tremendous insulation for a home, as well as transforming a considerable amount of carbon dioxide into oxygen. If you're interested in learning more about living roofs, Green Roofs is a very good resource online (see Resources, page 343).

CAPTURING RAINWATER
You also can earn as many as 4 LEED points for water efficiency by capturing rainwater—typically, by capturing rainwater that lands on

ENERGY MANAGEMENT

Not surprisingly, when it comes to conserving energy, the LEED for Homes Rating System rewards you for doing many of the things we've discussed in other chapters of this book. You certainly will want good—or better yet, great—insulation, along with great windows, great doors, and so on. You'll want a supertight envelope for your home.

You can also get considerable extra credit—as many as 34 points—for building a home that meets or exceeds the Energy Star for Homes requirements. That's right, not only are there Energy Star–qualified appliances and lights and windows and doors, there are Energy Star–qualified homes (see Resources, page 343). As

My rain barrel was one of the easiest cost-effective purchases I've made.

you would expect, these houses are 20 percent to 30 percent more energy efficient than
"standard" homes. And as you would expect,
they feature all of the Energy Star–qualified
equipment we've discussed in other chapters.

Much like the LEED Green Raters, there are
independent third-party Home Energy Raters
who go to houses, do inspections, and perform
tests to certify that homes qualify for the
Energy Star label.

You can earn up to 10 LEED points for putting in solar power.

The fact that this system has been around since 1995 made it easier for builders—primarily major builders of tract homes—to follow a logical pathway toward LEED certification. However, you also can get a single, custom-built house qualified as Energy Star. The process is not unlike the LEED certification process.

You can follow the Energy Star–qualification pathway through the energy efficiency part of the LEED certification process, or you can take another pathway. Quite logically, it involves doing most of the same things a builder would do in building an Energy Star–qualified house—

such as installing Energy Star–qualified air-conditioning and doors and lighting and so on. You can even get a ½ point for installing Energy Star–qualified ceiling fans (at least one per bedroom and one in the living room or family room).

Now, if you *do not* follow the Energy Star pathway through the LEED checklist, you can earn as many as 10 LEED points for putting in a "renewable electricity generation system," such as solar or wind power. According to the guidelines, you'll get 1 point for generating 3 percent of the amount of electricity a typical home would consume in a typical year. You'll get 2 points if you generate 6 percent, 3 points if you generate 9 percent, and so on.

The LEED program also encourages the use of solar to heat water, giving 2 or 3 points for a qualifying system (see page 281).

WATER EFFICIENCY

You know how important water conservation is to me. Well, it's very important in the LEED certification process as well.

You can get up to 3 LEED points for installing high-efficiency fittings and fixtures in your home. This includes faucets, showers, and low-flow toilets. Step up to very high-efficiency models and you can get a maximum of 6 points.

You also can get up to 5 LEED points for efforts you take to reuse water, such as

- capturing rainwater and using it for landscape irrigation or even using it inside your home according to local standards (up to 4 points)
- installing a gray water system for indoor use (see page 102 in Chapter 6) or for outdoor use (see page 214 in the following chapter; this can get you another point)

Or you can skip these two steps and participate in a municipal recycled water program, if there is such a program in your community.

Using municipal recycled water for your irrigation is good for 3 LEED points.

Landscaping is a big consideration when it comes to how much water you use, so the LEED guidelines also allow you to get up to 3 points for installing a high-efficiency irrigation system—or up to 4 points for reducing your irrigation needs by at least 45 percent compared with other homes in your area. (I'll go into landscaping and irrigation in more detail in Chapter 10, "Garden and Compost.")

INDOOR AIR QUALITY

Indoor air quality is another very important factor. In fact, there's a whole category called Indoor Environmental Quality in the LEED for Homes Rating System. One of the reasons for this is that you're creating a very airtight home. The envelope is going to allow very little air to enter from the outside. So you need to make a concerted effort to

- bring in fresh air
- vent anything that you don't want to breathe (like combustion gases from your water heater)
- install carbon monoxide detectors
- control indoor moisture levels to reduce the potential for mold and mildew
- have exhaust systems in all of your

bathrooms and in the kitchen

- balance the airflow of forced-air heating and cooling systems from room to room
- have a good air filtration system
- make sure the air from an attached garage is not entering your home
- control other indoor air contaminants, everything from fumes from the construction process to gunk you bring in on the soles of your shoes

The LEED rating system even provides a point for having a central vacuum system that's exhausted to the outdoors, and another point for having a built-in shoe removal and storage area, like a mudroom, near the entry to your home but separated from the living areas.

I'll go into more detail about flooring and paint and other materials that can off-gas and affect indoor air quality in Chapter 14, "Decorating and Cleaning Your Home," but the bottom line is to use the right materials. Stay away from urethanes. Stay away from volatile organic compounds, or VOCs. Keep away from toxic cleaning products.

If you avoid all these toxic elements when you build your home, you won't have an indoor-air quality issue. After all, the simple act of exiting and entering your house on a regular basis will bring in plenty of oxygen for you to live and breathe properly in your home. When you feel like you need more air, windows are easy to open and close again. You might even install a whole-house fan.

The bottom line is, if you're not using toxic

Installing double-paned windows can save you a lot on your energy bill.

materials in construction and not using toxic substances in your home, you're not going to have an indoor-air quality problem.

REMODELS AND ADDITIONS

The LEED for Homes Rating System makes a great checklist for new home construction, even if you decide not to go through the certification process. It's also a handy checklist to use as a guideline for a remodel.

But the USGBC has also collaborated on another program that's designed specifically for remodels and additions. Why is that? Simply because the options are different when you're talking about home improvement.

For starters, the home's location on the lot has already been decided. You're not likely to pick up your house and move it to a better spot or twist it to better catch prevailing winds or follow the path of the sun through the sky.

Remodeling projects also cover a pretty broad spectrum. They can range from something relatively mild like painting interior walls or changing the flooring in one room, to something more involved such as redesigning the kitchen, to something radical like completely gutting a house. They can involve work within an existing footprint, or they can involve an addition that's built from scratch, but that is still attached to an existing home.

All of these factors have been taken into consideration in designing the Regreen program (see Resources, page 344), which is a collaborative effort between the USGBC and the American Society of Interior Designers (ASID; see Resources, page 343). The focus of this program is just as comprehensive as the LEED for Homes guidelines. But in this case, the program provides a set of guidelines only. There's no rating system.

The Regreen guidelines have been custom tailored to handle the specific opportunities—and also the specific constraints—of a remodel, or even a relatively simple home-improvement project, such as getting a new air conditioner or choosing new windows. According to the Regreen folks:

Regreen addresses the major elements of any green renovation project, including the site of the home, water efficiency, energy and atmosphere, material and resources, and indoor environmental quality. The guidelines blend product selection, building systems integration and proven technologies into a seamless compilation of green strategies and case studies for the homeowner, builder and design professional.

The Regreen guidelines can be applied to a variety of home projects, from remodeling a kitchen to adding a major addition, from redoing a backyard to executing a gut rehab. Homeowners can either use the guidelines for their own do-it-yourself projects or visit a professional who can apply Regreen as a design guideline.

The emphasis here is on product selection—not recommending specific products, but helping you to make informed decisions.

RECYCLING THE OLD

If you're doing a remodel—or if you're tearing down an existing house and building a new one—there are so many wonderful choices available to you, not the least of which is choosing to make use of the materials from the demolition process in the new home. You can recycle the materials from your old space into your new space, quite literally.

The best use for those demolished materials—to get the highest LEED rating—would be to use them on-site in your own construction project. The next best option would be to provide them for use in someone else's project in a relatively close proximity. There's also Freecycle (see Resources, page 343), a nonprofit group that connects people who want to give away stuff with people who want to get free stuff. So if you have old sinks, old bathtubs, old mantelpieces, old floor tiles, old wood paneling, all kinds of stuff that comes out of a house, you go on the Freecycle website and post what you've got. The list goes out to people in your area, and somebody nearby is sure to want that stuff you no longer need. You may think that no one is going to want some of the things coming out of a demolition, but you'd be surprised. There's definitely someone who wants broken-up pieces of concrete driveway, if you can't use them on-site as I did on my property. I had to break up an old concrete path, and those broken pieces of concrete

reside on my property to this day as part of a new pathway in the front yard and another in the backyard. But if I couldn't use them, someone else would have! The goal is to make use of every single material from your demolition on-site or in the closest proximity available.

The other key aspect of recycling in any home-building or remodeling project, as I've mentioned, is using the highest recycled content possible. You can find a huge variety of recycled materials from sources all over the country. At the higher end, you can source pieces from antiques dealers. But all across the country there are also swap meets and flea markets and companies that specialize in architectural salvage. You can find reclaimed wood, used bricks, and used hardwood plank flooring from barns that have been torn down. It's even possible that the contractors and builder you choose have access to recyclables from other projects they're working on. You never know where you may be able to find just the right framing lumber or farmhouse sink or interior doors or drawer pulls. And you just might be able to save money in the process.

RESOURCES FOR STARTING A GREEN BUILDING PROJECT

Obviously, there are considerable resources available these days to help you get started on a green building project or a green remodeling project. In fact, green building has gone so mainstream that the National Association of Home Builders (NAHB; see Resources, page 344) makes it easy to find green builders near you.

The NAHB's National Green Building Program website includes a list of local and regional green building programs. The list, broken out by state, is easy to navigate and includes programs such as these:

- Build Green NH in New Hampshire
- Triad Valley Green Building Council in North Carolina
- Build Green Connecticut
- Indy Green Build in Indiana

Each of these programs has its own website, and each has links to local green home builders. Some also have their own certification programs, which may be similar to the LEED program, but which could be less expensive and which surely will be more regionally focused.

The NAHB also has come up with Model Green Home Building Guidelines, which were written by a group of builders, researchers, environmental experts, and designers to provide guidance for residential design, development, and construction. Much like the LEED guidelines, the NAHB guidelines cover seven areas, or guiding principles:

- lot design
- resource efficiency
- energy efficiency
- water efficiency
- indoor environmental quality

- homeowner education
- global impact

Like the LEED program, the NAHB guidelines also offer different levels of green building: in this case, bronze, silver, and gold. The group also is working on a National Green Building Standard.

Besides LEED and NAHB, there's Build It Green (see Resources, page 343), a nonprofit membership organization in California "whose mission is to promote healthy, energy-, and resource-efficient building practices in California," according to the group. You can use the Build It Green website for help in finding green building products, as well as certified green building professionals and even financing opportunities.

Another great resource is the green home energy audit company I mentioned in Chapter 1: Low Impact Living. Its website (see Resources, page 343) has some great links to green builders, green contractors and architects, as well as green interior designers.

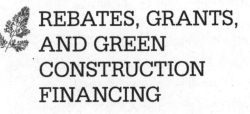

REBATES, GRANTS, AND GREEN CONSTRUCTION FINANCING

You certainly can finance green home building—or a green remodel—using traditional financing tools. But there are some special options available just for those of us who opt to go green. These are not just special loan programs. There are also rebates and grants to help directly offset the cost of building green, as well as tax credits to help partially offset those costs.

- You may be surprised to discover that giant lenders like Fannie Mae, Freddie Mac, and the FHA have gotten involved in green financing. They have all gotten involved with energy-efficiency mortgages, which allow you to incorporate the cost of energy-efficient improvements into a new loan or a refinance.

You also can find local financing options for building or remodeling in an environmentally friendly way. For example,

- There are special loan programs designed to help people purchase Energy Star–qualified homes by enabling you to qualify for a larger loan or reduced closing costs, since you will be paying lower utility bills by purchasing such a home.
- Smaller regional lenders, like Modern Earth Finance (see Resources, page 344), are developing green-specific programs for building and remodeling.
- Here in my area, Southern California Edison has a loan program that will finance 100 percent of the installation costs for efficient heating, ventilation, and air-conditioning (HVAC) equipment.
- In Nebraska, there's a state loan program that will cover the cost of installing energy-saving appliances, windows, HVAC, weather stripping, solar heating, wind power, and much more.

A number of websites offer current information about loans, grants, rebates, and tax credits in your area (see Resources, page 344).

With good financing, a green building project can become an absolute no-brainer. It's not a question of whether you believe in global warming or care about the crisis over oil prices. You literally could wind up with a home that's so energy efficient—perhaps one that even produces some of your own energy on-site—that the small difference in your monthly mortgage is completely offset by your lower utility bills. You could wind up cash-flow positive just by making green building decisions.

And not only do you come out ahead financially, you also wind up with a home that has a higher resale value—and that will sell faster than other houses, regardless of whether the real estate market is up or down. As Susan Colwell of My Green Cottage says, "We are reaching out to a lot of spec home builders and saying to them, 'You know, during this down market, a green home is going to sell faster. We'll teach you how to build this. We'll partner together on it. And you're not going to have to drop your prices so low."

Adding On

My house is only 1,585 square feet, and it has only two bedrooms and one and a half bathrooms—which is small for the three people who are living in it right now.

The rear of the house, which opens to the backyard, has the master bedroom in one corner, my office and Rachelle's office in the middle, and the kitchen and laundry room at the other corner. What I would like to do is take the house out farther into the backyard and expand those rooms, add a family room, transform a half bath into a full bath, and add another bedroom. Obviously, Rachelle's focus is the aesthetics of the indoor living space. Naturally, I'm focused on making sure that the remodel is done in the most environmentally friendly way possible. My priorities include the following:

- minimizing waste during the construction process and using local building materials
- recycling as much material as possible and using recycled materials from other sources whenever possible
- achieving a high level of insulation that protects the current building envelope I already have, so there's little or no increase in the heating and cooling requirements of my home
- using structural insulated panels (SIPs) for the new walls
- using the concrete area of the backyard for the expansion while protecting the vegetable garden and yard

Right now, these plans are in the computer-aided design (CAD) phase. Perhaps Rachelle and I will pull the trigger and get going on this project during the next season of my TV show, *Living with Ed.* If you want to see what challenges come up in the effort to build green—as well as in the effort to reach a compromise with a wife whose viewpoints are considerably different from my own—you'll have to tune in. I can promise you it will be entertaining, though quite likely at my expense.

10

GARDEN & COMPOST

Manufacturing Beauty & Food

NO BOOK ABOUT MAKING YOUR HOME GREENER would be complete without a chapter on the garden. Many of us are focused on indoor/outdoor living these days. We want beautiful views when we look out our windows, and we want a peaceful space outside where we can relax and entertain whenever the weather permits. We also want plants around our homes to take in carbon dioxide and produce oxygen. We want healthy air. And we also need plants to help reduce dust and prevent erosion, two very important aspects of being a good steward of our home's environment. Of course, we also want shade in the hot summer months, both so we can sit outside comfortably and so we can reduce our cooling bills and energy use.

I should start by mentioning that gardens can use an incredible amount of resources. And I don't just mean your time and energy tending to them. According to the U.S. Environmental Protection Agency's WaterSense program (see Resources, page 344), landscape irrigation wastes up to 1.5 billion gallons of water every day throughout the United States, which is why I'm also in favor of water-wise gardening. Choosing the right plants for your climate and getting rid of water hogs like lawns and nonnative plants is a smart move these days, when we really need to be focused on water conservation. You can also save water by watering your garden wisely. There are new technologies on the market that make this easier than ever before.

Growing food in your yard is a great way to use water and save energy.

Of course, I'm sure you realize that I'm in favor of organic gardening, of avoiding the use of toxic chemicals in the garden—or anywhere, for that matter. Of course, I'm also in favor of growing your own fruit and vegetables whenever you can. There's nothing like fresh-picked produce, and there's no better use of your resources than to grow something that will nourish you and your family and friends.

I'm also in favor of recycling. Making compost to nourish your garden is one of the best forms of recycling I can think of.

LOSE THE LAWN

One of the first things I did when I moved into my house was get rid of the lawn. A lawn is a luxury I can't afford to have in the desert locale where I live. Some of my neighbors run their sprinklers to water their lawns two times a day for several minutes at a stretch. That's a lot of water.

What do you get in return for doing what it takes to keep a lawn healthy and happy?

Something to eat? No. Something to cut and put in a vase to make your home look more lovely? No. You get nothing in return for all that water.

But you do get other expenses. If you have a lawn, you'll probably need to use some kind of chemical fertilizer. And if you have a lawn, you'll probably need to use some kind of pesticide. Those are the kinds of things I wouldn't put into the environment. I definitely do not want to put them into my own personal environment right near the fruit and vegetables that I plan to eat.

Also, if you have a lawn, you have to maintain it. You have to mow it and you have to edge it each week—or pay a gardener to do the same—using gas-guzzling lawn mowers and weed whackers.

My friend Chris Houchin of Quiet Garden Landscaping in Los Angeles is a totally different kind of gardener, who I value greatly. He's been landscaping for twenty years, and he takes care of my garden since I've been busy lately and I can't do all the work myself. Chris specializes in an environmentally friendly style of gardening.

Environmentally Friendly Tools

If your lawn does need mowing—if you go with one of the grasses that does get long and shaggy looking—then at least use a more environmentally friendly mower. The best choice would be to use a mower with a human-powered design. You know what I'm referring to—it's the old-fashioned push mower. If that's too much of a workout for you, then the next best choice would be a battery-powered or an electric mower. They're quiet and they don't produce any emissions at your house. You can also find electric weed whackers.

Now, electricity has to be generated somewhere, so there could be considerable emissions if your local utility is burning coal or burning waste or something. But an electric mower is particularly great if you're already producing your own electricity on-site or if you're buying clean, green electric power from your utility company. By all means, use electric then. Sure, you have to have a power cord, but it's the same as using a vacuum cleaner inside your house. In no time, you get used to having a cord.

And then for the rest of your gardening needs, you can use a rake, along with all of the other wonderful manually operated garden tools, from shovels to hoes.

He doesn't use any gasoline-powered equipment. Those gas-powered mowers that "regular" gardeners and plenty of homeowners use emit "forty-three times more pollution than even a car," according to Chris. "And that's not even including the two-cycle engines. You get a two-cycle weed whacker or a two-cycle blower and those emit up to eighty times the toxins, the fumes that an automobile emits. So it's quite significant." There's also the noise pollution to consider.

And don't forget the fuel that is burned and the emissions created by the gardener driving from house to house every day and then emitting more fumes and burning more fuel at each one of those stops. Don't get me wrong. I'm not trying to put gardeners out of business. But I would like to see them make more sustainable choices by working in some of the same changes I'm talking about in this chapter. Chris is even thinking about changing his company's vehicle to run on 100 percent biodiesel to be more environmentally friendly as he goes about his work.

DROUGHT-TOLERANT GRASS

First and foremost, I recommend removing your lawn. But if you absolutely cannot live without grass—if you feel that your children must have a lawn to play on or if you're a world-class croquet player or what-have-you—at least you can have a smaller patch of it. You don't have to dedicate the bulk of your property to lawn. Plus, you certainly can choose a type of grass that isn't a total water hog. There are more drought-tolerant grasses than what people typically plant. Chris points out that St. Augustine grass, Bermuda grass, and zoysia are quite drought tolerant, and they work well in the Los Angeles area. You can check with your local nursery or university extension office (see Resources, page 344) to find out which grasses are best suited for your environment.

So what are some other lawn options? A grass that doesn't require mowing or a ground cover like dichondra. There are many kinds of grass that will grow to just a few inches long. They provide a beautiful green grass area without the need for massive amounts of water and without the need for mowing and edging.

 AN ARTIFICIAL LAWN

Another option if you just can't live without a lawn is an artificial lawn. These lawns have come a long way since the earliest efforts. They look quite real. But unlike a real lawn, they stay green, they never need watering, they never need mowing, they never have a problem with bugs, and they never have a problem with weeds.

However, an artificial lawn is made from petroleum-based materials—nylon or polyethylene or polypropylene—so there is an envi-

The artificial grass in my yard is made from recycled plastic and rubber.

ronmental cost to manufacturing the stuff and trucking it and so on. But you could argue that if you absolutely have to have grass, an artificial lawn has a lower net environmental cost than the real thing.

My wife, Rachelle, insisted on having a small lawn area in the backyard for our daughter, Hayden, to play on. So I installed Riviera artificial grass from a company called AGL (see Resources, page 344). While it's made from polyethylene, this grass is 100 percent recyclable. The blades feel surprisingly soft, and they're a mixture of dark and light colors, so they look surprisingly real. AGL's artificial grass gets

installed with a cushioning material—what the company calls an infill system—and it's made from recycled materials, too. I find this artificial grass to be a much greener option than a real lawn in this desert climate where I live.

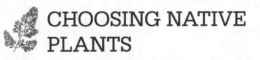 ## CHOOSING NATIVE PLANTS

So if you choose not to have grass—real or artificial—then what are the alternatives to a big, open lawn area? How about native plants?

My yard is still green without grass.

There's been a real push to landscape with native plants all over this country and indeed all over the world. In the prairie states, that could mean planting a meadow. In the desert southwest, it could mean planting cactus or succulents. But the choices are far broader than that. In most areas, you'll find a full range of native plant life, including:

- trees
- shrubs
- flowering perennials
- ferns
- vines
- grasses

Wherever you may live, variety is not likely to be a problem, as more and more nurseries cultivate native plants. Plus a big benefit of going with native varieties is they're far more likely to be grown locally, rather than trucked in from distant nurseries. That way, you're reducing emissions *and* you're supporting your local economy.

Native plants also have adapted to your climate. They've adapted to your area's average rainfall, the amount and intensity of the sunshine, the winds or lack thereof, and so on. You don't have to coddle native plants, as you do when, say, you're trying to grow tropical plants in the Northeast—or when you're trying to grow northeastern natives in the southwestern desert. Sure, if you have an unusually hot spell, natives will require more water than normal. But many natives can be planted and left alone once they've become established.

Native plants make your life easier *and* they conserve resources like water and soil amendments and fertilizer, since you don't have to try to change your soil into something it's not. You don't have to try to change your climate into something it's not. Plus, healthy plants are less susceptible to disease and to pests, so you won't be throwing out nearly as many dead plants or running around looking for environmentally friendly pesticides. Native plants also support local wildlife.

Your local university extension office will have information on plants native to your area. Many states also have their own dedicated native plant society. Or you can use some of the great resources online, including Plant-Native, Wild Ones, and eNature (see Resources, page 344).

 ## CLIMATE-SUITED OPTIONS

I realize that some people hate to be limited in their plant selection. They don't want to choose just from native plants, even if there are a hundred different flowering species available in their area. Actually, the State of California has more than 4,800 native species, including trees, shrubs, and other forms of plant life.

But still, if that just won't suffice, there's one other option that allows you to conserve resources. The next best choice, if you opt not to go 100 percent native, is to choose plants that come from a similar climate to yours. For instance, in Southern California, our climate is much like that of the Mediterranean. And so you see a lot of plants from similar climates—not just from the Mediterranean basin, but also from central Chile, the western cape of South Africa, and southern and southwestern Australia—thriving here.

Your area is also likely to share similar weather characteristics with distant locales. For instance, if you live in northern New England, your climate is considered hemiboreal (which technically means it's halfway between temperate and subarctic). In that case, plants from other hemiboreal areas, such as central Sweden, parts of Finland and Norway, eastern Poland, and much of Russia, should thrive in your area.

Again, local gardening clubs and societies are a great resource for this sort of information. Choosing plants from a similar climate anyplace else in the world can help you reduce your needs for water, soil amendments, pesticides, and so on.

PERENNIALS VS. ANNUALS

Another important point when it comes to water conservation is to choose perennials over annuals. Many gardeners enjoy the quick hit of color they get from planting annuals, but perennials are a far more water-wise gardening choice. Annuals typically come with very small root systems—or you may even be starting them from seed. In either case, they have to be watered often—sometimes twice a day when they're first planted. And they last only a few months. Then you toss them in the compost bin and start over with a new batch. They're labor intensive, water intensive, and often fertilizer intensive as well. In short, they're not the best use of resources.

SHADE TREES

Shade trees are valuable in making your garden comfortable and also in helping to reduce the cooling needs for your home. If you're not trying to get as much sun as possible on your roof for solar panels, then you just might want to go the other way and try to get as much shade as possible on your roof in the hot summertime. Shade trees can be an important part of a home's passive solar design.

As you know, the temperature in the shade is always dramatically cooler than the temperature in the sun, especially in the summertime, when the sun is much stronger. Shading your roof and shading your south- and west- and even east-facing windows can dramatically reduce your home's cooling needs. In fact, according to the California Energy Commission, "The temperature inside your home can increase as much as 20 degrees or more if east and west windows and walls are not shaded."

The key to this sort of passive solar landscaping is to choose deciduous trees—that is, trees that lose their leaves in the wintertime. That way, come late fall and winter, the branches will be bare. The sun will be able to shine right through when you want that solar radiation to help warm your house and reduce your heating costs. Of course, trees provide many other benefits as well, including shelter for local wildlife and increased property values.

 GROWING YOUR OWN FOOD

Now, as much as I love ornamental trees, my favorite use of gardening resources—time, energy, water, compost—is to grow food. I appreciate the beauty of ornamental plants, but growing ornamentals cannot contribute to your local community—your family, your neighbors, your friends, even your local food bank—in the way that growing fruits and vegetables can.

In my first book, I talked a lot about the value of fresh produce and the various plants

Growing your own fruits and vegetables saves you money at the grocery store—as well as saving the gasoline required to ship produce cross-country.

that I grow in my yard. I also talked about how important it is to eat food grown locally—about how much better it tastes, and how it saves resources compared with transporting food over vast distances.

Believe it or not, much of the food Americans eat has traveled 1,300 miles, on average. That's a lot of fossil fuel and a lot of emissions. When it comes to fruits and vegetables, this produce has to be able to withstand the rigors of transportation—being piled high in trucks—as well as the long time delay between being picked and being eaten.

If you've ever eaten a freshly picked peach, a freshly picked carrot, or a freshly picked ear of corn, you know it tastes vastly different from the stuff you buy at the supermarket. It has far, far more flavor. It has a more pleasing texture. It's juicier. It's better in every way, including nutritionally.

Once again, the key to responsible gardening is to plant fruit trees and vines and vegetables and herbs that do well in your climate. Fortunately, that has gotten much easier in recent years. Many companies have become interested in heirloom varieties of

Bill Nye's garden pests don't get a chance to do any damage, thanks to his solar-powered pest barrier.

fruits and vegetables, so now it's possible to buy seeds and even small plants that will thrive in a wide variety of geographies.

KEEPING PESTS AWAY

The biggest challenge with growing food in your garden actually can be getting to eat it yourself. Bugs, birds, rabbits, deer, and all manner of creatures will be quite glad to avail themselves of the smorgasbord you've set up in your yard.

So how do you keep away the pests without spraying toxic chemicals? You can use:

- **Beer.** Every gardener should have little trays or troughs in and around their garden where they can pour beer, since snails and slugs love beer. They crawl in the troughs and they die. It's an effective and inexpensive way to fight pests.
- **Beneficial insects.** Many beneficial insects, including praying mantises and ladybugs, will eat the insects that feed on your produce. You can buy them in local garden stores or online.
- **Sprays made with garlic oil, hot pepper, vinegar, castor oil, and rotten eggs.** These nontoxic bug repellents work on a variety of insects, including worms, aphids, spider mites, and white flies. Some also repel deer, rabbits, opossums, moles, voles, gophers, and moose.
- **Sprays that use bitter and smelly ingredients from grapes and other natural sources.** These are designed to keep birds from eating your crops. I enjoy having birds in my yard. Birds eat bugs, and they're an important part of the ecosystem. But birds can consume—or even just peck at and destroy—a considerable portion of your garden's bounty, particularly fruit.
- **Special nets.** You can put these over your plants to keep out birds if all else fails.
- **Solar-powered pest barriers.** A small solar panel produces electricity, which

the unit stores and then sends through a wire that you install around the edge of your flower or vegetable bed. If a rodent or other animal gets too close, the critter gets a mild electric shock—enough to send it elsewhere to eat.

Oftentimes you don't even need to buy a special product to get rid of pests. You can sometimes get rid of pesky insects just by spraying them with a stream from your garden hose.

WEED PREVENTION

Getting rid of your lawn is a great way to get rid of weeds. It's amazing how many different kinds of weeds thrive in a lawn—and how easily a gardener's mower can transport those weeds from house to house.

Another way to keep your weeding efforts to a minimum—and avoid the use of toxic chemicals to kill weeds—is to put in dense plantings. Weeds flourish where there's space and food and water. If you've got your yard pretty densely planted, there's little space for weeds to take hold.

What else can you do? You can use ground coverings like bark, river rock, gravel, even recycled glass or recycled rubber. Landscape fabric can help, too. By covering the bare soil in your garden beds or under your trees with

one or more of these materials, you'll make it tough for weeds to get a foothold. The best ground covers of this nature allow water to get through, so your plants can thrive but weeds' seeds cannot penetrate. All of these types of ground covers also help to hold in moisture, reducing your garden's water needs, so they're doubly good.

As for those few hardy weeds that do manage to pop up, the best way to get rid of them is to pull them by hand. You also may be able to kill weeds by pouring boiling water on them or spraying them with vinegar.

Once you've gotten rid of the weeds in your yard, you can discourage future offenders using one of the organic weed prevention products on the market. Many are made from corn gluten meal, and they're even safe to use on and around your vegetables.

HOW BEST TO WATER YOUR GARDEN

Even if you've planted water-wise plants that are appropriate for your climate, odds are they're still going to need some water sometimes, along with your fruit trees, fruiting vines, and vegetables.

According to the EPA's WaterSense program, more than half the water used to irrigate lawns and gardens is wasted. So how do you avoid wasting water? How do you deliver the right amount of irrigation in the most water-wise way?

Craig Borland, senior customer resource specialist of the Toro Company (see Resources, page 344), points out that all plants absorb water through their roots. So you really don't need to water their branches and their leaves.

Now, obviously, the traditional sprinkler system that waters things from the top down or from the sides in is not water-wise by any stretch of the imagination. It's watering the parts of plants that don't need water. Plus, a simple breeze can blow that precious water away from its intended destination. On a hot, dry day, a good portion of that water could evaporate before it ever reaches the ground, let alone your plants' root systems.

So the key is to design an irrigation system that best suits your landscape. When designing an irrigation system, you'll need to think about:

- **Zones.** Divide your garden into sections based on watering needs.
- **Water distribution method.** Do you want sprinklers or drip irrigation?
- **Run time.** How *long* do you want to water each zone?
- **Frequency.** How *often* do you want to water each zone?

I realize that your house may already have a sprinkler system installed. I'm not suggesting that you rip it out and start over. It may be enough to simply modify your system, along with your watering habits.

SETTING UP ZONES

Some of your plants need the same amount of water as others. The ideal is to group them together in your landscape, and to create zones in your irrigation system, so plants with the same water needs get watered together.

Also, some plants need to be watered differently from others. For instance, if you have a lawn, it has a relatively shallow root system, so it will need to be watered more often and for shorter periods of time than, say, a mature tree, which could have a root system that extends many feet down into the ground.

Another factor in setting up zones is the number of microclimates—and the number of different kinds of terrain—within your garden. Plants in the sun are likely to have different water requirements than plants in the shade. Plants in a boggy area or at the edge of a pond may not need any supplemental water at all, except in the most serious drought conditions. Plants in a windy area may need more water than plants that are sheltered by your home. Plants on a slope are going to have to be watered differently than plants in a low-lying area, etc.

CHOOSING A WATER DISTRIBUTION METHOD

When it comes to applying water to different parts of your yard, you have a few choices:

- **Spray heads,** the traditional-style sprinklers that spray water in a fixed pattern. These devices can spray water

Sample Costs and Paybacks: Smart Controller

So what does it cost to buy a smart controller? Right now, they range in price from $300 up to about $850 for a 24-station, 24-zone model, which is far more than the vast majority of us will ever need. Still, even at $300 or $400, a smart controller is not an insignificant investment.

However, you can wind up saving a lot of water—20 to 40 percent, typically, assuming you weren't underwatering your plants prior to the installation. So if you're saving $10, $20, or $30 a month on your water bill and saving some on your sewer charges as well possibly, a smart controller can pay for itself in a year or two.

One of these smart controllers also can do wonders to help out if you have an existing sprinkler system. It can help to optimize an older installation. So it can save you the considerable cost of digging out your old system and installing a whole new one.

Another thing to look into is rebates. Some water districts offer rebates to homeowners for installing this kind of technology, which can obviously help to offset your initial costs.

There's another consideration, too: Your plants will be happier with one of these systems. Craig says, "In July and August [2007], Los Angeles experienced probably the hottest sustainable days on record. And my system responded to that intense heat by providing more water to these plants during that timeframe to keep them alive. And that's where now the savings are not from water so much as by keeping the plants alive. A lot of people in my neighborhood lost their yard. Their plants died."

So there's a lot of money to be saved by not having to replace plants all the time, and by having healthier plants, which require less fertilizer and which are less susceptible to disease and pests.

all the way around the sprinkler—that is, in a 360-degree pattern. They can spray water just toward one side of the sprinkler—that is, in a 180-degree pattern. They can even spray in a 90-degree pattern or a 270-degree pattern. Many spray heads pop up when water starts flowing, then they retract when they're not in use. Craig says spray heads deliver roughly an inch and a half of water per hour, and they cover roughly a 15-foot square area.

- **Rotors,** which move, unlike fixed spray heads. Rotors spray water in a straight line, and the head of the sprinkler moves every few seconds. So water sprays in one place, then the head moves a bit and water sprays in the next area. Today, there are several different styles of rotors, including pop-up designs. Rotors usually send water over great distances. They typically are designed to be installed anywhere from 18 feet to 55 feet apart. They can rotate 360 degrees or cover a particular sweep of yard. Craig says rotors deliver roughly ¾ of an inch of water per hour, and they cover about a 30-foot square area.

- **Drip lines** put out far less water at a time. Usually, one long length of drip system tubing extends along the edge or through the middle of a bed or zone within your yard. Emitters are placed directly into that drip line, dripping water into the soil at intervals along

Choosing an Irrigation Professional

If choosing the right kind of irrigation system—let alone installing it—sounds like a daunting task, you may want to consult an irrigation professional. And if you're looking for someone who understands water-wise gardening, then the EPA's Water-Sense (see Resources, page 344) website is a good place to start. The site has state-by-state listings of WaterSense "partners"—people who have gone through a certification program. They've been trained in water-efficiency best practices.

Let me emphasize that the program doesn't just include designers and installers of irrigation systems. It also includes maintenance people, and with good reason. According to WaterSense, "If homeowners with irrigation systems hired WaterSense irrigation partners to perform regular maintenance, each household could reduce water used for irrigation by 15 percent, or about 9,000 gallons annually—that's the amount of water that would flow from a garden hose if it was left running for almost a whole day."

If you check things weekly or at least every couple of weeks, you can spot a problem and fix it before you wind up with a bunch of dead plants—or wind up wasting a whole lot of water.

the tubing. Or those emitters can be connected to smaller-diameter tubes, which then run directly to the base of each of your plants. Either way, the goal is for the water to go directly to each plant's root system, rather than covering a large surface area. The size of the emitter you choose will determine how much water flows through it over time. According to Craig, drip irrigation uses the least amount of water, applying ⅓ inch of water per hour or even as little as ¹⁄₂₀ inch per hour.

You'll want to use the same kind of water-application method throughout an entire zone for your irrigation system. For instance, a zone should have all spray heads or it should have all rotors.

If you have an existing sprinkler system, you can fine-tune it by changing the rotors or spray heads. You can choose heads that put out a lower volume of water, so you're putting less water to areas that need less water, for example. Or you can change from spray heads to rotors in some areas, so you're applying water more slowly over time, which makes it easier for the water to be absorbed by the soil, rather than running off. Drip irrigation has even less runoff potential. Plus, the water is applied right to the plants' roots, so you wind up using less water overall.

According to Craig, drip irrigation is the most economical in terms of materials costs. "Spray heads cost more than drip," he says. "Rotors cost more than spray heads."

You also have options within a drip irrigation system. For instance, you can install microsprinklers in your drip lines to water a grouping of plants all at one time. If you have a large or particularly densely planted yard, microsprinklers can be a more effective approach than installing a lot of tubing so you can reach every single plant with a drip emitter.

You also can install a drip irrigation system in which you bury soaker-type tubes. A soaker hose lets water escape from it slowly, so it can be good for watering a lawn or for watering a tree's roots. The benefit of burying a soaker hose is you don't have to worry about runoff or evaporation or wind blowing the water away from its intended target. These same qualities also make a buried soaker hose a good choice for sloping areas, where it can be a challenge to deliver water at a rate such that it can soak in, rather than simply run off down the slope, causing erosion problems.

RUN TIME AND FREQUENCY

Run time and frequency are the two other key factors in setting up your irrigation system. Ideally, you should use timers. You want to program your system—not just for your own convenience, but so you apply the right amount of water each time and you're not wasting water.

The proper run time and frequency will depend on the type of soil you have. For example, sandy soil absorbs water very quickly, but heavy clay absorbs water very slowly. "The number-one waste of water in our industry, hands down, is people applying water too fast for the soil to absorb it," says Craig. "That's what we call our *intake rate,* and it often is much lower than our application rate."

Run time also will depend on the kind of plants you're watering. Bedding plants have very shallow root systems, maybe only 2 inches deep. Lawns have roots that go maybe 6 inches deep. Established shrubs and larger perennials can have roots that go 6 inches or 12 inches deep, say. And some trees can have really deep root structures. So the key is to deliver water such that it will penetrate all the way down into the roots, but no more. Obviously you don't need to deliver as many inches of water to a lawn as you do to a tree.

Craig says he waters his garden in two irrigation applications of about six minutes each during the summer. And he waters it only every three days. He notes that his plants are healthier because he doesn't have any runoff. The water actually gets to soak in before the second application comes on. The water also is able to penetrate more deeply, so the roots can grow deeper. Deeper roots make for a healthier plant—and they allow for less frequent watering. Naturally, the ideal run time and frequency for your irrigation system is going to change with the weather.

RAIN SENSORS AND SMART CONTROLLERS

I used to call my wife, Rachelle, when I was on the road to tell her to shut off the sprinklers if it was raining. Obviously, I didn't want to waste water. But there are easier ways to regulate your irrigation so you don't have to go running outside in the middle of the night when you hear it raining. Or you don't have to stop and think, "Hey, this week has been cooler than normal for July, so I'd better dial back the amount of water I'm delivering to my flower beds."

If you already have a controller for your irrigation system, you may be able to add a rain sensor. When it senses that it's raining outside, it will automatically stop the irrigation cycle. Then, when the sensor dries out, the controller will go back to its regular irrigation program.

If your controller doesn't have a port where you can plug in a rain sensor, then you might want to consider installing a "smart" irrigation controller. As it turns out, there are two basic kinds of smart controllers:

- ones that use weather information
- ones that use moisture sensors in the soil

The smart controller that I have, which is from Toro, gets weather information wirelessly. So every day, my smart controller stops and thinks about the weather and it adjusts my garden's watering schedule accordingly.

More than just rain and heat, the weather factors also include humidity levels. If the air has very low humidity, water you apply will evaporate faster. If it's windy, the wind will dry out your plants. The controller also pays attention to whether it's cloudy or sunny and considers *evapotranspiration.* We all know what *evaporation* is. *Transpiration* refers to the amount of water coming out of a plant, its

Water captured in a rain barrel is great for spot irrigation in your yard.

leaves and its stem. "That changes radically between the summer and the winter," says Craig. So all of those weather variables, along with evapotranspiration rates, will affect how quickly your soil and your plants dry out, as well as how much of the water you're applying will actually soak into the soil.

The other kind of smart controller uses moisture sensors to tell it when to water. You place moisture sensors in the ground around the roots of some of your plants to keep track of the actual moisture content in your garden's soil. This new technology is so promising that the EPA's WaterSense program is looking at qualifying some of them, just as it has qualified certain high-performance low-flow showerheads and toilets and the like.

 ## COLLECTING RAINWATER

I'm a big fan of collecting rainwater for use in your garden. In fact, I talked about it a fair amount in my first book, and we did a pretty funny episode about it on my TV show, *Living with Ed*. The benefits of collecting rainwater are obvious:

- It's free.
- It's good for your garden.
- It reduces your need for water from other sources.
- If every homeowner collected rainwater for use in his or her yard, it

certainly would reduce our need for new water treatment plants.

The most common way to collect rainwater for garden use is to get some kind of storage tank—perhaps a recycled wine barrel or a purpose-built rainwater collection tank—and position it under a downspout from your rain gutters. Then, whenever it rains and water runs off your roof, you collect some of that water.

The nice thing about a purpose-built rain barrel is it will have a spigot or a faucet attachment near the bottom. That way, once you've collected rainwater, you can get it out of the barrel easily. You can fill a watering can, or, with the faucet attachment, you can even attach a hose to the barrel.

You can find rain barrels in all shapes and sizes and styles. Some look like stone. Some are made from plastic. Some people actually build custom tanks from galvanized steel for more of a rural, farm-vernacular look. Your typical rain barrel is either round or it has one flat side to fit flush against the wall of your house.

You can find really small rain barrels, which are good for use on terraces and balconies, since water is very heavy. But most rain barrels are somewhere in the 50- to 60-gallon range, with the upper limit usually around 100 gallons. If you get a lot of rain in your area, followed by long dry spells, you may want to invest in more storage capacity, perhaps even sinking a storage tank underground. These tanks usually range in size from a few hundred gallons up to thousands of gallons.

If you have some higher areas in your garden and you want to water them using a hose attached to your rain barrel, or if you decide to go with an underground tank, you're going to need a pump to get the water out to where you need it.

Rainwater can be very good for plants. Some gardeners swear that they need less water for their plants when they use rainwater instead of city water. However, rainwater generally is not safe to drink. After all, it has come off your roof and through your rain gutters. So there's a good chance it has come in contact with a variety of pollutants and grunge. Animal waste can be an issue, too, since all sorts of critters may spend some time on your roof.

Also, certain kinds of roofing materials can leach contaminants into rainwater. If your roof has wood shingles that have been chemically treated, or if you have asphalt roofing or cedar shingles, some experts recommend using the water you collect for lawns and ornamental plants *only*. Generally it's not wise to use collected rainwater on vegetable gardens or fruit trees.

If you're looking for rainwater collection supplies, my friend Lars Hundley has a company called Clean Air Gardening (see Resources, page 344) in Dallas, Texas, which specializes in environmentally friendly lawn and garden supplies. It sells all kinds of rainwater collection products, from rain barrels and pumps to downspout redirectors and even a dolly for a rain barrel to sit on so you can move it when it's full. Also, a German company called GRAF

makes complete rainwater collection, filtration, and pumping systems that feature underground storage tanks. You can find out more about those products through the company's U.S. distributor, Watts Radiant (see Resources, page 344). A couple of other great sources for information on collecting rainwater include Harvest H_2O (see Resources, page 344), which calls itself "the online rainwater harvesting community," and the American Rainwater Catchment Systems Association (see Resources, page 344).

 GRAY WATER IRRIGATION

You can collect rainwater for your garden's irrigation needs, or you can reuse some of the water you've already used in your house. I talked about gray water in Chapter 6, "Water Usage": what gray water is and why people have started using it, as well as ways people are using it *inside* their homes (see page 102). However, it is actually much more common— and more commonly legal, according to local building codes—to use gray water *outside,* for landscape irrigation.

Not surprisingly, states with a lot of hot and dry areas, such as Nevada and California, have been among the first to embrace the use of gray water for landscape irrigation. And with the recent droughts in other parts of the country, interest in gray water has been growing. My friend Buzz Boettcher from Gray Water Recycling Systems (GWRS; see Resources, page 344), which makes gray water systems for landscape irrigation, can help you figure out if a system is legal in your area. Or look online at the *Natural Home* website (see Resources, page 344).

To briefly rehash, here's how you use gray water: You capture the waste water that runs down your pipes from your shower, bathtub, bathroom sink, and clothes washer. This waste water is considered *gray water* (as opposed to *black water,* which is water from a toilet or urinal; water from your kitchen sink is also considered black water, typically, because that water can include not only ground-up food waste and grease but also bacteria you've washed off food, like e. Coli and salmonella). Instead of sending that used water into the sewer system or into your home's septic system, a separate set of pipes reroutes that water to a gray water system.

Now, people have been reusing water for millennia, but several companies have come out with engineered gray water systems that make it relatively easy—and safe—to use gray water in your garden. These systems include a storage tank, where the gray water is kept until you need it. GWRS's system also includes an overflow setup so when the gray water storage tank is full, any incoming gray water gets routed to a sewer system in order to prevent problems. The water always has someplace to go.

Some gray water systems require you to use a certain amount of chlorine to kill any bacteria in the tank. GWRS's system is different. Its tank is connected to a pump that sends the water through a series of particle and UV filters. When the water passes through the filters, it leaves behind most of its impurities—things like hair and lint that come along with the waste water from your clothes washer and your shower—as well as kills any harmful bacteria.

Buzz says that the filter in his company's system recycles the water to a level beyond gray water where it can be used in almost any irrigation application. And by using its pump and filtration process, the water can be kept in the storage tank safely for weeks.

UNDERGROUND DRIP

According to Steve Bilson from ReWater (see Resources, page 344), Arizona is the only state that lets you use traditional gray water *aboveground* in your irrigation system. You can install an aboveground drip system using gray water there. In other states, you can install a gray water drip irrigation system, but it has to be sunk *underground*. You have to trench and install the drip lines about 9 inches below the soil's surface. Nowhere are you allowed to spray gray water; it always has to be used as part of a drip system to carefully control where it goes.

You also have to use special drip system emitters with gray water, since gray water can contain suspended solids—larger particles than found in ordinary tap water—and those particles would clog ordinary emitters. So you need emitters with a larger-than-normal orifice.

You also need to position the underground drip lines fairly close together. Steve says the average is 18 inches on center. If you have a very dense type of soil, like hard clay, then you might run them a bit closer, like 16 inches on center. But 18 inches is the norm.

If you're using an underground gray water system like this, you'll need to do the same sort of things you'd do with any irrigation system: divide your garden into zones based on water needs, then use a controller to send the gray water to each zone for the appropriate length of time. ReWater's system comes with a controller that can accommodate up to twenty-one zones.

Here's how this system works: When gray water becomes available, the controller sends water out to each zone according to the programming. If it runs out of water, it stops the program and waits until someone in your house takes a shower or runs a load of laundry or creates more gray water some other way. When the system senses that there's enough gray water in the tank, it picks up where it left off, sending water out to different drip lines, to the different zones.

So, what happens if you don't create enough gray water during the day to water your yard? Or what happens if you go away for a few days? Does everything in your garden die?

Of course not. The ReWater system has been configured so that fresh water is also available. So if it reaches midnight and the controller was not able to run through the entire irrigation program, it will send fresh water to the remaining zones. And if someone happens to take a shower while the fresh water is being used, the controller will shut off the fresh water and finish the job with the new gray water coming in. So either way, your yard always gets the water it needs.

Obviously, reusing water from your home offers tremendous water savings. But using an underground drip system to water your yard takes that to a whole other level. "Underground drip is thirty to sixty percent more efficient than the best sprinkler system," Steve says. "In places where it's hot and dry and windy all the time, you can have up to sixty percent savings." With underground drip, you're going to have absolutely zero water evaporating before it soaks into the soil.

INSTALLING A GRAY WATER DRIP SYSTEM

Obviously, a gray water irrigation system has a lot of appeal. It's going to save you a lot of money on water, especially if you have a sizable yard and live in an area where your local utility charges a high price for water. And a gray water irrigation also can save you money on a sewer bill, depending on your locale and how your local utility handles billing.

The only real potential drawback to a gray water drip irrigation system is installing it— both the plumbing for the gray water system and the underground drip irrigation lines. In new construction, gray water landscape irrigation is a no-brainer. You can build the house with the properly routed plumbing lines in place, and you can design a landscape and then

GRAY WATER AND RAINWATER
RECYCLING SYSTEM SCHEMATIC

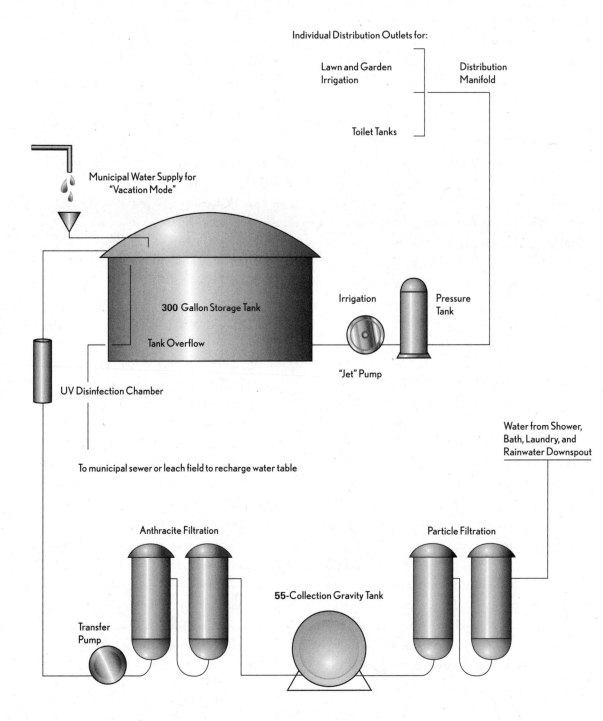

Individual Distribution Outlets for:

Lawn and Garden
Irrigation

Distribution
Manifold

Toilet Tanks

Municipal Water Supply for
"Vacation Mode"

300 Gallon Storage Tank

Irrigation

Pressure
Tank

Tank Overflow

"Jet" Pump

UV Disinfection Chamber

Water from Shower,
Bath, Laundry, and
Rainwater Downspout

To municipal sewer or leach field to recharge water table

Anthracite Filtration

Particle Filtration

55-Collection Gravity Tank

Transfer
Pump

place all the drip lines underground before a single plant goes in. But if you have an existing house with traditional plumbing, you may or may not be a good candidate for gray water. If your house is on a slab, then all the plumbing lines have been set into that concrete. You'd literally need to rip up your flooring and get a jackhammer to add a gray water system. That's certainly more work than most people are willing to do. On the other hand, if your home was built on a raised foundation, then you can make changes to the plumbing relatively easily—definitely for any rooms on the first floor and possibly for second-story rooms as well.

The same goes for an already landscaped yard. If you have a bare yard—if this is the first time you're installing any kind of landscaping and irrigation—then it's not such a big deal to dig trenches to add a gray water irrigation system. But if you have plants in place and you don't want to kill them, it's going to be really challenging to dig around their root systems to install a gray water system.

PURPLE PIPE WATER

There's a new way to use gray water for landscape irrigation that allows a more traditional aboveground use. Buzz Boettcher of Gray Water Recycling Systems in Southern California is taking an approach to residential gray water that is very much like the way cities "recycle" water.

When cities recycle water, they predominantly use it for landscape irrigation—like the irrigation on the sides of freeways and other public land areas. This water is commonly called *purple pipe water*, so named because it is delivered in special purple pipes. The color-coded pipes ensure that everyone knows this water is not potable. You can't drink it. But it's not regular gray water, either. It has been highly filtered.

Now, when reclaimed water gets filtered to a certain degree—when it's been filtered to the California Department of Public Health Title 22 standard for recycled water, for example—you no longer have to apply that water through underground drip irrigation only. You can apply the water through an aboveground sprinkler system.

So Buzz has developed a residential gray water system that filters water to this standard using an advanced multistage purification process. He uses three particle filters for water clarity and a UV light chamber to kill bacteria. Once Buzz gains approval from the State of California and other states for this system, he can offer another option for gray water irrigation—and one that's much easier in a retrofit situation. With this new gray water setup, you actually will be able to use your existing sprinkler system to irrigate with gray water. You won't have to do any trenching and digging and disturbing of plant roots.

Using gray water is a brilliant way to recycle at home. And there's another type of garden-oriented recycling that's also among my favorite eco-friendly practices—in fact, it's one I've been practicing for years—and that's making your own compost.

WHAT CAN YOU TOSS INTO THE COMPOST BIN?
Compostable Materials

- ❑ Algae, seaweed, and lake moss
- ❑ Ashes from untreated, unpainted wood
- ❑ Beverages, kitchen rinse water
- ❑ Bread, rice, and pasta
- ❑ Cardboard
- ❑ Coffee grounds and filters
- ❑ Compost activator
- ❑ Cornstalks, corn cobs
- ❑ Dryer lint
- ❑ Eggshells
- ❑ Fruit scraps
- ❑ Grains
- ❑ Grass clippings
- ❑ Hair
- ❑ Leaves
- ❑ Manure (horse, cow, pig, sheep, goat, chicken, rabbit)
- ❑ Newspaper
- ❑ Pine needles and cones

- ❑ Sawdust and wood shavings (untreated wood)
- ❑ Tea bags
- ❑ Vegetable scraps
- ❑ Weeds
- ❑ Yard and garden debris

OPPOSITE: With a compost tumbler, there's no constant shoveling or mixing of a compost pile.

LEFT: These designs are durable and can hold up to 90 gallons of materials.

BOTTOM: Round bins work fast to break down material into rich compost.

Municipal Composting

You don't necessarily have to make compost yourself. Some cities will pick up your yard waste curbside. They give you a special bin, then they pick up that yard waste and create compost on a much larger, municipal scale. In my area, we have a green bin, and you can put all kinds of yard waste and also kitchen scraps from fruit and vegetables into it. Then the waste is processed and turned into soil amendments.

Having your city make compost is certainly the easiest approach. You barely have to do a thing, aside from sorting your trash into the correct bin. If you don't have that option, you can bring your compostable materials to someone else. Perhaps your kids' school has a garden and makes its own compost, or perhaps there's a community garden in your area.

Some cities use yard waste in their landfills. They spread a layer of yard waste over the trash to keep down the vermin, to keep seagulls and rats and other critters from being a problem at the landfill, and to keep the smell down, so people who live downwind of the landfill don't have to suffer with a stench from it. Obviously, this is not nearly as green a use of this organic material as creating compost, but it is better than using perfectly good topsoil to do the same job.

Regardless of where it ends up, the best use of your yard waste and kitchen scraps is to create compost—either at your home, at another site nearby, or through a municipal composting program.

 THE VALUE OF COMPOST

Making compost is the best thing you can do for your soil. Gardeners call the stuff *black gold* because it's rich, black, superfertile humus—the same stuff you find on a forest floor. It enriches your soil, so it's great to mix in with dirt from your yard whenever you're putting new plants into the ground. I use it every time I plant vegetables in my garden. Compost also makes a perfect, balanced mulch and fertilizer, which is why I spread it around the base of my fruit trees at least a couple of times a year.

If you have clay soil, like I do, compost will help to loosen it up and allow water to penetrate better. It also helps sandy soils to retain water better, rather than letting the water drain right through. And it helps to aerate all kinds of soils, making your garden more fertile and providing a healthy environment for your

When done properly, your compost should not have any bad odor.

plant's roots and for beneficial creatures, from earthworms to microorganisms in the soil.

Composting also reduces the amount of waste going into landfills. It's a little-known fact but, according to Lars Hundley of Clean Air Gardening, most landfills are completely sealed off. Therefore the organic matter that goes into landfills does not decompose, as it does in a compost pile, so it can't enrich the soil in the landfill. It's just wasting space—as much as a third of the space in many landfills—and it's wasting nutrients that could be benefiting your soil. So, creating compost saves space in landfills. It cuts down on the amount of fossil fuel burned and emissions created in trucking that organic matter to landfills. And it provides a huge benefit for your garden. Composting is a win-win-win situation, environmentally speaking.

I spoke to Lars recently about all the different ways you can make rich, nutritious compost for your yard, with minimal effort and no odor. That's right. One of the most common misconceptions about compost is that it's smelly, but it's not. Compost should just smell earthy.

MAKING YOUR OWN COMPOST

What I do is make my own compost, and I hope many of you will do the same. In spite of what you may have been led to believe, compost is incredibly easy to make.

Lars suggests keeping a little sealable container, like a Tupperware container, next to your kitchen sink. And you just throw your fruit and vegetable scraps in there while you're cooking. Then you just take the container outside and toss the kitchen scraps into your compost bin (more on bins and other options in a moment). I do this once a day and it only takes a minute.

The key is to keep your compost somewhere convenient. Since it's not going to smell, you don't have to worry about having it near the house. Ideally, you want to keep it someplace close to your kitchen so you'll really use it. If it's too far away, you'll find a million reasons not to walk out there and toss your kitchen scraps into the bin.

If you're cutting off the end of a piece celery, just toss that in the container. Toss in the husk and the silk from an ear of corn. Toss in the greens from the end of your carrots. If you peel an orange or a banana, throw the peel in there. If you core an apple, toss that in. If you've got the stems left from a bunch of grapes or the greens from the end of strawberries, toss them all in.

You also will want to throw a bunch of yard waste into the compost bin. I don't mean tree branches or anything too big, even twigs, because they'll really slow down the compost process. In fact, you may want to shred leaves—or drive over a big pile of leaves with your lawn mower—before you put them in the compost bin, so they break down more quickly.

Also, when it comes to kitchen scraps, you want to avoid meat and dairy and fish and really fatty things, like salad dressing. You don't want to throw those kinds of things into your compost bin. Now, they *can* be composted, but they're not recommended for a home compost bin. That's partly because they'll attract critters—rats and raccoons and squirrels and the like—and also because they can cause your compost bin to smell. They get putrid as they break down, so you—and your neighbors—definitely don't want that stuff in your compost heap.

HOW COMPOSTING WORKS

So, how do all those yard trimmings and kitchen scraps become something that's good for your garden? They break down. They literally decompose. They turn into humus, that rich, dark material that you want to mix into your soil.

That transformation requires oxygen and it also requires hundreds of different organisms. Bugs and microbes, bacteria and fungi break down that organic matter. They feed on it, and that's what creates compost.

So if you see bugs in your compost, that's a good thing. Bugs are there to work, to help break down the compost. Especially earthworms. Earthworms are a great sign in a compost pile—or in a yard, for that matter.

The real key to the composting process is to have a good mix of materials. You don't want to have a compost bin filled with nothing but grass clippings or nothing but banana peels. You want a mix of different things.

That's because some of those things will be rich in nitrogen and some of those things will be rich in carbon. The nitrogen-rich materials are considered *green* matter—things like grass clippings or kitchen scraps. And the

carbon-rich materials are considered *brown* matter—things like dead leaves or straw or hay or newspaper. And as long as you have some kind of balance—it doesn't have to be a perfect ratio—as long as you've got a mix of both green and brown materials, you'll wind up with good, rich compost.

DIFFERENT WAYS TO COMPOST

You can compost in a bunch of different ways. The most common options are to:

- **Trench.** With this method, you literally dig a hole in your yard and throw all your compostable stuff in the hole. Then you cover it up and you never have to touch it again. Those food scraps attract earthworms and microbes in the soil, which feast on those scraps and turn it into compost. This is a great technique if you have a problem spot in your yard. Maybe you have an area where plants just don't want to grow. Once you've created compost in that spot, it's going to be incredibly fertile and ready for you to plant. You can even use this technique if you're going to be planting vegetables in a raised bed.

- **Compost bin.** A bin is an appealing way to compost because it's enclosed, so you don't have to worry about animals getting into it. Plus, it's manageable and tidy looking. You can use the compost wherever you need it in your yard.

- **Compost pile.** With this method you literally make a heap in your yard. The big benefit of a pile is that it can get really hot inside. It's a big mass, and heat helps make compost break down faster. It makes it ready to use sooner. Inside the middle of a big compost pile, temperatures can get up to maybe 150 degrees F. The only drawback here is that you can't just toss everything on top of the pile and walk away. Some things will need to be buried in the pile so you don't attract critters or even have a problem with your dog or your cat getting into the stuff you toss on the compost heap.

There are times you'll see plastic sheeting covering a compost pile. Some people do this to help keep the temperatures high, if they're having a problem along those lines. Others use a plastic sheet to keep out too much water if they live in a rainy area. And some people use it just to keep animals from getting into the scraps they've thrown on the pile. The need for this simply depends on your geographical situation, and you may not need to cover your pile at all.

If you choose to use a compost bin instead of making a pile in your yard, you can select from many shapes and styles, including a tumbler. It's mounted on a stand, and you put your stuff into the bin and then literally turn a handle and tumble the materials around. "When you tumble them, it's doing two things: It's mixing the compost and it's aerating the compost to make sure there's plenty of oxygen in there," says Lars Hundley. "Those are the two keys to composting quickly. Well, that along with having a good mix of materials. So with the tumbler, you can often compost really quickly, plus it's just convenient. You don't have to use a pitchfork to mix it up. You don't have to use one of those composting tools. You just basically throw it in, you flip it around, and you're standing the whole time."

Lars says you don't even need to get a compost starter to get your bin or pile going. You just need a shovelful of dirt, and eventually, everything will turn into rich compost.

Naturally, the material at the bottom of the pile or at the bottom of your compost bin will be the material that has decomposed the most. So when you're ready to start using that compost, you'll want to use the material at the bottom first.

POSITIONING YOUR COMPOST

So, should you put your compost bin or your compost pile in the sun or the shade or does it even matter? Most of the time, this is not a big deal. But if you live in a more extreme climate—someplace where it gets really cold in the winter or really hot in the summer—then it's worth thinking about where you position your compost.

As I mentioned, heat is good in a compost pile. You want it to heat up and stay hot. So if you live in a cold area—or even someplace near the ocean that never gets very hot—

then having your compost in the sun is a wise choice.

Now, in the wintertime, if it gets below freezing, your compost is going to go dormant. The composting process will stop. But once the weather warms up again, the process will take right off. Having your compost pile in the sun will help it heat up again that much faster. Still, even when it's dormant, you can keep throwing stuff on your compost heap in the winter. It won't break down, but the cold weather will make sure it doesn't smell either. So you can continue composting all year-round. Then when you're ready to start gardening again in the springtime, the stuff at the bottom of your compost pile will be ready to use.

So what if you live in a hot climate? Well, you need a certain amount of moisture in your compost. If compost dries out, it will stop decomposing. It will stop breaking down. If you live in Arizona or New Mexico or anyplace hot and dry, then you may want to put your compost in a shady spot. Or you can add some water periodically to make sure the compost doesn't dry out. But you don't want to add too much water. Compost doesn't need to be wet. Lars says it actually is supposed to have the same dampness as a wrung-out sponge.

Obviously, if you live in a rainy area, dry compost won't be a problem, but you actually could wind up with a muddy mess if you aren't careful. In that case, you'll probably want to choose a compost container with a lid on it, so you don't let in a whole lot of rainwater.

Also, if you decide to make a compost pile, rather than using a bin, then you want that pile to be on dirt or grass. You don't want to start a compost pile on a patio or on asphalt. You want those beneficial microbes and worms and such in the dirt to have access to your compost.

WORM COMPOSTING

There's another type of composting that's typically done inside, and that's what's called *worm composting*. "It's as easy or easier than traditional composting," says Lars. "Actually, it's more suitable for breaking down things like kitchen scraps—your eggshells, your coffee grounds, your banana peels and apple cores and things like that. It doesn't really work for leaves and grass clippings and garden waste."

And it can be done on a really small scale—say if you live in a condo or an apartment. "Basically, what happens is you can buy worms over the Internet. They'll send them to you in the mail. And then you can put them right in your bin that you have prepared. And you'll basically just have a few layers of damp newspaper at the bottom, and then you want to put [in] some shredded newspaper and a little bit of dirt to get it going. And then you put your worms in there and you start putting your materials in there. And the worms can eat their own body weight worth of stuff."

Once the compost is ready, you can scoop it out and use it for your houseplants or for plants on your patio or in your yard. And if you want to use all of the compost at one time, you just strain it so you keep the worms. Then you put those worms back in the bin with more newspaper and dirt and kitchen scraps and start the process all over again.

USING COMPOST

I use compost whenever I plant vegetables, and I use it as mulch and fertilizer for my fruit trees. You also can use it on houseplants. You can put it in your flower beds. You can use it under your shrubs. You can use it on grass, if you choose to have a lawn.

What you'll soon find, once you start composting, is that there's never enough. Compost is so good for your garden, you'll always want more. That's partly because there's a lot of shrinkage. When you throw your yard waste and your kitchen scraps into the compost bin, you don't get the same exact amount of finished compost back. Actually, you get much less. As Lars says, the volume reduces as the material breaks down.

If you want more, you could buy bags of compost at your local nursery, but that may not be the best choice. Now, you don't have to worry about chemicals or anything like that. "If it's a bag of compost, then it usually is organic," says Lars. "But the issue with the bagged compost is that often they're made primarily of one material. Like they'll be made from cotton stalks or from chicken poop or something like that, where they're really rich in just one material. Whereas compost you make yourself or municipal compost has a wider mix of materials, so it's typically a little bit better."

Once you start gardening in a more water-wise way, you should notice some real savings on your water bill and possibly even your sewer bill. Plus, choosing plants better suited to your climate should save you the time and expense of replacing dead plants and the hassles of dealing with pests and disease. Also, a few properly placed shade trees can help you save on cooling costs.

This kind of garden is as good for the environment as it is for your pocketbook. Native and climate-appropriate plants create a great habitat for local wildlife. They transform carbon dioxide into oxygen. They beautify your property and your neighbors' views. Great landscaping increases a home's value, as well. And if you add edibles into the picture, then you're talking about healthier, tastier food for you and your family. Bottom line: A well-thought-out garden can improve your quality of life in many, many ways.

Installing a Hybrid Gray Water System

I'm going to be installing a gray water system at my home. It will collect water from the bathtub, the shower, the bathroom sinks, and the clothes washer, and then I will use that water for landscape irrigation in both my front yard and my backyard.

Now, this is really a two-part project. The first part is making the change to the irrigation system in the front and back yards for a gray water irrigation system. This may require running new irrigation lines with different spray heads or drip emitters, as well as putting in a filtration and pumping system. Of course, I'll also have to change my home's plumbing to redirect the gray water to the filtration system and storage tank.

That's part one. The second part will make this a hybrid system. I'm planning to install an expanded rainwater collection system. Right now, I just have one 50-gallon rain barrel under one of my downspouts. I plan to expand the system to capture rain from additional downspouts and to store all the rainwater in an underground storage system. I'm looking at an underground cistern or tank as the storage device, probably in the 500-gallon range. That would accomplish two things, actually. It would allow me to store a lot more than 50 gallons of rainwater, and it would allow me to get rid of the ugly orange rainwater storage barrel that my wife so vocally despises.

The trick will be to connect the two systems, so the gray water and rainwater can both flow into and be filtered by one common system. I have no doubt the brilliant engineering minds from Gray Water Recycling Systems can help me make this happen. See the diagram of the water-recycling system developed by them on page 218.

SECTION III
MANAGE

Continuing to Refine &
Improve Your Life & Reduce
Your Carbon Footprint

Some people think that I've done every-thing there is to do in terms of conserva-tion and production . . . that Ed Begley finding a new green project would be like buying a gift for the man who has everything. But life is always changing and technology is always changing, so there are always new things to do and new processes to manage. I am con-stantly refining my life, looking for new ways to do things cheaper and with less environmental impact.

In just the last several years, I've done many projects at home using resources that weren't available to me in the 1980s or 1990s. I recently put in a new fence made of a combination of recycled wood and plastic; this is a material that wasn't previously avail-able. I recently installed some new kitchen appliances with a new level of Energy Star efficiency not previously available to me. Because of all the changes I've made to my home, includ-ing many of the conservation-oriented changes I talked about in the first sec-tion of this book, I was able to install a new, efficient, and much smaller air-conditioning unit. I also discov-ered—and installed—a new style of home heating system.

Managing your life and your carbon footprint means reading. It means stay-ing current on new technology and new developments in resource management. It means applying these new technolo-gies and using new methods to measure results. It also means finding the things that are right for you and your home and getting the most bang for your buck. When you manage the process correctly, it really can be life changing.

11

HEATING YOUR HOME

**Choosing the Best System
for Your House**

HEATING AND COOLING ACCOUNTS FOR MORE THAN half of the energy used in most homes. So clearly it pays to insulate your house and choose windows and doors that will reduce your heating and cooling needs. Not only do those steps reduce the amount of money you spend on heating and cooling, they also have a major effect on the *size* of the heating and cooling system you need. If you're considering shopping for a new heating and cooling system, I cannot overstate the importance of taking care of your home's insulation and window and door needs first. Unless your heater or air conditioner has suddenly died, it's very important to make every effort to conserve (see Section 1) before you shop for a new heating and air-conditioning system.

When it comes to heating and cooling your home, you have many choices. There's no one right answer in terms of what sort of system is the best or the most environmentally friendly. Instead, you've got to make that choice based on:

- where your home is located
- how large your home is
- what your current system is, if you're doing a retrofit (e.g., is it vented?)
- the amount of space around your home that you have to work with
- what you can afford to do relative to payback

You'll have to consider all of these variables. Then you can begin to make a decision by eliminating the systems that won't work for your needs. Once you've narrowed the selection, you can consider price and, quite simply, personal preference.

In this chapter, I'll talk about your options for heating a home; then in the next chapter I'll cover cooling. It's important to point out that in most homes across the United States—in homes with central heating and cooling—the two systems share quite a few components, including a blower and ductwork.

Even if your home doesn't need heat—or if it doesn't need A/C—I still recommend that you read both this chapter and the next one, because there is quite a bit of overlap in the systems. Also, I've taken care not to repeat vital information, so, for instance, you'll find the information on choosing a contractor, proper ductwork sizing, split vs. packaged systems, and multizone systems in the next chapter, "Cooling Your Home."

HEATING 101: FORCED AIR VS. RADIANT HEAT

Most homes in the United States are heated with either a furnace or a boiler. A furnace heats *air* and uses a blower, or air handler, to distribute that air through ductwork. This is what's known as *forced-air heating.* It's also considered part of a *central heat* system, since the heat is made in one central location and then distributed throughout the house.

So a furnace heats air, while a boiler heats *water.* The boiler either makes hot water or it makes steam, and then a pump usually distributes that hot water or steam through pipes that have been run throughout the house. Most boiler-based heating systems are considered *radiant heating,* as opposed to forced air. Rather than blowing hot air throughout your house, they distribute hot water and allow it to *radiate* heat into the rooms.

Of course, there are exceptions to the rule. Some boiler systems use a coil to heat air and then distribute that hot air throughout the house. But as a general rule, boilers are part of a radiant heating system, and furnaces—as well as heat pumps—are part of a forced-air heating system.

BASICS OF HEATING AND REFRIGERATION

Many, but not all, types of heating and cooling systems employ some type of refrigerant, for example Freon, so here's a quick overview of how that process works.

The magic of refrigeration works by taking some sort of refrigerant and squeezing it. Whenever you squeeze or compress something, you raise its temperature. So heating, ventilation, and air-conditioning (HVAC) systems either make the refrigerant very hot by compressing it, or they make it very cold by depressurizing it.

In the wintertime, your HVAC system squeezes the refrigerant and makes it hotter. The system blows air across the hot refrigerant, heating the air, and then the system circulates that hot air through your house.

According to my friend Bruce Ritchey, president/CEO of Water Furnace (see Resources, page 344), whatever sort of forced-air heating system you install, it's going to blow air that's about 100 degrees F to warm your home. And whatever kind of cooling system you install, it's going to blow air that's about 50 degrees F to cool your home.

LOCATION AND FUELS

All HVAC systems require some sort of fuel to operate. The type of fuel you choose is going to depend, in large part, on where you live.

Why does your geographic location matter? There are two main reasons:

- fuel availability
- energy costs

For starters, different regions have different sorts of heating fuels available. You also may want to take into consideration the type of fuel that is powering your current heating system. You may be using:

- electricity
- natural gas
- propane
- heating oil

Because the rates for each of these power sources varies dramatically from state to state and from region to region within many states, the decision as to which type of fuel to use can vary dramatically. For instance, if you live in Idaho, where you can get inexpensive electricity that's green, as noted on page 140, then it may make perfect sense for you to use electricity for heating.

You also might want to seriously consider electric heating if you've installed solar or wind power and you're generating a fair amount of clean, green electricity on-site.

If you live in an area where electricity is generated by burning coal or by burning waste, then it certainly makes environmental sense to investigate cleaner, greener alternatives to electricity.

And if you live in an area where electric rates are sky high, then it makes financial sense to investigate alternative fuels, especially natural gas, for heating.

So again, there's no one right answer. The "greenest" solution is entirely dependent on your particular situation. Every single home in America potentially could have a different "greenest" solution.

 GAS FURNACES

Most of the heating in the United States is done with gas furnaces. About 3 million new gas furnaces are sold every year, both for new construction and as replacement units for existing homes.

I had a gas furnace in my home for many, many years. With natural gas prices being low for decades, a natural gas–powered furnace has made a lot of financial sense for people who have access to natural gas. While natural gas obviously is a fossil fuel, it happens to be one of the cleanest-burning fuels there is. So it can be considered a green option.

But natural gas isn't so cheap anymore. Now people who've relied on natural gas without thinking about it for their whole lives are considering other options.

One thing to bear in mind as you look at the escalating price of natural gas is the cost of alternative fuels. If you live in an area, as I do, where electricity is charged on a tiered system—where you can buy so much electricity at a low rate, but then if you use any more electricity, your rate jumps up to the next, much higher tier—it might make sense to stick with natural gas. If using natural gas for heating keeps you from jumping up to that next tier for electric rates, it can be a very wise choice.

HOW A GAS FURNACE WORKS

Not all conventional furnaces burn natural gas; some also can burn propane to create heat, and some can burn heating oil. Furnaces essentially have four components:

- a burner, which literally burns the fuel to heat a refrigerant

- a flue, which vents the exhaust from the burner's combustion process
- a heat exchanger, through which the refrigerant travels
- a blower, which blows air across the heat exchanger and then sends it through the ducts in your house

Now, as it turns out, there are three styles of gas furnace today:

- **Conventional furnaces** work in the way I just described, and they draw some additional air from your home into the flue, which helps to reduce the temperature of the very hot exhaust gases before they exit through a chimney. These are the old, low-efficiency models.
- **Induced draft furnaces** are quite similar, but they draw air through two different openings—one on the front of the furnace and another at the flue— which serves to create a natural draft effect, and that increases the efficiency of the furnace. These are considered midefficiency designs.
- **Condensing furnaces** are the most efficient because they actually take advantage of the fact that exhaust gases from the combustion process are hot: They use a second heat exchanger to capture some of that heat and use it to heat your home. There's another benefit to this design, too: Once that

heat has been extracted from the exhaust, it's much cooler, so it can be vented through a plastic pipe and out through a side wall in your home (as with the vent for a gas clothes dryer), rather than having to exit through a flue and a chimney. This makes installation more flexible and potentially more economical.

COMPARISON SHOPPING

Fortunately, you don't have to memorize the different kinds of gas furnaces. There are easier ways to comparison shop. Here are a few factors to consider:

- efficiency
- size
- comfort

To get the best out of your gas furnace, choose one that has the Energy Star rating.

With gas prices such as they are, it's certainly important to start by looking at the efficiency of your existing natural gas furnace, if that's what you have. And when you're considering new furnaces, it's easy to compare their efficiency. That's because all gas furnaces are given an annual fuel utilization efficiency (AFUE) rating. The higher this number is, the better. So an AFUE of 80 simply means 80 percent of the fuel—say, natural gas—being burned is being turned into heat for your home.

As with many things around the home, from toilets to showerheads, there are government-mandated efficiency ratings. All gas furnaces being installed today must have

a minimum AFUE rating of 78, but some homes have older gas furnaces with AFUEs as low as 60. That means just 60 percent of the heat made by your system goes into your home, and the other 40 percent winds up being vented outdoors.

Seventy-eight is the minimum required AFUE rating today, but you can find much more efficient furnaces on the market, furnaces with ratings in the 80s and 90s. To receive the Energy Star qualification, a natural gas furnace must have an AFUE of 90 or better. Right now, one of the most efficient gas furnaces on the market is the Trane XV-95. It has an AFUE rating of up to 96.7. According to my friend Randy Scott, vice president of product systems management at Trane, that 96.7 percent efficiency rating is good for a 20 percent savings in energy costs over a 78 AFUE unit. That's a big difference and definitely worth considering.

Another key consideration when selecting a gas furnace is size. When you get a quote on a new gas furnace, typically a contractor will visit your home and perform a *load calculation*. This helps determine the right size unit based on your particular home's *heat loss* during cold weather and *heat gains* during warm weather.

You don't want to oversize the system, since it will cycle on and off a lot more often than it should, which is hard on the equipment. You'll wind up having to replace equipment prematurely. A too-large system also will be noisier than necessary.

Obviously, you don't want to undersize the system either. A system that's too small just won't be able to keep your home comfortable. Also, that system will be overworked, so it most likely will die a premature death from excessive wear and tear.

Another factor that can really affect comfort is fan speed. Some gas furnaces have a fan that operates at a fixed speed, while others have a variable-speed fan. Most of the time, these variable-speed fans will operate at a lower speed, so you get a constant, even flow of warm air throughout your house. This helps to reduce energy use as well as noise. One reason it reduces energy use is that the heater isn't cycling on and off all the time. Think of it like driving

a car: You get better gas mileage when you operate at a steady, slower speed than when you're driving in stop-and-go traffic. Furnaces with variable-speed fans also can pick up the tempo when the temperature outside becomes particularly cold, so they make sure your home stays warm enough.

Furnaces also require regular maintenance. You'll want to have a heating professional check your system once a year to be sure everything is still working properly and safely.

BOILERS AND RADIANT HEATING

As I mentioned, most houses in the United States are heated by either furnaces or boilers. Boilers tend to be most common in the Northeast and the Upper Midwest, and you also see them at many ski resort areas with serious snowfall, and often in places without access to natural gas.

In most boiler-based heating systems, the boiler heats water either to make hot water or to make steam, and then a pump distributes that hot water or steam through pipes that have been run throughout the house.

Steam boilers are much less common these days than they once were, in part because they're inherently less efficient than hot water boilers. Obviously, they have to operate at a hotter temperature to turn water into steam. But if you have an existing steam boiler, it is possible to replace it with a new, high-efficiency model.

For the most part, boilers today create hot water, and then they

- distribute the hot water via pipes to baseboard radiators in each room
- or they distribute the hot water through pipes under the floor in each room in what is known as radiant floor heating

In both cases, the heat is being distributed at floor level, and since heat rises, this is a sensible way to heat a home. It can keep floors, feet, and furniture warmer than can a forced-air system, which commonly has ducts blowing warm air from openings high up on your walls or in your ceiling. With forced-air heating, the hot air rises and tends to stay at ceiling level. Perhaps you've noticed as you sit in your home in the wintertime that your body is comfortable, but your feet get cold. Radiant heating experts point out that the hot air coming right off the floor keeps rooms warm at the level of the people in the room.

If you or someone in your household has allergies, another big benefit of a radiant heat system is the lack of airflow. You're not constantly blowing air through the house, stirring up dust, pollen, pet dander, and germs.

As you would expect, to heat water a boiler has to burn some sort of fuel, typically

- natural gas
- propane, or
- heating oil

Because something is being burned, as with a furnace, a boiler requires a flue to exhaust the byproducts of combustion.

Also like furnaces, boilers are rated for their annual fuel utilization efficiency (AFUE). The minimum AFUE rating allowed by the government for boilers today is 80 percent (75 percent for a steam boiler). There are also Energy Star–qualified hot water boilers, which have a minimum AFUE of 85 percent, and you can find even more efficient models on the market. My friend Jonathan Payne, who's a product manager at Bryant Heating & Cooling Systems (see Resources, page 344), says less than six years ago, boilers were just starting to get up to 90 percent AFUE ratings. Now, you can find boilers with AFUE ratings of 95 percent, which puts them in the same efficiency range as gas furnaces.

The big advantage that a forced-air heating system has over a typical boiler system is cost. If you've never had heat before, installing a forced-air heating system with ducting, in most cases, will be easier and quite a bit less expensive than installing a boiler with copper piping or flex tubing running throughout your home. In a retrofit situation, if you do opt to go with a boiler, it's obviously much easier—and more economical—to run copper piping and install radiators in each room than it is to rip up your flooring and install flex tubing, then install new flooring so you can have radiant floor heating.

It's also very rare to see radiant floor heating on anything but the first floor of a home.

Two-story houses usually employ a sort of hybrid system: radiant floor heating on the lower level and forced-air heating on the upper level. In this case, the same boiler is used for both parts of the heating system. To create hot air for the upper floor (or floors), air is blown across a coil that contains hot fluid, much like an automotive radiator. While this may sound like an unnecessarily complicated installation, remember that most homes with this sort of setup also will have central air-conditioning, which is always a forced-air installation. So you'd need that ducting upstairs anyway.

RADIANT FLOOR HEATING

Ordinarily, radiant floor heating is considered an option for new home construction or for additions. In fact, because of the very labor-intensive—and therefore very costly—installation, radiant floor heating is often recommended as a single-room option, such as in a bathroom with tile or stone floors.

In the case of new construction or a room addition, the tubing to run hot water under the floor often is mounted into a concrete slab foundation. That thick layer of concrete helps hold in the heat and then release it slowly over time, so it becomes a key part of your home's heating system. This is what's known as a *wet* installation.

If you're doing a retrofit or if your home has a raised foundation, it's possible to do a sort of milder wet installation. In this case, tubing can be installed in a thin layer of concrete over an existing foundation or subfloor.

Now, the other option is a *dry* installation. In this case, the tubing gets installed in an airspace below the flooring material. This type of installation usually creates a system that's not as efficient, but it's far easier to install.

Still another radiant heating option is using electricity to heat your floors. Several companies now offer electric heating mats that can be installed under flooring materials to heat one room or an entire home. These mats skip the boiler entirely and provide 100 percent electric heating.

ELECTRIC HEATERS

The good news is electric resistance heating is very efficient. It converts very close to 100 percent of the electricity used into heat. However, if you're getting your electricity from a utility company that generates electricity in one of the old-fashioned ways—by burning coal or oil or gas—that part of the process is very *inefficient*. Only about 30 percent of the energy from the fuel that's burned gets converted into electricity. So again, where you get your electricity—and how much you pay for it—will determine whether you will want to consider electric heating.

If you do want to consider electric heating, you have several options:

- electric furnaces
- electric boilers
- baseboard heaters
- wall heaters
- portable heaters (also known as space heaters)
- radiant heating
- heat pumps

ELECTRIC FURNACES AND BOILERS

As you might expect, an electric furnace works much like a gas or oil furnace, except it doesn't involve combustion. Instead of burning fuel to heat up a refrigerant, electricity does the job by heating electric resistance coils.

The big benefits to an electric furnace, compared with a gas or oil model, are

- the equipment is often less expensive
- you don't need a flue or a chimney, so the furnace can be installed virtually anywhere in your home
- it's a more economical installation
- it doesn't require regular maintenance

The big drawback with electric furnaces, when compared with other *electric* heating options, is that they require more energy to heat your home. It takes energy to circulate that heated air through ductwork.

Electric boilers are much less common than natural gas–, propane-, and heating oil–fueled boilers, but they are available. Again, since there is no combustion, they don't require a flue, so they can be installed anywhere. They also tend to be smaller than other types of boilers. Some models will even fit in a closet.

The AFUE ratings for electric boilers and furnaces range from 95 percent to 100 percent. The lower ratings typically are for boilers and furnaces that get installed outdoors, because they lose heat to the outside air. As I mentioned, electric heat is very efficient, but it also traditionally has been very expensive.

BASEBOARD HEATERS

Baseboard heaters are a single-room electric heating option. You can install a baseboard heater in just one room in your house, or you can install one in every single room. Each will have its own thermostat, so you can control the room's temperature.

Baseboard heaters are particularly popular for

- home additions, since you can add as much heat as you need for the new space
- adding heat to a home that has never had central heating before, which means there's no existing ductwork.

Baseboard heaters run at low radiant temperatures and are kid friendly.

Installing ducting—particularly in a home on a slab foundation with a shallow roofline—can sometimes be a real challenge, and it's certainly a considerable expense.

- rooms that are not used very often, so you don't waste money—and energy—heating a space unnecessarily
- homes in which some people like a much warmer space and some people prefer a much cooler space, since each room has its own thermostat and can be set to its own individual temperature
- homes where one room just doesn't get warm enough from the central heating system

You've probably seen baseboard heaters in hotel rooms. They're also popular in retirement homes because each resident can choose his or her own room temperature.

Baseboard heaters are very simple devices. They normally get mounted against an outside wall of the house just above floor level, and they stick out only about 3 inches into the room. Cool air at floor level is drawn into the unit. A simple electric heating core warms that air, which is then allowed to rise out of the baseboard heater and move into the room. In other words, they use convection to heat a room. And because they have no moving parts, they're considered maintenance-free.

Now the real difference between baseboard heating units comes in *how* they heat the air. Some have an open heating element, not unlike a toaster. Others use a recirculating heat transfer fluid and a finned design, like an automotive radiator. The latter style, what's called a *hydronic* baseboard heater, usually is quieter, more durable, and better able to maintain a consistent temperature in a room.

WALL HEATERS

Like a baseboard heater, a wall heater is a single-room heating option. But while a baseboard heater gets mounted in front of a wall, a wall heater actually gets mounted *into* a wall. Most are designed to fit between the studs in a home, which are usually spaced 16 inches on center, so these heaters are relatively small. You can install one wall heater in a smaller room, or you can install two wall heaters that are controlled by a single thermostat to heat larger rooms or to heat oddly shaped rooms.

A wall heater will have an electric heating element inside and a reflective material on the wall side to make sure that the heat moves toward the room you want to warm. Most wall heaters also have a fan inside to help circulate that heat.

Unlike a baseboard heater, a wall heater should be mounted on an interior wall. That's because it can be challenging to insulate an outside wall properly when you have a heater mounted into it, and you know how important proper insulation is.

PORTABLE HEATERS

If you have just one room that's too cold—or just one person in the house who's always cold—a portable electric heater may be just what you need.

Some people do use space heaters as the sole heating source in a home, but this typically only makes sense from an efficiency standpoint if you plan to heat just one room at a time. Using space heaters as your only form of heat is also a safety concern. According to the U.S. Consumer Product Safety Commission, more than 25,000 residential fires each year are related to the use of space heaters. So if you do purchase a space heater, by all means make sure it's a new model with all the appropriate safety features.

Space heaters come in a wide variety of shapes and sizes, including the following:

- your basic, old-fashioned design with open coils like a toaster and a grill on the front
- oscillating models that look like a fan and that actually include a built-in fan to distribute the heat
- flat-panel wall-mount units (they don't get mounted *into* a wall, but rather *onto* one)

- convection models that are designed to heat a whole room and that also feature a fan to move that heat outward
- portable baseboard heaters that plug into any wall electrical outlet

Space heaters that use open coils typically are not as efficient as models that use a heat transfer liquid. The latter will retain and radiate heat longer, providing a more constant temperature in the area, and they won't have to cycle on and off as frequently.

 AN AIR-TO-AIR HEAT PUMP

For electric-powered wholehouse heating, a heat pump system usually is the best choice. There are two different kinds of heat pumps on the market today:

- air-to-air heat pumps
- geothermal heat pumps

An air-to-air heat pump essentially is an air conditioner that has a reversing valve inside, so it can also make heat. It can cool your home, and it can heat your home—at least in some climates.

An air-to-air heat pump actually works a lot like a refrigerator. The refrigerator takes heat out of the food you put into it—as well as the air inside the refrigerator—and it uses a coil

setup on the back to exhaust that heat into your kitchen.

So in the summertime, a heat pump works like a refrigerator, taking heat out of your home and exhausting it to the outside. In the wintertime, it does the opposite: It takes heat from the air outside and it uses that heat to warm up your home. To do this, it uses two heat exchange coils, a hot coil and a cold coil. The cold coil absorbs heat, and the hot coil dissipates heat.

There are two parts to the system: an indoor unit and an outdoor unit. The outdoor unit looks virtually identical to a traditional air-conditioning unit mounted in your backyard or in your side yard. There's a refrigerant inside the outdoor unit. And when you're in heating mode, the heat pump controls the refrigerant temperature so that it's lower than the temperature of the outside air. That way, heat will transfer *from* the outside air *to* the refrigerant. If it's 40 degrees outside, that refrigerant will be cooled to 30 degrees or 27 degrees, and the warmer outside air will heat up the refrigerant.

Then that heated refrigerant goes into your house, traveling through what's known as the *loop*. The indoor part of the heat pump system is the *air handler*, which looks kind of like a gas furnace. In this part of the system, the refrigerant gets squeezed by a compressor. Squeezing it increases the temperature dramatically, up to 220 degrees F. The hot refrigerant gets moved into a coil. The system blows air across that coil to heat it, then it circulates the hot air through your home.

AIR-TO-AIR HEAT PUMP

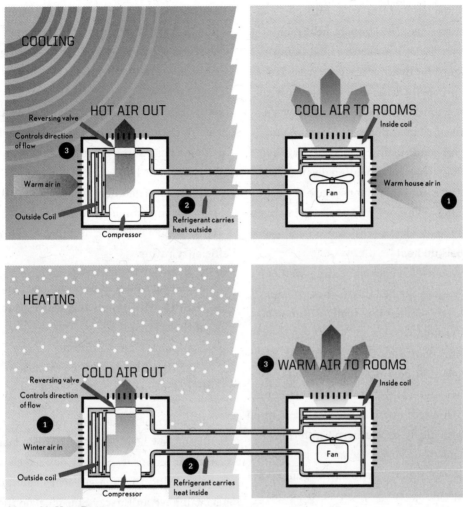

COOLING

HOT AIR OUT

Reversing valve
Controls direction of flow **3**

Warm air in

Outside Coil

Compressor

2 Refrigerant carries heat outside

COOL AIR TO ROOMS

Inside coil

Fan

Warm house air in **1**

HEATING

COLD AIR OUT

Reversing valve
Controls direction of flow **1**

Winter air in

Outside coil

Compressor

2 Refrigerant carries heat inside

3 WARM AIR TO ROOMS

Inside coil

Fan

Air-to-Air Heat Pump

KEY CONSIDERATIONS

Before you decide on an air-to-air heat pump, you'll want to consider these factors:

- electric rates in your area, since heat pumps use electricity to operate
- if it's going to be a retrofit to an existing home, is the system actually installable? Running the loop is usually the tricky part, but adding ductwork to a home that doesn't have it can be a challenge, as well.
- if wintertime temperatures often drop below freezing in your area

I spoke with my friend Duane Hallowell, president and CEO of Hallowell International (see Resources, page 344), about heat pumps. Duane says, "Today's air-source heat pump isn't designed for heating performances. It's designed primarily as an air conditioner with a secondary function of heat. With a conventional air-source heat pump, you're going to use it for air-conditioning primarily, and then you're going to use it for heating down to freezing conditions. And then chances are the heat pump's going to shut off, and you're going to go to a fossil fuel or electric resistance heat, [some kind of] backup heat."

Now, if you need a backup heating system, that may negate the benefit of a heat pump for your home—unless it is really a standout choice for cooling.

But Duane points out that heat pumps are the *dominant* heating source below the Mason-Dixon line, and they're also more popular than you might guess in the western United States, particularly in Southern California. Many people who think they have a traditional air conditioner actually have a heat pump. The reason heat pumps are popular in these climates is because it stays above freezing—above 32 degrees F—for most if not all of the year.

A heat pump is a really efficient heating and cooling choice in this sort of climate because it's a single installation. You don't need both a furnace for heat and an air conditioner for cool. You've got one single system handling both your heating and cooling needs. Also, you don't need a flue.

And it's a really efficient system overall. Heat pumps actually can provide output that's equal to four times the energy that you put into them—since they're literally *moving* heat, rather than *creating* heat.

Any home can be a good candidate for a heat pump if you're currently using electric heat. You also will want to at least consider an air-to-air heat pump if you're using propane or oil to heat your home, and if you're not a good candidate for a geothermal heat pump, which I'll go into in just a moment.

Heat pumps have two different kinds of efficiency ratings:

- a heating seasonal performance factor (HSPF), which rates the heating part of the system
- a seasonal energy efficiency ratio (SEER), which rates the system's cooling efficiency

The government has mandated a minimum HSPF for new heat pumps of 7.7. The most efficient heat pumps available today have an HSPF between 8 and 10. High-efficiency heat pumps also will have an Energy Star label on the front, showing both SEER and HSPF ratings.

NEW DESIGNS

Newer heat pump designs offer a few enhancements over traditional models, including

- two-speed compressors, which enable them to cycle on and off less frequently and to increase compressor life

- variable-speed fans, which increase comfort, minimize draftiness, and make systems more efficient overall
- the ability to also heat water for a home (see Chapter 13, "Heating Water," for more about this)
- reverse cycle chillers

A heat pump system with a reverse cycle chiller is quite different from a standard system. In this case, the heat pump either heats or cools water that is stored in a large, insulated tank. That water is then used with a fan coil system to create hot or cold air, which can be sent through normal forced-air ductwork. However, this sort of setup offers another option, as well: It can be used with radiant floor heating, literally sending that hot water through the flex tubing in a home's floors.

The reverse cycle chiller also solves one of the common problems with heat pumps: They sometimes blow cold air when they're in heating mode because they have to periodically go into a defrost cycle to defrost the coils outside. Heat pumps with a large water storage tank can use the heat being held in that water to blow hot air, even when they're operating in defrost mode.

There's also a new type of air-to-air heat pump that is designed specifically for cold climates. Duane and his business partner, David Shaw of Shaw Engineering Associates, were looking for ways to make a heat pump work better in a cold climate. Their company,

Hallowell International, has taken the standard air-source heat pump and made some changes.

"David Shaw actually conceived an idea as early as 1981 and brought it to life in 1995 called 'boosted compression,'" says Duane. "With a conventional air-source heat pump, you would lose your ability to absorb heat, traditionally at thirty-two degrees Fahrenheit, or about the freezing condition outside. . . . But there's plenty of usable energy in the air all the way down to absolute zero. . . . [With boosted compression], we can absorb heat and transfer it into a house at temperatures across the United States and Canada down to minus forty-six below zero. . . . We rate our system down to minus thirty below zero, while still maintaining coefficients of performance above a two, or two times the energy that you'd see out of resistance heating elements."

This sort of system is worth considering if you live in a northern climate or anywhere with a serious need for heat.

MINI-SPLIT HEAT PUMPS

Now, a typical air-to-air heat pump system will feature ductwork, just like a furnace-based central heating system. But there's another way to go: You can install a mini-split heat pump. It's like a standard air-source heat pump, in that it has two parts to the system: the outdoor compressor/condenser unit and the indoor air handler. But there are some big differences.

Unlike a standard air-to-air heat pump, a mini-split system

- features no ductwork
- has an air handler that heats (and cools) just one room in a home
- has a single outdoor unit that can work with as many as four indoor air handlers
- has a separate thermostat for each of those indoor air handlers, so it's easy to control the temperature of rooms individually
- is quite easy to install; usually all you have to do is run a single conduit through a wall to connect the indoor and outdoor components, so it's a good option for retrofits, as well as for additions

You also have a choice of air handler location. It can be

- mounted on a wall
- hung from a ceiling
- set into a dropped ceiling
- freestanding on the floor

This makes installation easier and more flexible than some other options.

The biggest drawback with mini-split heat pumps is the cost for the amount of heating (and cooling) they provide. In spite of their flexibility, they can be dramatically more expensive to install than a central heating system if you're looking for whole house heating.

 # GEOTHERMAL HEAT PUMPS

I've covered air-to-air heat pumps—both standard and mini-split designs—but there's another type of heat pump on the market: a geothermal heat pump, which is a little bit different from an air-source design. Actually, the components of the system inside the house are the same. You're either blowing hot air or cold air: 100-degree air in the wintertime, and 50-degree air in the summertime. The difference in these pumps is what's found *outside*. With a geothermal heat pump, you don't have an outdoor unit. There's no box outside with a fan. Instead, you have hundreds of feet of pipe buried 5 feet or more beneath the ground in your backyard.

Now, why would this system be preferable? Well, wherever you may be in North America, the ground—not at the surface level, but a few feet below—is going to be 60 degrees F, give or take 5 degrees. So the ground is going to be maybe 55 degrees F in northern Minnesota, and it's going to be around 65 degrees F in Florida, but there's not a whole lot of temperature variation.

The ground with that nice, stable temperature actually makes a much better heat transfer medium than air. Instead of having to battle 26 degree outdoor air or 0 degree outdoor air and trying to get heat, you've got a 60 degree base, and that means your heating system can be much more efficient.

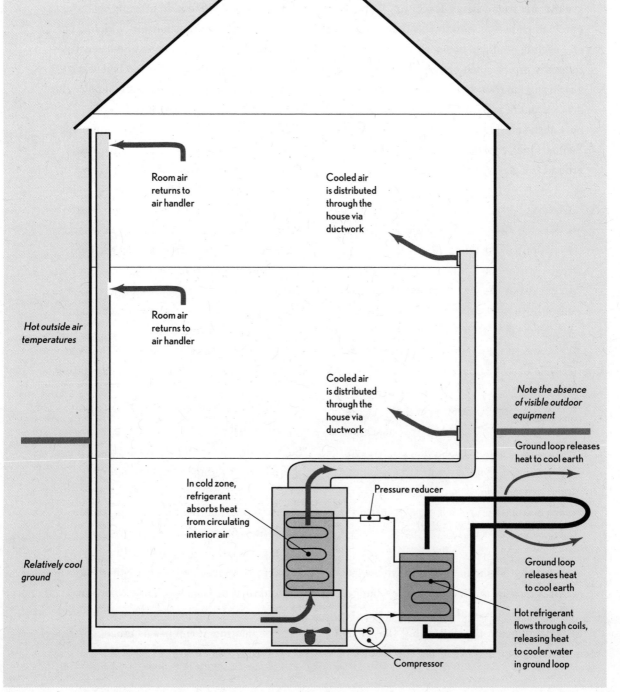

RESIDENTIAL
GEOEXCHANGE SYSTEM
(COOLING MODE)

Room air
returns to
air handler

Cooled air
is distributed
through the
house via
ductwork

Hot outside air
temperatures

Room air
returns to
air handler

Cooled air
is distributed
through the
house via
ductwork

Note the absence
of visible outdoor
equipment

Ground loop releases
heat to cool earth

In cold zone,
refrigerant
absorbs heat
from circulating
interior air

Pressure reducer

Relatively cool
ground

Ground loop
releases heat
to cool earth

Hot refrigerant
flows through coils,
releasing heat
to cooler water
in ground loop

Compressor

The other efficiency with a geothermal heat pump comes from the natural moisture in the ground. My friend Bruce Ritchey of Water Furnace, which has been in the geothermal heating and cooling products business since 1981 (the company pretty much pioneered the residential geothermal market here in the United States; geothermal heat pumps actually are a major part of the market in Sweden, Finland, and Switzerland), explains why moisture in the ground is a good thing.

What we do is use the first law of thermodynamics that says that heat always goes from hot to cold. So, to illustrate that, if you take a poker and put it in the fire, it starts to get red at the tip, and that heat goes toward the cold part of the poker. Any time you have heat, it's going to go from hot to cold. And you can't destroy heat. Heat can only be moved. It goes from one spot to the next.

So, you know how the tip of that poker is glowing red hot? If you take that poker and say, "Okay, I've got to cool that off," and you start blowing on it, you've got to blow a long time to get it cool. If you take that same poker and you stick it into a bucket of water, just like that it cools down.

In exactly the same way, earth with a lot of water content is a terrific heat exchanger. That's why geothermal systems use the ground instead of the air. Basically, what they're doing is they're absorbing heat *from* the ground in the wintertime and they're putting heat *into* the ground in the summertime.

Bruce says, "We're kind of using the ground as a huge solar storage battery, which is basically the whole principle here. Solar energy— fifty percent of it—gets trapped below the earth's surface. So we're basically doing solar energy, whether it's sunshiny or not."

So how does a geothermal heat pump use that consistent underground temperature? By running water with a little antifreeze in it through pipes. "It's like a great, big radiator," says Bruce. "It's the same principle, only instead of blowing air across it, you're letting the moisture in the ground carry the heat away and absorb it [for cooling]. . . . And then inside, we have a refrigeration compressor just like you have outdoors on an air conditioner. Ours is indoor in that box. And again, it's using refrigerant to take the heat out of that water or to put heat into that water that's circulating."

ADVANTAGES OF A GEOTHERMAL HEAT PUMP

So what are the relative advantages of a geothermal heat pump? There are many.

- A geothermal heat pump uses 25 percent to 50 percent less energy than a traditional heating and cooling system. Compared with an air-to-air heat pump, it uses as much as 44 percent less energy. And compared with electric heating, it can use as much as 72 percent less energy.

RESIDENTIAL
GEOEXCHANGE SYSTEM
(HEATING MODE)

Room air
returns to
air handler

Warmed air
is distributed
through the
house via
ductwork

Room air
returns to
air handler

*Cold outside air
temperatures*

Warmed air
is distributed
through the
house via
ductwork

In hot zone,
refrigerant
gives up heat
to circulating
interior air

Pressure reducer

Ground loop absorbs
heat from warm earth

Ground loop
absorbs heat
from warm
earth

*Relatively
warm ground*

Cold refrigerant
flows through coils,
absorbing heat from
warmer water in
ground loop

Compressor

Sample Cost and Payback Analysis: Geothermal Pump

The cost of the *equipment* is about the same, whether you're looking at an HVAC system that has a gas furnace and a traditional air conditioner or an HVAC system that uses either an air-to-air heat pump or a geothermal heat pump. According to Bruce Ritchey, the cost of that equipment—whichever way you choose to go—is really within about a hundred bucks. There's no big difference.

Now, the actual *installation* in a brand-new house—or an older house that does not yet have central heat—is actually cheaper with a heat pump than with a gas furnace because you don't have to install a flue.

The disadvantage to a geothermal heat pump is installers have to dig a trench in your backyard to put the pipes in the ground. That's labor-intensive, and labor costs money. Installing that piping will cost between $1,000 and $4,000 *per ton* of air-conditioning. According to Bruce, his company typically installs a 4-ton unit. That translates into a cost of $4,000 to $16,000 more to install a geothermal heat pump system than a traditional HVAC system. Why such a big price range? Because it's easier to bury the pipes underground in some backyards than it is in others.

If you've got a big backyard with lots of space, the installer can use a backhoe and dig a trench and lay the piping, which will probably cost you about $1,500 a ton. What if your house is right next door to another one and you can't fit a backhoe through the side yard? Or what if you have a very small backyard, as so many homes do these days? Then the installer will have to come in with a horizontal boring machine or with a well driller and put in vertical bores. According to Bruce, that's going to cost you about $4,000 a ton. And if your home was built on solid granite or something equally impenetrable, then geothermal heating and cooling really isn't an option. It would be beyond cost-prohibitive.

When it comes to *new construction,* where the cost for the system gets rolled into a mortgage, Bruce says a geothermal heating/cooling setup is definitely a "cash flow positive" proposition. "What it's going to cost you on your mortgage is dramatically less than the amount of money you're going to save every month on your heating and air-conditioning and water heating bill. The system saves you a couple hundred dollars a year on the cost of heating water.

- It cuts the *peak* energy draw by half on a building. If you're installing solar, that means you can get away with a dramatically smaller solar installation.
- The EPA says putting in a geothermal heat pump system is the environmental equivalent of taking one-half of a car off the road *permanently*.
- It offers three stages of heat, so it provides a much more even temperature than many other heating devices.
- On the outside of the house, you don't have one of those big boxes like you have for a regular AC or an air-to-air heat pump. So you don't get the noise and you don't have the eyesore in your yard.
- Inside, the system is quieter; you shouldn't even be aware of it starting and stopping.
- It provides better humidity removal than other systems in the summertime.
- It's extremely efficient because of that consistent ground temperature, which is roughly 60 degrees F.
- You get free hot water. (More on this in Chapter 13, "Heating Water.")
- The average life of a geothermal heat pump system is twenty years. Compare that with twelve to fifteen years for a typical air conditioner and about fourteen years for an air-to-air heat pump.
- The only maintenance required is changing the filter. Compare that with

"On a 7 percent mortgage, you're talking about $7 a month for $1,000. So let's say there's a $10,000 difference in the cost of this system, which would be pretty high for new construction. So that'll cost you $70 a month more."

According to Bruce, a geothermal system will help you save about $100 a month on your utility bills, when compared with a traditional, efficient system—for instance, a 90 percent efficiency furnace with an air conditioner that has an efficiency rating of 13 SEER. If you compare geothermal with a high-efficiency air-to-air heat pump, you're still going to save about $90 or so each month in heating and cooling costs and the cost of heating water.

Now, if you're in an area where you're heating with fuel oil or propane or straight electric, Bruce says the savings will be even more dramatic: "You're talking $200 to $300 a month savings."

So for new construction, you can pretty much count on being cash-flow positive with a geothermal heating and cooling system. With retrofits, the numbers depend on your specific backyard.

a traditional gas furnace and an air conditioner, which require two service calls per year, one for each system.

- An air-to-air heat pump has to be defrosted just like a refrigerator, because when it's 40 degrees outside and you're running the coil at 28, frost forms on the coil and after a while it can't transfer any heat. So you have to reverse the system, and that causes some loss of efficiency. Because a geothermal heat pump is underground, the coils never get frosty.

It definitely makes sense to at least consider geothermal heating if you live someplace with long, cold winters. It also can be a wise choice in areas that have major cooling needs.

 # WOOD-BURNING STOVES AND HEATERS

There are certain parts of the country, and the world, in which wood can be an economical source of heat and energy. I'm certainly not in favor of cutting down trees in order to heat your home. But if you have a source of downed wood that has no other practical use—if the wood cannot be used as lumber or to make furniture or to reuse in a responsible fashion—then it can make sense to investigate wood-burning stoves and heaters.

Even if you live in an area rich with wood resources, it's still very important to find the most efficient way to make heat from that downed wood. If you've ever lived in a house with a wood-burning fireplace, you know a fireplace does not give off a whole lot of heat. You have to sit directly in front of the fireplace to feel the warmth.

You've probably also noticed that you can really smell wood that burns from a fire. That smell is a sure sign that there are serious emissions resulting from burning wood in a traditional open-masonry fireplace. In fact, traditional fireplaces create considerable air pollution. They're not an environmentally friendly way to heat a house.

However, there are high-efficiency fireplaces and fireplace inserts on the market that are EPA approved. An insert can literally be placed into a traditional open-masonry fireplace to convert it into a more efficient design. The insert uses the chimney you already have, and it transforms your fireplace into a type of woodstove. It's important to have a professional handle this installation, so the insert is installed safely and in an airtight fashion.

There are also some new fireplace designs on the market that still let you enjoy the view of the wood being burned, as well as providing heat with low emissions. These new designs draw in air from your room and heat it. The warmed air is then vented right back into the same room or routed through ductwork to other parts of your home.

Another way to burn wood and heat your

home is by using a woodstove. Some of the newer designs on the market have efficiencies in the 70 percent to 80 percent range.

If you're seriously considering burning wood as your primary heat source, I would recommend investigating masonry heaters, which are also sometimes called Russian or Siberian or Finnish fireplaces. These freestanding heaters are made from masonry, rather than metal, which enables the fire to burn much hotter. This not only creates more heat but also reduces emissions. Masonry stoves are often 90 percent efficient and produce minimal emissions, plus you only have to build a small fire once or twice a day to heat your house. The only real drawback—besides a price point of $5,000 or more for a large model—is that these heaters take a while to warm up your home. You need to plan ahead for heating.

 ## PELLET STOVES

You'll go through a considerable amount of fuel if you're burning wood to create heat. So you might want to consider another option: pellets. You can use pellets in masonry heaters or in heating appliances, including fireplace inserts, designed especially for burning them. The pellets pretty much look like rabbit feed. And they can be made from many different materials, including:

- sawdust
- wood chips
- bark
- paper
- agricultural waste

Obviously, I do not recommend burning pellets made from virgin materials. But you can find pellets made from recycled materials or from agricultural waste, both of which can be environmentally friendly choices—*if* you choose a clean-burning pellet stove or heater.

Burning pellets is usually a much easier lifestyle choice than burning wood. They don't require you to tend the fire several times a day to keep your home warm. Instead, pellet stoves have a hopper that automatically feeds pellets into the fire. You determine the feed rate based on your heating needs. You'll find different-size hoppers, ranging up to about 136 pounds.

Pellet stoves do require some electricity to operate. Also, a professional installation is very important, and you may want to purchase a maintenance/service contract since pellet stoves are rather complicated and they do require routine maintenance.

 ## TURNING HOT WATER INTO HEAT

I briefly mentioned that you can get free hot water from a geothermal heat pump. But you can also go the other way: You can use the hot water that your water heater produces to heat your home.

Basically, an air handler gets connected to your home's water heater. This unit is just like the heater in your car. It has a big radiator that hot water runs through—a series of tiny coils, really—and a fan blows air across the radiator, heating the air. That hot air then gets circulated through the regular ducting in your house. There are a lot of benefits to this setup:

- It's easy to install.
- You don't need a flue, since there's no combustion taking place.
- You don't need any gas piping.
- The unit itself is smaller than a typical gas furnace. It can be installed above a ceiling, in a closet, in an attic, or even recessed into a wall.
- Outside temperatures have no effect on your heating system's efficiency.
- You can opt for a heating-only model or for one that also includes cooling coils.

The unit does need to be professionally installed, and you will need to make sure that your water heater is adequately sized to serve both purposes.

If your heating bill has been getting you all hot and bothered, it's probably time to investigate alternatives. Obviously, you have a lot of choices, both in terms of fuel and in terms of heating system designs.

Again, there's no one right, green way to go. Geothermal is a great choice for some homes.

My Aqua-Therm has helped me cut my natural gas bills by 40 percent.

Radiant floor heating is great for others. A more traditional setup is still the best option in many situations. Maybe all you and your family need is a space heater.

The key is to investigate fuel prices and investigate installation costs for different types of systems. That way, you can make an informed decision about what's greenest environmentally and also what's greenest financially in your particular situation.

Using a Water Heater to Heat My House

After I finished sealing off my home's basement as part of my insulation project, it left me with a problem: There was no more air circulating in my basement.

Now, why is this a problem? Because I have two devices in my basement that require air. One is the gas water heater that augments my solar hot water, and the other is my gas furnace. Both of those natural gas devices require air to breathe. Additionally, neither one is particularly efficient. This made me realize that it was time to redesign the boiler room of the S.S. *Begley*.

First, I dealt with the hot water issue. I've had solar hot water in this house since 1990 and I have long since been paid back on my investment. But, solar hot water is not *always* hot. There are cloudy days as well as days when Rachelle takes a twenty-minute shower. So, I have a backup system—a natural gas–powered water heater—when the solar setup can't supply enough to meet my total needs.

However, that gas water heater was just a standard one. So I replaced it with an A. O. Smith Vertex 100 super-insulated water heater (see Resources, page 344). It's the most efficient natural gas water heater on the market today. It's 96 percent thermal efficient. It far outperforms any standard system. In addition, because it's a sealed system, it takes its air and exhausts its air through 3-inch pipes going all the way out of the sealed basement. So, bingo! No more air required.

But I still had to consider the furnace. I decided to remove my regular gas furnace that I had been using to heat my home and replace it with a unit called the Aqua Therm from First Company (see Resources, page 344). The Aqua Therm takes 130 degree F hot water from the Vertex water heater and circulates it through a series of tiny coils while a blower creates the hot forced air.

So now I have not only eliminated the need for air in my basement but also completely eliminated an entire natural gas device—my furnace—and everything is running off one superefficient gas water heating device. My natural gas bill for the first sixty days of this new system dropped by 50 percent. I can't wait for next winter!

12

COOLING YOUR HOME

**Finding the Best System to Fit
Your Particular Situation**

AS I MENTIONED AT THE BEGINNING OF CHAPTER 11, "Heating Your Home," there is no one right choice when it comes to heating and cooling systems. The cleanest, greenest choice is situational. You have to choose the best option for your situation based on where you live, your climate, your home's construction type, and so on.

At least when it comes to cooling, there's one less variable to consider: All of the current cooling options are powered by electricity, so it's simply a matter of choosing the most efficient option that works in your situation and within your budget.

When I say "cooling your home," I'm sure many of you instantly think about air-conditioning. But there are other cooling options, as well—some of which can use far less energy to cool a house. In this chapter, we'll look at:

- home ventilation systems
- evaporative coolers (also known as swamp coolers)
- central air-conditioning
- heat pumps
- room and portable air-conditioning units

NATURAL VENTILATION

Of course the simplest form of ventilation is to open your windows and doors and let a natural breeze cool your home. If you live near the coast, ocean breezes are perfect for ventilation. But even inland, if you live in a temperate climate—or if the temperatures drop after dark where you live—cross-ventilation can be enough to cool your home, at least some of the time.

If you're wondering why people always talk about *cross*-ventilation, it's easy to understand. Wind blows into the windows on one side of your home, and the vacuum effect draws warmer inside air out the windows on the opposite side. It literally creates a breeze *through* your house.

If you're building a home or if you're adding on, it certainly makes sense to position doors and windows to take advantage of any prevailing breezes—to literally orient your home into the wind so you can encourage natural cooling. You also can use landscaping to direct airflow into your windows. You can use windbreaks—such as a wall or a row of trees or shrubs—to redirect the prevailing wind and point it toward your home's windows.

If you have a two-story house, you also can take advantage of what's called the *chimney effect*. When you open windows on the ground floor or in the basement, cooler outside air comes in. As my friend Bruce Ritchey of Water Furnace explained in the last chapter,

heat always moves toward cool. So that cooler outside air gets warmed by the hotter air inside your house. Because heat rises, when you open the windows upstairs, the warmer air from downstairs travels up and out those upstairs windows.

All of this airflow does more than just cool the air inside your house, it also cools your body. One of the reasons a breeze feels so cooling, whether you're indoors or outdoors, is because of *convection*. As cool air moves across your warm body, that air absorbs some of your body heat. The now-hotter air rises, and cooler air moves in, again absorbing heat from your body and rising. The faster the hot air rises and the cool air flows in—literally the faster the airflow—the cooler you feel. This is the *wind chill* effect.

CEILING FANS

If the air tends to be awfully still where you live, then you can create your own man-made breezes using fans. Of the various fan designs on the market, ceiling fans are the most effective at cooling a home. The fan itself often uses the same amount of energy as a 100-watt incandescent lightbulb or less—even as low as 10 watts—which is nothing compared with a traditional air conditioner.

What ceiling fans do is create a wind chill factor, so you feel much cooler at a given

The size of your room determines the length of the fan blades. Larger rooms require larger blades.

temperature. Typically, you can raise the temperature setting on your air conditioner by 6 degrees F and still feel just as comfortable if you use a ceiling fan. In fact, Hunter Fan Company (see Resources, page 345) recently commissioned a study using very sophisticated energy rater software programs. They found that using ceiling fans with a 6-degree thermostat change enabled homeowners in all different parts of the country—Boston; Washington, D.C.; Fort Myers, Florida; Chicago—to literally save hundreds of dollars each year on their energy bills.

My friend Jim Gallman, vice president of brand marketing at Hunter, says most of the fans these days come 90 percent preassembled, and they're an easy do-it-yourself installation. You don't need an electrician to install one.

Considering that you can buy a ceiling fan for as little as $70, you can easily purchase three fans—say, for your bedrooms and for your family room or living room—and the fans will pay for themselves in energy savings within the first year. This is a no-brainer move.

Naturally, you'll want to choose high-quality, energy-efficient ceiling fans. Fortunately, all you have to do is look for the Energy Star label. Ceiling fan/light combinations that are Energy Star qualified are about 50 percent more efficient than nonqualified models.

Of course, you'll want to choose the correct size ceiling fan and install it properly. The number of blades on a fan is more of an aesthetic issue, but the length of the blades is important. "If you're able to visualize air coming down from that central fan, it blows outward in a cone. And you want a wider cone for a wider room, or a smaller one for a smaller room," Jim says. "When you get to rooms, for example, that are 20 foot by 20 foot or larger, you really want to go with a larger fan blade, 56 inches or higher. When you get into a midtier room, 14×14 up to 20×20 or 18×20, somewhere in that range, you can drop down to a midtier, which is somewhere between 52-inch and 54-inch blades. Then you can go down to anywhere from a 30-inch to a 48-inch fan for rooms that are smaller."

The other key, according to Jim, is to position that fan about 8 feet from the floor. So you could install the fan flush up against the ceiling (what the industry calls a *flush-mount* or *hugger* design), or you could use a *down rod* to hang the fan farther from the ceiling, so you get it the right distance above the floor.

Jim makes another great point, too: If you have a room with high ceilings, a ceiling fan can help reduce your heating needs. Because heat rises, it can wind up at the top of a room with a high ceiling. By running your ceiling fan on the low speed (and often by reversing the direction it spins), you can circulate the warm air. So you can change your thermostat setting from 72 degrees F to 68 degrees F in the winter, for example, and be just as comfortable.

CIRCULATING AND WINDOW FANS

Of course, there are many other types of fans besides ceiling fans. You can find fans that are designed to

- sit or stand on the floor
- sit on a tabletop
- mount on a wall
- hang in a doorway
- mount in a window
- suspend from the ceiling

All of these fans help to produce the wind chill effect. Many are quite powerful, able to move air as far as 65 feet—which might be more than most of us need inside our homes, but it can certainly make a garage or workshop much more comfortable in the summertime.

You'll find that some fans are fixed, so they blow air in just one direction. Others oscillate, turning back and forth to improve airflow throughout a room. Most fans also have multiple speed settings.

For home cooling, window fans are probably the most sophisticated offerings. They typically are reversible, so you can use them to exhaust hot inside air to the outside or to bring cool outside air in. If you want to do both at the same time, there are dual designs, too.

Some window fans include a thermostat. So, for instance, if you're using the fan to keep your bedroom cool at night, once the temperature in your room reaches a preset level, that fan will automatically shut off. You don't have to get up when you're freezing at 4 a.m. and stumble over to the window to turn off the fan. (You may find some higher-end floor-mount or tabletop fans with a thermostat, as well.)

When you're shopping for a window fan, look for an Energy Star–qualified model, since it will move air about 20 percent more efficiently than nonqualified designs.

WHOLE-HOUSE FANS

Ceiling fans and circulating fans certainly can help to bring cool outside air into your home, but there's another option that's much, much faster: a whole-house fan.

A typical whole-house fan gets installed in your attic, and it extends through your ceiling. When you're ready to use it, you simply open all the windows—and ideally the doors, too—in your house. Then you flip the switch, and the powerful fan draws cool outside air into your home and up through the attic. Vents in the attic then allow warmer air to exit.

A whole-house fan typically measures 24 or 30 inches across. You'll want to have it

professionally installed, because you may need to cut through ceiling joists during the process, and you'll certainly want to make sure it's framed in properly. You also may have to add more attic vents to allow for sufficient airflow.

Typically, people use a whole-house fan to quickly cool down a house later in the day, such as when they get home from school or work if the temperatures outside have dropped. A whole-house fan is a fast and effective way to bring in the cooler outside air and get rid of the heat that's built up in your house. Then, once the house has cooled down sufficiently—usually within a very short time—the whole-house fan is turned off and cross-ventilation continues to keep the home cool.

There are some drawbacks to a whole-house fan, however, such as these:

- They often can be quite loud.
- Most are belt-driven, which means they need regular maintenance of the belt.
- You have to cut a hole in the ceiling of your house to install one, which means there will be no insulation in that portion of the attic.

Some of the newer whole-house fans on the market have been designed to address these concerns. Some are much quieter. Some use multiple fans, instead of one large fan. Some are maintenance-free. And some feature an insulated, built-in door on the backside of the fan, which closes to seal off the attic from your house when the fan is not being used.

All of these ventilation techniques work very well in a dry climate, but they're not effective in really hot, humid climates, particularly in areas where there is very little temperature difference between daytime and nighttime.

EVAPORATIVE COOLERS

Another cooling option in a dry climate is an evaporative cooler, also known as a swamp cooler. Evaporative coolers use a lot less electricity than traditional air-conditioning units—perhaps 75 percent less—plus they cost only about half as much to install, which explains why they're very popular in industrial buildings.

If you've ever been on a patio that's cooled by misters, or if you've ever noticed how much cooler the air is near a waterfall, then you've experienced evaporative cooling. When water droplets evaporate, they lower the temperature of surrounding air considerably.

A typical home evaporative cooler takes advantage of this effect. It takes warm outside air and uses a blower to direct that air over water-saturated pads. The pads cool the air anywhere from 15 to 40 degrees F. Then the cool air is sent into your home through one central outlet, or it can be directed into individual rooms through ductwork.

When using an evaporative cooler, you will need to open some windows—or have another way to vent air out of your house. There are two reasons for this:

- **Humidity.** As you might guess, an evaporative cooler adds considerable humidity to the air that's coming into your home, which is why it's never recommended for anything but a dry climate. If you keep all of your windows closed while an evaporative cooler is operating, you'll wind up with a lot of relative humidity inside your home—as high as 80 percent.
- **Quantity of airflow.** Evaporative coolers also send a considerable amount of air into a home, so it's important to give the hot air that was already in the house someplace to go.

The key is to open windows on the leeward side of your house, which is just the opposite of your goal with ventilation. In this case, you do not want hot outside air blowing into your home. Instead, you want to open windows on the other side of the house and allow the hot inside air to exhaust out; it will literally get pushed out the windows by the steady flow of cool air from the evaporative cooler.

If you don't open the windows wide enough, you'll know. You'll start fogging up windows and mirrors inside the house. And if you open the windows too much, you'll know too, since hot outside air will start coming in.

One of the benefits of an evaporative cooler is that it provides a steady flow of fresh air. A traditional central air-conditioning system recirculates the air that's already in your house. An evaporative cooler keeps cooling fresh outside air. So that can improve your home's air quality. The key is to make sure your evaporative cooler is fitted with a filter (which is usually an optional accessory) to reduce the amount of dust and pollen and other allergens coming into your home.

Evaporative coolers have been popular in hot, dry areas like the western and mountain states, including such cities as Phoenix, Denver, Salt Lake City, and Albuquerque.

Obviously, there are some drawbacks to evaporative coolers, including the following:

- increased humidity
- on really hot days, they will not cool a home as much as an air conditioner would
- having to keep some windows open (a safety concern) or having to install ducts to exhaust hot air from inside your home up into your attic—which, in turn, may require additional vents to exhaust hot air out of the attic
- the potential for roof leaks. Evaporative coolers typically have been mounted on the roof—what's called a down-flow design—but experts now are recommending the installation of horizontal-flow units on the ground, which certainly eliminates the possibility of roof leaks.
- the need for maintenance about once a month, including draining and

cleaning the cooler, as well as replacing the pads twice each cooling season. While you can do most of the required maintenance yourself, it does increase the hassle factor.
- most important, the continual use of a fairly substantial quantity of water. This is a very serious consideration, especially in areas like Los Angeles where water comes at such a high cost in so many ways.

So far, I've focused on how a typical evaporative cooler works, what is known as a *direct* evaporative cooler. There's also another type of system known as an *indirect* evaporative cooler. In this case, the system uses a heat exchanger (again, like a radiator), so the humid air never actually enters your home.

There are also newer designs that are two-stage evaporative coolers. They have an indirect stage and a direct stage. These models are more efficient. They tend to lower air temperatures quite a bit, so they're better suited for really hot climates. Plus, they increase indoor humidity less than direct designs, usually to between 50 percent and 70 percent relative humidity.

Choosing a Contractor

Retail pricing for HVAC systems is wide ranging and depends in large part on where you live, but Randy from Trane says an average is anywhere between $7,000 and $10,000 to install or retrofit your home with a new high-efficiency heating *and* cooling system. This is a big investment. The key is to do it right with the right contractor.

"In order to really get at lowering your energy cost and addressing the green elements we've discussed," says Randy, "there're three elements related just to the heating and cooling system. Number one is the ductwork. Number two is the system. And number three is the installation of that system. So those three things all have to be done correctly in order to get the energy-rated performance."

I can't emphasize strongly enough that proper installation is vital for optimum efficiency. An air-conditioning system that's installed improperly will be dramatically less efficient than its ratings would imply. Installing an air-conditioning system is *not* a DIY job. This is a job that should be handled by a trained professional.

Most people will get quotes from two or three different contractors. If a contractor visits your home, asks you the square footage of your house, and then whips out a calculator and gives you an estimate from that, send him on his way.

It is *vital* that the contractor you choose performs a proper load calculation. The contractor should use computer software to do some number crunching. He should ask you for some key information to enter into that software program, so he can recommend the right system for your home.

The important questions include:

- What is your home's square footage?
- What is the type of construction (e.g., wood frame)?
- What is the R-value of your attic insulation and your wall insulation?
- Do you have a crawl space or a basement? If so, what is the R-value of any insulation down there?
- Do you have single-pane, dual-pane, or triple-pane windows? He may even ask for more details, such as if they're gas filled or if they have a low-e coating.
- At what temperature do you normally set your thermostat for heating?
- At what temperature do you normally set your thermostat for cooling?
- What are the ceiling heights in various rooms?
- How many people live in your home?

The contractor should take some measurements to determine the exterior wall space and the size of the windows. He'll pay attention to the type of window treatments you have. He'll note how many skylights and fireplaces you have. He'll also consider the orientation of your house. If you have a southern exposure with many windows, that can really affect your cooling needs. Or perhaps you have a porch or an awning to help block some of the summer sun, so it doesn't shine right into your home. He'll also take into account whether you're located in a hot climate, a cold climate, a humid area, and so on.

All of these factors make a real difference in terms of the size of the system you need, as well as the size of the ductwork running to each room. And speaking of ductwork, if you have an existing system, the contractor should inspect your ductwork. He'll go into the attic or into the crawl space and check out the size of the ducting and also to see if your ducting is crushed or leaking or otherwise compromised.

Once he has input all of the information into his computer program, then he should be able to accurately determine the size of the heating and cooling system you need. He should be able to tell you something like, "Your home needs a 100,000 BTU furnace and a four-ton air-conditioning unit." And the size of the system will vary based on all of those very specific details about your home as well as on the kind of system you choose—whether you're looking at a heat pump for heating and cooling or an air conditioner and a gas furnace or what-have-you.

Naturally, an oversize air conditioner is not as efficient as a properly sized unit. In a humid climate, an oversize air conditioner is an especially big problem, because it won't remove enough moisture from the air. Obviously, an undersized air conditioner is also a problem. It just won't be able to reach a comfortable temperature on really hot days. The key is to install the right size unit.

When it comes to air conditioner size, they're rated in terms of output capacity. A 1-ton air conditioner will have the capacity—the capability—to remove 12,000 BTUs worth of heat from inside your house. Home air conditioners usually range in size from 1 ton to 5 tons.

The size of the system also will depend on the efficiency of the units in question, and you may have to ask about that. The contractor is probably used to people being more concerned with price than efficiency. So don't be afraid to ask about the specifics of the equipment he's recommending, including the SEER.

AIR CONDITIONERS

The ventilation systems and evaporative coolers that I've already mentioned are only suitable for dry climates. So what if you live in a humid area? Well, air conditioners are not only suitable for humid climates, part of the way they *condition* the air is by removing humidity. Air conditioners can make living in a humid climate much more comfortable, even if you don't have a profound need for cooling. Of course, they work quite well in dry climates and in-between areas, too.

Two out of every three homes in the United States has an air conditioner. And the Department of Energy says air conditioners use 5 percent of *all* of the electricity produced in the United States. That's a lot of energy. The potential for savings by upgrading an older air conditioner to a newer, more efficient model is huge—in the 20 percent to 50 percent range if you take some of the other steps I've mentioned to help keep your home cool.

Now, there are actually four kinds of air conditioners:

- central air conditioners, which use ductwork to circulate the cold air throughout your house
- ductless minisplit air conditioners
- individual room air conditioners, which typically are mounted in a window or a wall
- portable air conditioners

In this chapter, I'll focus on central air conditioning systems since that's what most people will choose for their homes. But I will touch on the other options, as well.

HOW AIR CONDITIONERS WORK

At the most basic level, an air conditioner takes the heat out of the air *inside* your home and transfers it to the air *outside* by using:

- a cold indoor coil, also known as an evaporator
- a hot outdoor coil, also known as a condenser
- a liquid refrigerant
- a pump, also known as a compressor

These coils look like what you'd find on the back of a refrigerator. The S-shaped metal tubes are usually made from copper, and they have little fins on the outside, which are usually made from aluminum to help transfer heat as air blows across them.

So inside the house, the compressor literally compresses a refrigerant, turning it into a very hot gas (see page 234 in Chapter 11 for more on the magic of refrigeration). The compressor then pumps that gas through tubing to your hot outdoor coil. That coil is called a condenser because it allows the heat from the refrigerant to transfer to the cooler outside air. As that heat transfers, the refrigerant returns to a liquid state. It condenses. The liquid refrigerant then flows back into the house. There, the pressure on the refrigerant is reduced and it cools off very quickly. It then travels through the evaporator coil. Warm air from inside your house gets blown across the indoor coil. That air cools off by transferring its heat to the refrigerant. The refrigerant changes again from a liquid to a gaseous state—that is, it literally evaporates—and the process starts again.

CENTRAL AIR CONDITIONERS

In addition to the components I just listed, a central air conditioner also will have a system of ductwork to direct cooled air to the various rooms in your house. It's called a *central air conditioner* because the cool air is created in one central location, then it's distributed throughout your house.

The ductwork doesn't have to reach into every room in your home. But every room that has a duct leading to it will have a *register*, or *grille*. It might be located high on a wall, low on a wall, or set into the floor or ceiling. Wherever it is located, that register can be adjusted to direct the air toward a particular part of the room, and it also can be closed to restrict airflow to that room when cooling (or heating) is not needed.

The system also will have a return duct (or ducts) to take air out of your home. A return duct is usually installed in the ceiling—often in a hallway—since the air is warmer at ceiling level because heat rises. The return duct then directs that warmer air back into the air-conditioning system for cooling.

Certain features can make some air conditioners more comfortable to live with than others. You'll want to look for such things as:

- **A variable-speed air handler.** According to my friend Randy Scott, vice president of product systems management at Trane (see Resources, page 345), a system with a variable-speed fan will be more efficient than a system with a single-speed fan. Again, it's like driving at a slow and steady pace versus driving in stop-and-go traffic. Most of the time, the variable-speed fan will operate at a lower speed, so it will be quieter, and it will operate for longer periods of time. (A single-speed fan will cycle on and off much more frequently.) The slow and steady approach helps to keep the temperature more stable in your home, and it also provides more air circulation and better air filtration. Another, perhaps surprising benefit is humidity reduction. One of Trane's units actually can remove up to 24 gallons of water per day from the air inside a house. That's a lot of humidity! The idea is to have the system running at 50 percent of its capacity most of the time, and then on really hot days, it steps up to 100 percent output.
- **A quiet unit.** Central air conditioners are rated for loudness, in decibels (dB), so it's easy to compare units.
- **A fan-only switch.** This lets you use the system for ventilation, saving money and saving energy. For instance, if you live in an area that has cooler temperatures at night, a fan-only switch

will allow you to open the windows and use the air handler to circulate that cooler outside air throughout the house.

- **A filter check light.** A unit with this feature will keep track of how many hours the system has been running and notify you when it's time to change the air filter. This keeps the unit running at its most efficient levels, which again saves energy and money, plus it keeps the air quality higher inside your home.

- **An automatic fan delay.** This keeps the fan running for a few minutes after your home has reached the desired temperature and the A/C compressor has turned off. Because the indoor coil is still cold, the fan blows that extra cold air. It literally takes advantage of the money you've already spent on cooling the coil, giving you some nearly free A/C.

HYBRIDIZING YOUR AIR CONDITIONER

Running a central air conditioner system is costly, especially if you live in an area with very hot summers. I've found something that can make any central air-conditioning unit into a kind of hybrid. It's an evaporative cooling add-on that makes the air conditioner itself more efficient in dry climates. It's called Cool-N-Save (see Resources, page 345), and it attaches to any freestanding air conditioner. It actually surrounds the outside unit with

misters. And as I mentioned in the section on evaporative cooling, water evaporating can lower the temperature of air dramatically. In this case, the temperature around your air conditioner can drop as much as 30 degrees.

If you live in an area with extreme heat, as I do, this is a serious benefit. Where I am, in the San Fernando Valley, temperatures regularly rise above 100 degrees F in the summertime, and we've seen temperatures as high as 117. An air conditioner can have a real problem transferring heat to such hot outside air. By lowering the outside air temperature around the air conditioner dramatically, the Cool-N-Save makes any A/C unit's life easier, thus saving energy.

The Pre-Cooling system is easy to install.

So how does it work? When your air conditioner kicks on, the fan for the condenser comes on, too. That fan blows heat out of the unit, and the hot air blowing raises a flap on the Cool-N-Save control valve. This tells the Cool-N-Save to turn on the misters. Simple, right? In fact, this gadget is so simple that you can install it yourself in five minutes without using any tools. This is the same sort of technology that big industrial users of air-conditioning have been employing for years. It's just the first time this idea has been adapted for home use in a cost-effective, easy-to-install way.

HEAT PUMPS

Now, as I mentioned in the last chapter, heat pumps are very much like air conditioners (see Resources, page 244). In fact, the two systems' outdoor units are virtually indistinguishable. The big difference is that a heat pump will have a reversing valve inside so that it not only produces cool air, it also can produce heat. I even mentioned in the last chapter that many people think they have an air conditioner outside, when what they actually have is a heat pump.

Because they're so similar, the choice between an air conditioner and a heat pump usually boils down to what sort of system you're choosing to heat your home.

According to Bruce Ritchey, you also might want to consider a *geothermal* heat pump (see page 248) for your cooling needs if you live in an area with extreme heat. He says, "Any normal air conditioner has trouble anytime it gets over 115 degrees. So if you've got an air conditioner sitting on a roof in Las Vegas or Phoenix, when it gets very hot, they really struggle to be able to get rid of the heat to the air. On a rooftop in Las Vegas, you could hit 140 degrees, and you just can't get the heat transfer that you need in an air-to-air unit. So that's a real challenge in those very, very hot, hot climates."

Now, a geothermal heat pump doesn't try to transfer heat to the air. It transfers heat to the ground, which again ranges in temperature from 55 to 65 degrees F in most of the United States. So this sort of cooling system can remain quite efficient regardless of the outside air temperatures.

EFFICIENCY RATINGS

All air conditioners and heat pumps are rated for efficiency. So if you're on the fence about whether or not to upgrade your current unit, consider this. According to the U.S. Department of Energy (DOE; see Resources, page 345): "Today's best [central] air conditioners use 30 percent to 50 percent less energy to produce the same amount of cooling as air conditioners made in the mid-1970s. Even if your air conditioner is only 10 years old, you may save 20 percent to 40 percent of your cooling energy costs by replacing it with a newer, more efficient model."

Both central air conditioners and heat pumps are rated according to their seasonal energy efficiency ratio (SEER). The SEER compares the total BTU (British thermal unit) output of a particular central air conditioner or heat pump over the course of the cooling season with the total amount of electricity required to run it during that season (measured in watt-hours). The higher this number, the better.

Randy Scott at Trane says, "You can think of SEER kind of like miles per gallon in your car; simple analogy. The higher the miles per gallon, obviously, the less fuel cost and the more miles you could travel. It's very similar with a SEER rating." For a given amount of electricity, an air conditioner with a higher SEER rating will provide more efficient cooling.

The government has mandated a minimum SEER for central air conditioners and heat pumps of 13. The Department of Energy says an air conditioner with a SEER of 13 is 30 percent more efficient than a unit with the previous minimum SEER of 10. Older central air conditioners may have a SEER as low as 6.

You also can find Energy Star–qualified split system air conditioners, which have a minimum SEER of 14.5. You can even find air conditioners on the market with SEER ratings as high as 20. According to Randy, going from a unit with an 8 SEER to one with a 20 SEER can reduce your energy consumption by almost 60 percent.

Both air-to-air and geothermal heat pumps will have a SEER efficiency rating, too. According to the Department of Energy, if you replace an old, 1970s-era central heat pump that has a SEER of 6 with a new unit that has a SEER of 12, you will literally cut by half the amount of energy you use for cooling. And that's with a SEER of 12. Today's most efficient heat pumps have a SEER in the 14 to 18 range.

There's also another efficiency rating applied to *central* air conditioners, and it's the *only* rating for room air conditioners. This is the EER, or energy efficiency ratio. The EER is a rating of how efficient the cooling system is in real time—how much energy is consumed compared with how much heat removal is taking place at a given moment in time and at a particular outside temperature. The Department of Energy actually calls EER a "high-temperature rating": an indicator of how efficient the unit is when outside air temperatures are at their hottest. The higher the EER, the better. With central air conditioners, you'll want to look for an EER that's higher than 11.6.

SPLIT VERSUS PACKAGED SYSTEMS

In Chapter 11 and thus far in this chapter, I've talked about several types of HVAC systems that have both indoor and outdoor components—systems with indoor furnaces and outdoor air-conditioning units, as well as systems with indoor air handlers and outdoor heat pumps. These are called *split systems*. They're split, in that part of the system is inside and part of the system is outside.

There is another option: a *packaged system*. A packaged system has just one unit outside. There is no indoor component. Everything is contained within that box outdoors, whether you opt for a heat pump system or a furnace/air conditioner system or a hybrid, which includes both a heat pump and a furnace (for colder climates, where a heat pump requires a supplemental backup heating system).

A packaged system may seem like a better design, since it doesn't take up any floor space in your home. However, according to Randy at Trane, these systems are typically not as efficient as a split system, with SEER ratings of up to 16.60. They're generally installed in certain parts of the country where this type of design is required by building code, or where it's required by a sort of regional expectation. People who live in these areas—and builders who build in these areas—simply install packaged systems because it best fits the application. If you live in one of these areas and you're considering investing in a new HVAC system, I'd recommend investigating a split system for maximum energy efficiency.

Also, if your house doesn't have air-conditioning right now but it does have a furnace—that is, if you do have central heat—then a traditional split system will be the more economical choice, compared with a packaged system.

DUCTWORK

It's important to note that if your home has central heating and central air-conditioning—or if you're planning to install them—these systems will share the same ductwork. That's why experts are so adamant about the importance of installing a *matched* system. If you size the ducting for cooling, it may not be sufficient to meet your heating needs. And if you size it for heating, it may not be sufficient to meet your cooling needs. The key is to create a single system that can meet all of your needs.

I've lived in places with both central air-conditioning and heat where one room is always too hot or too cold. Sometimes one room gets too much A/C and heat, or another room never gets enough. This problem results from ductwork. You can pretty much rest assured that one of two common causes is at fault:

1. Either the ductwork is not of sufficient diameter to provide the proper amount of airflow to that room to begin with.
2. Or the airflow to that room has been reduced because the duct has been crushed or it's leaking (as much as 20 percent to 30 percent of heating and cooling gets lost to the attic or the crawlspace of many homes because of leaky ducting).

Actually, there's a third potential reason that does not have to do with ductwork. It's possible that the home's A/C or heating unit is undersized and cannot deliver enough airflow to make the longer runs to some of the rooms. So choosing the right size heating and cooling units is critical to a system's success, whether you're doing a new installation or a retrofit. And so is installing properly sized ducting. If you want to be comfortable in every room in your home, you need the correct size ducting.

DUCTLESS MINI-SPLIT AIR CONDITIONERS

If ductwork is not an option—say, your house has a slab foundation and a very shallow roofline or a flat roof without enough attic space to run ducting—then there's another option: You can install a ductless mini-split air conditioner. These units also are popular for additions, in lieu of upgrading the home's entire air-conditioning system.

Ductless mini-split air conditioners are very much like the ductless mini-split heat pumps I described in the Chapter 11 (see page 247). Like a regular split system, they have an indoor component (the air handler) and an outdoor component. And a single outdoor unit can be connected to as many as four indoor air handlers, so you can use this sort of system to cool larger rooms or even several rooms in a house. Again, each air handler will have its own thermostat.

The biggest drawback when it comes to ductless mini-split air conditioners is cost. They typically run about 30 percent more than a regular central air-conditioning system, and they could be as much as double the price of a similar-capacity window-unit air conditioner.

TWO-ZONE SYSTEMS

You've probably been in some homes where there are two separate thermostats. I don't mean one thermostat for the heat and one for the cooling. I mean homes where the central HVAC system has been divided into two zones. This is most common in two-story homes. Since heat rises, the upstairs in a two-story home often is warmer than the downstairs, so a dual-zone system makes sense so that you're not cooling the already cool downstairs when you really just want to cool the warmer upstairs rooms.

A two-zone system also makes a lot of sense for the way we live, even in a single-story home. Some people set up a two-zone system so that the bedrooms are in one zone and the living areas are in a different zone. That way, when everyone is home and awake, you can have the system on and cooling (or heating) the living areas. Shortly before people start going to bed, you can have the other zone's cooling kick up a notch and bring the temperatures down to a comfortable level for sleeping. Then while everyone is asleep, you can let the living areas warm up and focus just on cooling the bedrooms until it's time for folks to get up in the morning.

It's like using a programmable thermostat only twice as good: In this case, you have two programmable thermostats to tailor which parts of the home are heated and cooled based on your lifestyle and needs.

Sometimes, a two-zone system features two separate air conditioners, one for each zone, and sometimes it features just one system with a way to deflect the airflow where it's needed. For larger homes—4,000-square-foot homes and bigger—it almost always makes sense to have separate systems for each zone.

When you're setting up a two-zone system, there can be more cost involved in terms of the equipment. But you also have the potential to buy two smaller, less expensive units, which will make a big difference. Plus, you often can save considerable energy by targeting your heating and cooling as needed. Most new homes use a two-zone system.

ROOM AIR CONDITIONERS

Most of this chapter focuses on central air conditioners, but there is another option: the room air conditioner. A room air conditioner gets mounted in a window or a wall. In either case, one side of the air conditioner is positioned inside your room and the other is outside your home. This is because the air conditioner will extract heat out of your room and exhaust it to the outside.

It's also best to position a room air conditioner on the east or north side of your home, so it won't be in direct sun. Direct sunlight can reduce a unit's efficiency as much as 10 percent.

Even when installed in a good location, room air conditioners are not as efficient as central air conditioners, so they generally are not considered a great choice for whole house cooling. But they can be an efficient option if you only need to cool one room, such as an addition.

As I mentioned earlier, room air conditioners have an energy efficiency rating (EER). The Department of Energy says, "If you own a 1970s-vintage room air conditioner with an EER of 5 and you replace it with a new one with an EER of 10, you will cut your air conditioning energy costs in half."

With room air conditioners, you want to look for an EER of 10 or higher. Also look for the Energy Star label. Energy Star–qualified units use 10 percent less energy than nonqualified models.

Of course, the other important number, when it comes to room air conditioners, is cooling capacity, which again is measured in BTUs.

These air conditioners will range from 5,500 BTUs up to 14,000 BTUs, or more than a ton of cooling capacity. Now, bigger is not necessarily better when it comes to room air conditioners. A smaller unit that runs for a longer period of time will actually do a better job of uniformly cooling a room and removing humidity than a big unit that cycles on and off more frequently.

As a general rule, you can figure that you need 20 BTUs per square foot of room size. But there are other variables to consider, including your climate, how high your ceilings are, if the unit will be in the shade or the sun and so on. You can use the Cooling Load Estimate Form on the Association of Home Appliance Manufacturers' consumer website (see Resources, page 345) to help you choose the right-size room air conditioner for your needs.

You also will want to look for a room air conditioner with a 24-hour timer, so you can program it to turn on or off when you need it. A timer will help you cool a room *before* you get home. With a room air conditioner, you'll get better efficiency and more comfort if you cool a room slowly, rather than cranking it up to the maximum setting to try to cool the room after you're in it.

A room air conditioner's size will determine its electrical needs:

- Small units can be plugged into any 120-volt outlet in a home that has 15- or 20-amp service, as long as you don't have any other major appliances on that particular circuit.

- Medium-size units (over 7.5 amps), will require their own dedicated 120-volt circuit, so you'll need an electrician to help you connect one properly.
- Large units actually will require 240-volt service, so you'll need the services of an electrician at the electrical panel and in the room to install a special outlet.

PORTABLE AIR CONDITIONERS

Portable air conditioners are mounted on wheels and can be rolled from room to room. These units are most appropriate for people who can't mount a room air conditioner in a window or wall for whatever reason. The ability to use a single unit in whichever room you're occupying at the time is appealing. However, portables often are not as effective at cooling a room as window-mounted units, and they can be more expensive, too.

Most portable units have an exhaust hose that you stick out through a window to exhaust hot air to the outside. A *window venting kit* has an opening for the hose and then blocks off the rest of the window opening. Nonetheless, this setup often allows hot outside air to leak into your room, which can offset much of these units' cooling ability. Some portable air conditioners have two hoses, one to exhaust hot air and one to bring in outside air to cool the condenser coils; this design may be more efficient than single-hose setups.

Portable air conditioners do condition the air—that is, they do remove moisture, and that water usually winds up in a drain tank. Now, some portables will use that water to help cool the condenser coils and some will drain that water through an exhaust hose. But with many other portables, you need to empty the drain tank once or twice daily. So portables can have a higher hassle factor than window- and wall-mount air conditioners.

Some portables are also combination machines: Some are both heaters and air conditioners, while others are both air conditioners and dehumidifiers.

If your current air conditioner isn't cooling your house sufficiently—or if your electricity bills are still too high in the summertime, even after you've installed a programmable thermostat and improved your insulation and changed to dual-pane windows and the like—then odds are you're ready for a new A/C unit. Choosing a high-efficiency model can make your life more comfortable and help you save considerable energy over time.

But don't forget the other steps you can take, especially installing ceiling fans. It's incredible what a difference the wind chill factor can make in reducing your home's air-conditioning needs—and at a fraction of the price. That's really managing resources wisely.

Sample Costs and Paybacks:
Air Conditioners

As you may have guessed, my new air-conditioning installation was not inexpensive. Not only did I replace my air conditioner outside, I also replaced all of my ductwork in the best possible way, with extra steps taken to verify that everything was working properly. As you know, extra steps take more time, and contractors always translate time into money. So with all the time and all the new equipment that went into my cooling system installation, the total bill came to $13,900.

However, I should start saving considerable energy. I changed from an older 4-ton air conditioner to a new, more efficient 1.5-ton unit. I also installed great, new, properly sealed ductwork that delivers the right amount of air to each room, so I'm not over-cooling some rooms just so that I can make other rooms comfortable. And, of course, I've got the much better insulation throughout my house.

So with all of these increases in efficiency, I should be cutting my electricity use in half during the summertime.

At current electric rates, that means the system will take about ten years to pay for itself in energy cost savings. But as I've said before, electric rates are only going to go up, and they're going to go up dramatically. As that happens, my wait time to hit the break-even point will get shorter and shorter.

Now one thing I should mention is that I wound up installing a 13 SEER air conditioner. This is probably surprising. It may even be shocking. Here I am, the guy who's telling you to get Energy Star everything, and I went for an air conditioner that does not have an Energy Star qualification. But I did this for the same reason you may choose to: *I did this because of cost.* The price difference between a 13 SEER unit like mine and a 14 SEER Energy Star–qualified unit was $500. And as little as I actually use my A/C, as small as my house is and as efficient as it is now, it would have taken me a long time to recoup that additional $500 investment. It would have extended my payback period beyond ten years. And it wouldn't have saved me nearly as much energy as many of the other steps I took, some of which cost quite a bit less in fact, such as improving the seals around my doors and windows.

ED'S PROJECT

Change the
Air Conditioning Unit

My new 1.5-ton air conditioner keeps the house just as cool as the 4-ton unit did.

You've already heard about several aspects of my whole home-improvement marathon. The next leg of that marathon was cooling. Now that my home is far, far better insulated (see Chapter 4) my air conditioner was actually quite a bit oversize for what we needed.

I had a contractor come out and do all of the analysis I described in this chapter. He recommended switching from my old 4-ton air conditioner to a new, more efficient 1.5-ton unit. Now that's a huge change! A 1.5-ton air conditioner is a really small unit. Most people have 4-ton air conditioners for their home. But I have a small house by most people's standards—certainly by Hollywood's standards. My house is only 1,585 square feet and it has a very tight envelope. Thanks to the doors and windows that I've installed and the new weather stripping and the extra insulation, my home's envelope is supertight. So I was able to install a much smaller air conditioner than even I expected.

The contractor who installed my new air conditioner also recommended changing over all of the ductwork in my house to new R8 flex ducting. That ductwork runs through the basement, under the house. The registers are located in the floor. So this contractor went through the house and installed all new registers. And even more importantly, he installed all new floor boots. These boots seal the ducting to the grilles.

To be sure the entire new system of ductwork was sealed properly, he used another one of my favorite tools, a Duct Blaster electronic duct tester (see Resources, page 345). This verified that the new ductwork was sealed to the highest standard, below 3 percent of the cooling system's airflow capacity.

He also went through and tested the air pressure in each room to make sure it was properly balanced. If the pressure had been too high in one or more of the rooms, he would have had to go through the house and make some changes, such as installing *transfer grilles,* which literally help transfer air from room to room, or even undercutting interior doors.

When you're talking to prospective contractors, you can ask them if they do these things, too. Will they take the extra steps like using a Duct Blaster and testing the air pressure in each room to make sure your system is functioning absolutely properly? Be certain the answer is yes.

13

HEATING WATER

Choosing the Most Economical,
the Most Livable, & the Most
Eco-friendly Water Heating System
for Your Home

THE WAY YOU GET MOST PEOPLE'S ATTENTION, including mine, is by attacking their pocketbook. I had been living with my father for most of my teen years. I moved out when I was eighteen and started paying my own utility bills. I took note and began to turn down the thermostat and take other similar measures to save money.

It wasn't 'til the early 1970s that hot water got my attention. I lived in a studio apartment near Santa Monica Boulevard and Western Avenue in Hollywood. My rent was $75 a month. There was an electric hotplate, an electric refrigerator, and electric lights, plus all the other appliances I had plugged in. The only natural gas device in this studio apartment was a water heater. Natural gas was used just to heat water, yet I noticed this bill was $14 a month. That was a lot of money in the early 1970s for a water heater for a single man.

Once I realized the bill was so high, I turned down the thermostat on my water heater and got instant relief. The next bill was $8. So I turned the thermostat down further. And the bill went to $6. I eventually found myself using about a dollar's worth of natural gas a month, because I turned the water heater thermostat right to the middle mark between hot and cold. And yet it was still warm enough for a shower. This is how I learned about hot water and waste. And it made me think about other ways to heat water, too. I yearned for the day when I could have my own house where I could install solar panels and heat water from the sun.

TYPES OF WATER HEATERS

There are several different ways to heat water for taking showers and baths, doing laundry, running the dishwasher, and washing your hands. You have a broader choice of water heater styles than many people realize, including:

- **Solar water heaters.** You can install one or more solar panels up on your roof to heat water.
- **Conventional storage tank water heaters.** Most people in the United States have this kind of water heater sitting in their laundry room, in their garage, in a closet, or in a small shed against the side of their house.
- **Tankless water heaters,** also known as on-demand or instantaneous water heaters. They've become less expensive and more efficient, so they're certainly worth considering in certain situations.
- **Heat pumps.** If you choose a geothermal heat pump or certain types of air-source heat pumps to heat your home, you also can use the system to heat your water.
- **Tankless coil and indirect water heaters.** These systems also use your home's heating system to heat your water, though they do it differently from heat pumps.

So let's look at these various options and see which one makes sense for your situation.

SOLAR HOT WATER

If you know the way I live, you can guess that solar is my first choice for heating water. I have solar hot water in my home today. In fact, every home I've owned since 1984 has had solar hot water in it. I find it to be a fairly simple and elegant way to heat water. Now you may be saying, "Simple and elegant, sure, but how exactly does solar work for heating your home's water?" Well, there are a couple of different ways: direct and indirect. I have a direct system.

With direct, you have a cold-water line that comes into your house. You take that cold-water line and you run it up to a glazed solar panel on your roof. That panel typically has black tubing inside of it, and the water runs through the tubing. You position the panel as you would any solar panel (see Chapter 7), which ideally faces directly toward the south. When the sun strikes the panel, the water in the tubing gets very, very hot. It can get up to 150 or 160 degrees F. Then the water gets passed to a storage tank. The tank could be on your roof or at ground level. It might even be inside your home.

In my case, I have a fairly simple solar hot water system that has a 4×10 panel. There's a sensor in the panel that monitors the temperature of the water. It compares that temperature against another temperature sensor that's inside my water storage tank. When the water in the panel is hotter than the water in the

Bill Nye's solar hot-water tank is just one part of his hot-water system.

storage tank, a small energy-efficient pump is put into motion. A circuit is completed. The pump runs and puts that hotter water from the panel into the tank. Then when the water in the tank hits the same temperature as the water in the panel, the pump shuts back off again and you save power.

It cools off at night where I live. So, how does the water in the storage tank stay hot all night long, if you're not adding more hot water? The tank is very, very well insulated. It's insulated enough so the water can stay hot until the next morning. You also choose the size of your storage tank. You can have a 20-gallon tank or

a 40-gallon tank, even on your roof. Or if you have a lot of space, you could have an 80- or a 100-gallon tank on the ground or in your basement or garage.

This is how a direct circulation system works, and it works very well in places where temperatures rarely drop below freezing. Of course, in cold climates, running household water in pipes up onto your roof is a bad idea in the wintertime. You'd run the risk of that water freezing and the pipes bursting. So there's another style of solar water heating system: an indirect system.

In an indirect system, the pump does not circulate the actual water used in your household, but instead it circulates a fluid that won't freeze. That fluid is used for heat transfer, just like in an air-conditioning system or in many types of home heating systems. That heat transfer fluid travels up onto your roof and into the solar panels. There, it gets hot. Then the hot fluid travels through a heat exchanger to transfer the heat to your home's water. It essentially adds an extra step to the process, but it's the safe way to have solar hot water in colder climates.

A BACKUP SYSTEM FOR SOLAR

If you're a single person or part of a couple who takes modest showers, you can reasonably get by with just the solar hot water during the sunnier times of the year, certainly the summer and indeed the spring and fall. You should have 40, 60, 80, or 100 gallons, depending on the size of the storage tank you install.

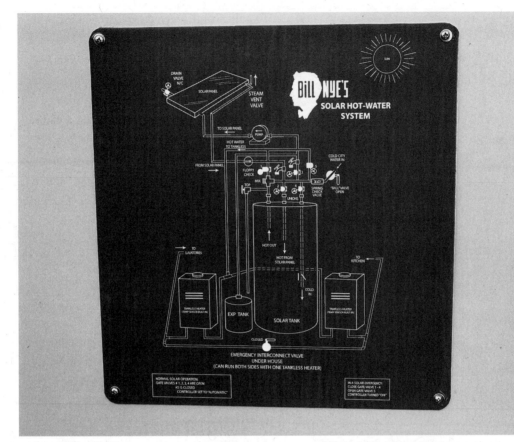

Bill's hot-water-system diagram shows the process of heating the water directly from the sun.

But, if you have a cloudy period, or if you have three or more people in the household who are taking longer showers, etc., you'll want to have some sort of a backup water-heating system. Actually, I would recommend a backup system for everyone but a Spartan living alone.

For the backup system, you have options:

- You can get a two-tank system, where the solar hot water is stored in one tank, which is connected to a conventional storage tank water heater.

- You can install a one-tank system, where the backup storage tank water heater does double-duty as the storage tank for your solar-heated water.

- You can install a storage tank for your solar-heated water and then a tankless-style water heating system as backup.

I have a two-tank system at my house, which gives me more capacity for my family's needs. Here's how it works.

As people in your house start using hot water, the water coming into the traditional water heater from the solar storage tank is nice and hot. But eventually as people shower and run the dishwasher and the washing machine, the water going into the backup water heater isn't hot anymore. Or maybe it's been raining and cloudy for a few days. Either way, that backup heater will engage. Once the water in the backup heater gets below a certain threshold—whatever temperature setting you've chosen—the backup unit will kick in to heat water to the desired temperature.

For you, it's a seamless operation. You don't have to switch back and forth between solar and a conventional backup system. It's all taken care of automatically.

Here's the beautiful thing about a solar system to heat your water. Water comes in from the street at usually 55 to 60 degrees F—even colder in the winter in some parts of the country. Even on a cloudy day, the solar unit is going to heat the water to 78 to 82 degrees F. It heats it a certain amount, so a standard water heater is going to have that much less work to do. The solar water heater literally preheats your water. So, much of the time, the backup system doesn't have to do any work at all, and when it does have to kick in, it still doesn't have to work as hard as it would to heat cold water coming in off the street. You reap the benefits of water being heated entirely by the sun much of the time, and then whenever your backup system is needed, you're spending less on fuel to heat the water the rest of the way.

This is why I encourage solar power to heat water. Solar is number one in my water heating hierarchy.

FUELING A WATER HEATER

If you don't have a good site for solar—i.e., too much shading or a flat roof that already leaks—or if you have budgetary issues that preclude the use of solar to heat your water right now, or even if you do install solar but still need a backup system, then you'll have to choose the type of fuel used for that water heater.

You actually have several choices:

- **Natural gas.** Natural gas is a very efficient way to heat water. Indeed the majority of people in the country are heating it in this manner.
- **Electricity.** Electricity is another good way to heat water in many different conditions.
- **Propane.** There are many people who do not have a natural gas line running to their town or their rural area, so they have a propane tank on their property. And that propane is used to cook their food and also to heat their water.
- **Heating oil.** In other parts of the country, heating oil is used in place of propane.

As with heating a home, there's no one right choice when it comes to fuel for a water heater. The best option for your home will have to do with

- your access to these various fuels
- the costs of fuels in your area
- how electricity is made in your area or in your home (e.g., do you have solar or wind power on-site, or do you have access to inexpensive, clean, green electricity?)
- your home's location and orientation (should you even consider solar for heating water?)
- your finances
- your tolerance for a longer or shorter payback period for your initial investment
- whether you're buying a new water heater because your old one just died, so you need it *right now,* or whether you can spend some time contemplating your options and doing a different type of installation rather than a straight replacement

CONVENTIONAL STORAGE TANK WATER HEATERS

A conventional storage tank–style water heater is what most people picture when I say "water heater." It has a storage tank to hold the water you'll need during peak demand times, when someone is taking a shower and doing laundry and washing dishes. Those tanks usually range in size from 20 gallons up to 80 gallons. Cold water flows into the storage tank at the bottom, so it can be heated.

With natural gas, propane, and heating oil–fueled water heaters, you heat the water the same way you would boil water in a teakettle. The storage tank has a flame at the bottom. It also has a chimney and a flue tube. Some larger models will even have more than one flue tube.

The flue tube leads from the combustion area at the bottom of the water heater all the way up through the tank. And the hot gases from the combustion process pass through the flue tube, so they can transfer heat to the water. Now, some of the heat you produce by burning natural gas or propane or heating oil goes into the water, and some of the heat goes out the chimney.

A conventional tank–style water heater that's powered by electricity is quite similar, but you don't need a chimney or a flue since there's no combustion taking place. You're not burning anything to make heat. Instead, you use electricity to heat elements, and those elements transfer heat to the water. So an electric tank water heater is an easier, more flexible installation, in terms of location and labor, since an electric water heater doesn't need a chimney.

Again, you choose the temperature setting for the water heater—usually low, medium, or high. Most people stay away from the very hot setting for safety reasons. You don't want anyone to get scalded. There's a temperature sensor inside the tank, and when it determines that the water is cooler than your desired temperature, the heater kicks on—either the burner or the electric heating element—to heat up your water.

It's important to point out that water heaters can use some energy, that they can burn some fuel, even when you aren't using any hot water. The storage tanks are very well insulated these days, but there's still going to be some standby heat loss. So the water heater will cycle on and off even when you aren't using any water. The better insulated the tank, the less this will happen, so the Department of Energy (see Resources, page 345) recommends looking for a water heater that has an R-value (just like the R-value for insulation, which measures thermal resistance) of R-12 or higher.

My friend Scott Bateman, president and owner of Bateman Water Heating Engineering Inc. in Los Angeles (see Resources, page 345), which has been in the business for about forty years now, says there were some improvements in combustion-type water heater efficiency in the 1980s because manufacturers began to use a flue baffle. "It's kind of like a twisted piece of metal that the exhaust gases have to wrap around to get out," says Scott. Basically, that baffle keeps the hot exhaust gases in the tank area longer, so they can transfer more heat to the water before they head out the chimney.

EFFICIENCY RATINGS

All storage tank water heaters sold in the United States have to have an EnergyGuide label on them. That label will tell you the unit's

- **Energy factor.** The higher this number is, the better. It's based on three things:
  1. **Recovery efficiency**—that is, how much of the energy you use actually goes into heating your water. The ideal here would be 100 percent, but that's not yet possible.
  2. **Standby heat losses**—how much heat is lost when the water is just sitting in the tank. This is calculated as a percentage, on a per-hour basis.
  3. **Cycling losses**—which measures heat lost as the water cycles through the tank or through any necessary pipes on the way in and out of the tank.
- **First hour rating.** This is the number of gallons of hot water the unit can provide per hour, assuming it's starting out with a full tank of water that's already hot.

The first hour rating is very important in choosing a water heater, since it will tell you if a unit can actually meet your household's demands. If you have five people in your home and all of you take a shower in the morning, plus you do some dishes and maybe you throw a load of laundry in the washing machine before you leave for work, obviously you're going to need a lot more hot water at one time than a single person who showers in the morning and does laundry in the evening.

Also pay close attention to the water heater's recovery efficiency. That number is very important from an energy-usage standpoint. Let's say you're considering a water heater that has a recovery efficiency, or a thermal efficiency, of 75 percent. In simplified terms, for every dollar you spend to power that water heater, you're getting 75¢ worth of hot water.

Electric water heaters are close to 100 percent efficient, which sounds great. But you have to ask, how efficient is the source of electricity in your area? Do you live in Idaho, where you get clean, green, inexpensive electricity made at a hydroelectric power plant? Or is your local utility burning coal to make power?

Natural gas water heaters have gotten very close to 100 percent efficiency. You can find plenty of water heaters in the 75 percent and 80 percent efficiency range. But we're also seeing water heaters well into the 90 percent range. Also, natural gas still costs far less than electricity in many areas, so I'm very much in favor of natural gas for heating water.

The super-high-efficiency natural gas water heaters that I've mentioned—the ones up in the mid- to high 90s for recovery ratings—use some different technology to reach those higher levels of efficiency. Remember, higher efficiency means more of the heat that's created gets transferred to your home's water, rather than being wasted.

Scott explains that one way these water heaters become more efficient is by keeping the hot gases inside the flue tube for a much longer time. "The engineering problem behind this is when the [hot gas] is in contact with those [heat transfer] surfaces longer, it actually cools those gases a lot more," says Scott. "Then you have a problem with exhausting the by-products out through the vent. Because heat rises. But if you get below a certain temperature, it won't make its way through the vent anymore, and then you have a problem getting most of the combustion by-products out of the heater.

"So the major design change was to put a fan-assisted burner on the water heater that can help force this gas and air mixture through the flue tubes and out through the vent. That way, you can keep the heat in the water heater longer and still get those gases out of the heater safely.

"The other by-product is condensation. The longer you keep the heat in the water heater flue tube, as that gas cools down, it condensates. It's kind of like having a glass of ice water sitting on your table and you get little droplets of water on the outside of the glass. That's what happens inside these high-efficiency water heaters. You actually get water droplets building up on the inside of these flue tubes. Of course that has to be drained and taken out of the heater. So the technology has changed, redesigning that whole flue tube area so that you could drain this condensation out of the heater. And that's really where we're at today."

CHOOSING THE RIGHT SIZE WATER HEATER

If you choose a storage tank–style water heater —or solar hot water with a storage tank—you certainly don't want to get a tank that's too small for your household, because you'll never have enough hot water for your peak demand times. A water heater that's too big is less of a problem, but still, you'll be paying to heat—and maintain the temperature of—more water than you need. And that's not efficient.

As water heat manufacturer A. O. Smith's literature explains: "All water heaters are designed to supply a minimum of 60 percent of the total tank volume before the hot water supply drops 30 degrees Fahrenheit. To explain this further, a 50-gallon water heater set at 120 degrees Fahrenheit would supply a minimum of 30 gallons of hot water before the 30th gallon measures 90 degrees in temperature.

"The normal shower temperature is about 105 degrees Fahrenheit. The average showerhead will consume about 1.5 gallons per minute of hot water from the water heater; an average shower of 10 minutes uses 15 gallons. As the hot water supply is being used, the temperature drops. At 20 minutes of shower time, the hot water supply is less than 105 degrees Fahrenheit."

So, if you have two people showering in the morning for ten minutes each within a fairly short timeframe, then you need a water heater that's larger than 50 gallons, or there won't be enough hot water. Plus, you won't have any hot water left over to run the dishwasher, wash a load of laundry, or fill a pot at the kitchen sink.

So how do you determine the right-size water heater? It's going to depend on several factors, including these:

- how much space you have
- what sort of fuel you prefer to use
- how many people live in your home
- how long those people stay in the shower
- the number of baths or showers that will be happening in a given timeframe
- the number of oversize bathtubs you might be filling, such as garden tubs or whirlpool tubs, and just how many gallons of water the tubs hold

Another way to get a feel for how much water you use is to visit the Department of Energy's Energy Efficiency and Renewable Energy website (see Resources, page 345). In the section on storage tank–style water heaters, you'll find a worksheet to help you estimate your peak demand—again, this goes back to your first hour rating needs—for hot water.

TANKLESS WATER HEATERS

Another alternative to traditional storage tank water heaters is a tankless water heater, also known as an *on-demand* or *instantaneous* water heater. These tankless designs first came to market in the United States back in the early to mid-1980s, but they've actually been around for almost a hundred years. In Europe and Asia, tankless water heaters are the most common design, in part because homes just don't have the space for a traditional storage tank.

Back when tankless water heaters first came to market in this country, they were marketed to high-end homes. They were very expensive. Today, they can still be more expensive than conventional tank-style water heaters, but they've come down to a level where many more homeowners can at least consider them.

You can use a tankless water heater as your sole water heater in the house, or you can use it as a backup system for a solar water heater.

So how does a tankless design work? Essentially, when you turn on the hot water at a faucet or in your shower or when you turn on the dishwasher, that action tells the tankless water heater to start heating water. So cold water flows into the tankless water heater, where a heating element heats that water. Rather than being stored in a tank, the hot water flows directly through the tankless water heater and into your pipes, then out through your faucet or showerhead or dishwasher. When you turn off the shower or the tap, the water heater turns off, too. It runs only when you need hot water, which is where the *on-demand* name comes from. Tankless water heaters can operate off of natural gas or electricity. In the case of electric tankless water heaters, electricity heats a burner that then heats the water. A natural gas model will have a gas burner,

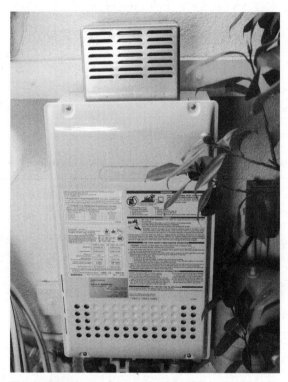

This tankless water heater can be used as the sole heater or as a supplement to solar.

much like a storage tank–style water heater. It may have a pilot light that stays lit all the time, which does use some energy, or it could have an intermittent ignition device (IID), kind of like the spark ignition on some ovens and stoves. IID models will use somewhat less energy.

There are some real benefits to tankless designs, including:

- space savings
- the elimination of standby heat loss
- endless hot water, or so the manufacturers say

There is a lot more flexibility in terms of installation location for a tankless system. That's because it's smaller and lighter. Water weighs 8 pounds per gallon. So a 40-gallon storage tank water heater, which is relatively small, will hold *320 pounds* worth of water, plus the weight of the water heater itself. You also don't need floor space for a tankless water heater. You can mount it on a wall, which adds installation flexibility.

However, you usually do have to wait a little longer—about ten to twenty seconds longer—for hot water to come from a tankless water heater rather than from a tank-style design. That's because there isn't hot water stored and ready.

Today's tankless water heaters are much more efficient than the ones installed in the 1980s. Scott says you can see efficiencies of up to 90 percent on some tankless designs today.

But are they really capable of providing limitless hot water? That depends on how much water you need at one time. Most tankless designs can flow between 2 gallons and 5 gallons of water per minute. That's usually enough for one person to take a shower at a time. But if you turn on the clothes washer or the dishwasher—or if someone else cranks up a shower in another bathroom—either the water won't be as hot as you want or you'll wind up with no hot water at all.

Some people also experience what's called a *cold water sandwich* with tankless water heaters. The water runs hot and then cold and then hot again. Needless to say, this can be a challenge for many people to live with.

There is a way to avoid running out of hot water if two people are showering simultaneously or if you want to be able to run the dishwasher and shower at the same time: You can install more than one tankless water heater. What people often do in temperate climates is install one tankless water heater outside the bathroom, just mounted on the outside wall of your house, and then they install another one outside the kitchen, for example. In colder climates, where freezing pipes are an issue, the tankless heater can be mounted inside.

When you have more than one tankless water heater, you wind up with a shorter run of piping from the water heater to your shower or your sink, so there will be less heat loss from the water traveling through those pipes. But of course you have the added expense of purchasing and installing two water heaters, not to mention the additional run of plumbing pipes. If it's a natural gas model, you've got additional gas pipes and you've got to vent the exhaust gases from combustion. This is the typical approach in Europe and Asia, where houses normally have two or three tankless water heaters.

To choose the right size tankless water heater (or heaters), again you need to consider your peak demand needs, since tankless models are rated according to the number of gallons they flow per minute. The idea is to choose one that flows at a high enough rate that you really will experience unlimited hot water, if at all possible based on your household's peak needs.

Install a Super-High-Efficiency Water Heater

You already know from Chapter 11 on heating that I recently installed a new water heater. It's a super-high-efficiency model from A. O. Smith (see Resources, page 345). I chose the Vertex natural gas water heater for my backup system to go with my solar hot water, and the Vertex also is part of my home's heating system (see page 257).

This water heater is quite different from most of the models on the market. First of all, the burner is on the top, not the bottom. That's a big change compared with conventional tank–style designs.

The Vertex also has a blower to help get the by-products of combustion to leave the water heater. And it's fully condensing. Since the burner is on top, the hot exhaust gases don't travel *up* through a standard flue in the center of this water heater. Instead, they go down, but not straight down. They pass through a coil that spirals through the water. It's called a *helical coil heat exchanger.* And it holds the heat in much longer than a traditional 75 percent or 80 percent efficient water heater. This is a 96 percent thermal efficient device, which is a very good number for heating water.

The Vertex also has been designed to be environmentally friendly in another important way. It produces very low emissions of NOx, or oxides of nitrogen. Because something is being burned to heat water in most water heaters, there are emissions from the combustion process. This Vertex model actually complies with the ultra-low NOx emission standards that are supposed to be implemented in 2012. So it's ahead of the curve in terms of being clean and green.

From a day-to-day usability perspective, it acts like a bigger water heater than its size would suggest, which is another great benefit. According to A. O. Smith, "The Vertex delivers hot water output that exceeds a seventy-five-gallon atmospheric gas water heater. In fact, the fully condensing Vertex design is so advanced, it can deliver continuous hot water for shower after shower . . . a continuous flow of over four gallons per minute."

I did pay more to have an efficient water heater—maybe twice as much as for a less efficient natural gas model.

- A regular storage tank water heater that's 70 to 75 percent efficient costs somewhere around $300 to $600.
- A tankless water heater that's 80 to 84 percent efficient with an electronic ignition costs $1,000 to $2,000.
- The Vertex, which is 96 percent efficient, costs somewhere between $1,500 and $2,500.

It's important to point out that the cost of the water heater itself is not the whole story. There are installation costs, too. The total *installed* cost for these different kinds of models can vary a lot. For example, if you're doing a retrofit of a tankless model, you normally will have to do some special venting, and you usually will need an upgraded gas line, which often takes the total installed cost to more than $4,000. For the A. O. Smith Vertex, you'll have to add a power connection and a condensate drain, beyond the standard tank–style installation steps.

So the payback is longer, clearly, on the more efficient options. But based on the efficiency alone, if you can afford to pay for a few years of water heating bills in advance, the Vertex clearly is the best option in the long term.

Again, I needed the extra water heating capacity because this unit works with an Aqua Therm from First Company (see Resources, page 345) to heat my home in the wintertime. So the fact that the A. O. Smith Vertex provides greater livability in terms of hot water flow rates than many other designs was really important. In fact, in my household, the Vertex has been able to provide limitless hot water. So those were all important considerations in my decision, and I've been very pleased with the outcome so far.

FREE HOT WATER FROM HEAT PUMPS

One of the big benefits of installing a geothermal heat pump for heating and cooling (see pages 248 and 269) is free hot water.

When the geothermal heat pump is being used to cool your house in the summertime, the by-product of cooling is heat. That heat has to go somewhere. So all of that heat can go out through the geothermal system's pipes and get transferred into the ground in your backyard. Or you can put some of it to good use: to heat water for your home.

In that case, a heat exchanger takes the heat from the geothermal system's water and transfers it to the water for your home. The system can do that in one of three ways. You can

- have a water heater installed as part of your geothermal heat pump installation
- use an existing storage tank–style water heater and retrofit the geothermal heat pump's water-heating equipment to it
- use the geothermal heat pump's water-heating equipment with an on-demand, tankless water heater

In other words, heating your household's water becomes the first step in the process of cooling down the water that was used to air-condition your house. So basically, you get free hot water all summer long.

Then in the wintertime, the system is set up to heat your house first and foremost, as it should be. But when the heat pump is not busy heating your house, it's still able to use the ground outside to gather heat, and it can use that heat to heat water for you, too.

My friend Bruce Ritchey, president/CEO of Water Furnace, which has been in the geothermal heating and cooling products business since 1981, says, "We're able to heat water a lot more efficiently than you could with gas, oil, propane, or electric." If you have a house with a high demand for hot water, that's a real bonus, and that bonus could be significant.

"It's huge in places like hotels where they have a lot of use for laundry and for dishes and those types of things," says Bruce, "or spas, you know, where they need a lot of water heated. Or in Acapulco or someplace where they're in air-conditioning [mode] all the time but they also need large quantities of hot water, it's a way to get all of that hot water free. So you not only have a very inexpensive source of heating or cooling, you also have free hot water."

For a long time, this has been a big benefit of geothermal heat pumps over air-to-air heat pumps. But now some of the new high-efficiency air-source heat pumps also can heat your household's water, via these two options:

- **Desuperheater.** Some air-source heat pumps—and even some new more deluxe air conditioners—have a feature called a *desuperheater*. It takes some of the heat that the heat pump needs to get rid of when it's in cooling mode and uses that heat to heat water. According to the Department of Energy (DOE), "A desuperheater-equipped heat pump can heat water two to three times more efficiently than an ordinary electric water heater." Now, this is only in cooling mode with air-source heat pumps—and obviously with air conditioners, it's going to work only when you're trying to cool off your home.

- **Reverse Cycle Chiller.** Other air-source heat pumps have a *reverse cycle chiller* (RCC), which actually heats or cools a large storage tank filled with water as part of the home's heating and cooling process. If you get a heat pump with a reverse cycle chiller, you can also choose to install a *refrigeration heat reclaimer* (RHR). This way, the heat pump can heat your home's water not just when it's in cooling mode, but also when it's in heating mode. The DOE says, "The combined RCC and RHR system costs about twenty-five percent more than a standard heat pump of similar size. The simple payback on the additional cost in areas where natural gas is not available is in about two to three years."

In short, either a geothermal or an air-to-air heat pump is a particularly good option if you live in an area where electricity is your only fuel—or your best fuel option—for heating water.

TANKLESS COIL AND INDIRECT WATER HEATERS

There's another water-heating option that's similar to the heat pump scenario. You can have either a tankless coil water heater or an indirect water heater tied into your home's space heating system.

The tankless coil water heater works much like any other tankless water heater, except that it relies on your home's furnace or boiler to heat the water. So when you turn on the hot water at your faucet or in your shower, the water flows through a heating coil or a heat exchanger in that furnace or boiler. Either electricity or natural gas fuels it.

This kind of a tankless coil system is great for heating water during the wintertime, when you're using your home's space-heating system on a regular basis. It's not so great in the summer. But if you live in a part of the world where you've got the heat running most of the year, it's an option worth considering.

The other choice—often the more efficient choice—is an indirect water heater, which uses a storage tank and which can be fueled by natural gas, propane, heating oil, or electricity. In this case, your furnace or boiler heats a fluid. That fluid then gets circulated into a heat exchanger inside a heavily insulated water storage tank. The hot fluid transfers its heat to your household's water, and your furnace or boiler doesn't have to cycle on and off ver often. It can be an efficient choice if you have a very efficient furnace or boiler, and is an option worth considering.

Much like heating and cooling your home, you have many choices when it comes to how you heat water. Now, I recognize that solar hot water is not right for everybody, but it's by far the top choice in my water-heating hierarchy. I love using the power of the sun to heat water, as well as to preheat water, if the solar water heating system isn't quite sufficient on its own.

Next in line in my hierarchy is a super-efficient natural gas water heater. Or, if you've chosen a geothermal heat pump or an air-source heat pump for your home's heating and cooling needs, then it's really hard to beat free hot water from your home's HVAC system.

Once again, there's no one right solution here. Only you can determine the greenest choice—and the best financial move—in your particular situation.

BASIC DOMESTIC HOT WATER SOLAR SYSTEM

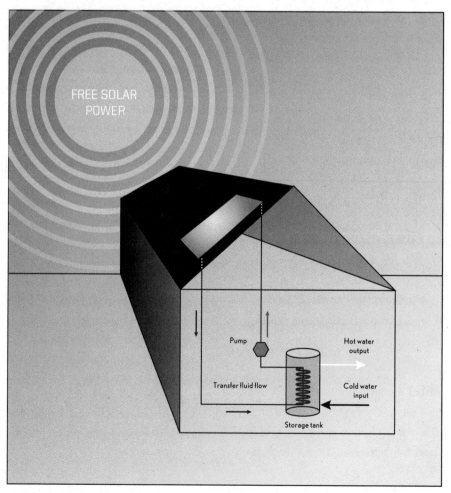

This illustration shows how the sun heats the water in your home.

Sample Costs and Paybacks:
Solar Hot Water

When I put in a solar water heating system in my house, in 1990, it was $2,500, which is pretty cheap. It would cost double that today. For just one glazed solar panel, a tank, and the install, it would easily cost $5,000 or perhaps more. For an entire installation, including a backup system, you could wind up paying $10,000 or quite a bit more.

So the payback considerations are similar to a solar electric installation. Paramount among them would be

- the fuel you use for heating water now
- the price you pay for that fuel
- if tax incentives or rebates are available in your area

You can find out about tax incentives and rebates for solar hot water online, on some of the same websites I've mentioned earlier, including GreenMadeSimple and DSIRE (see Resources, page 345). Enter your ZIP code and the sites will tell you what sort of options are available in your area. The DSIRE site also includes things like special local loan programs and grant programs.

As a general rule of thumb, if you get a quote for a system that costs about $4,000—or with tax incentives and rebates the cost of your system comes down to about $4,000—then you're looking at a payback period of six or seven years, compared with exclusively using natural gas for water heating.

If you can wait a while to reach breakeven—if you can look at it as paying in advance for your hot water—then the other thing to bear in mind is that a solar hot water system will last a lot longer than a conventional water-heating system. Also, a solar water-heating system will add value to your home in a way that other water-heating options will not.

If you're building from scratch or if you're remodeling—if you're able to get a long-term loan to finance your solar hot water installation—then you can be cash-flow positive right away, in many cases. If the solar hot water adds $10, $15, or $20 to your monthly mortgage payment, you may well be saving more than that on your water-heating costs from day one.

14

DECORATING & CLEANING YOUR HOME

Choosing Materials that Will Make Your Home Beautiful, Healthy, & Green

I CERTAINLY COULD WRITE AN ENTIRE BOOK JUST about decorating your home in an eco-conscious way. There are so many materials to choose from, and so many aspects of those materials to cover. To keep it concise, I'll focus in this chapter on some of the biggest areas when it comes to interior design. Biggest in terms of investment. Biggest in terms of square footage covered. Biggest in terms of your home's style and beauty. And also biggest in terms of impact on its indoor air quality and its environmental friendliness.

In short, I'll focus on flooring, countertops, cabinets, and paint. And I'll also cover the key concerns when it comes to cleaning your home, since cleaning products seriously affect your indoor air quality and your health.

Bamboo flooring comes in many different shades and styles. It's both an environmentally and aesthetically smart choice.

 FLOORING

When it comes time to decorate your home, one of the biggest choices you'll make is flooring. Of course, flooring is about far more than style. Flooring is also a key environmental choice. You can choose flooring materials from local sources or from distant sources. You can choose renewable resources or scarce resources. You can choose recycled materials or virgin materials. Plus, flooring can seriously affect the air quality inside your home. So let's take a look at flooring materials that are available today and consider their environmental and health aspects—materials such as these:

- wood
- bamboo
- cork
- tile
- stone
- concrete
- linoleum
- carpet
- other recycled flooring options

WOOD

There are three different kinds of wood flooring: solid wood, engineered wood, and laminates. Solid wood flooring is just what it sounds like: flooring that's made from solid pieces of wood. It's all wood, all the way through. I have solid wood floors in most of my house because that's the way it was built. I chose to stay with this material because I really like it. But I also chose to keep the wood floors because they were already there. Removing them would have required energy—both in terms of the effort involved in the process and in terms of the energy required to obtain new materials, to process them and then to install them.

There are choices within solid wood flooring. You can buy strips, which are usually 1½, 2¼, or 3¼ inches wide. You can buy planks, which are typically 3, 4, 5, or 6 inches wide, or you can buy parquet, which is small pieces of wood that have been put together to form a pattern.

If you're looking to install a wood floor, you'll want to look for FSC (Forest Stewardship Council; see Resources, page 346) certified lumber. You'll want wood from a forest that was managed in a sustainable, environmentally friendly way.

The important question is, *where* is the wood coming from? Obviously, there's an environmental cost to transporting lumber over great distances. That's why the LEED for Homes Rating System rewards you for using materials that come from within 500 miles of your home. Also, some solid woods are harder than others, so if you can't stand the look of minor dents and dings, you'll want to choose a hardwood.

Another really green option, when it comes to wood flooring, is using recycled wood. You can find previously used flooring. You can find wood from old barns that have been torn down. There are lots of reclaimed wood options these days, and that's a really good choice to make.

The other key component is the finish. You certainly don't want to buy an environmentally conscious local or reclaimed solid wood flooring material and then apply a toxic finish. You want to make sure the finish contains no VOCs (volatile organic compounds, see page 302) and no toxins whatsoever. You don't want wood with a finish that's going to off-gas and create a problem in your home.

ENGINEERED WOOD FLOORING

With engineered wood flooring, thin pieces of wood are pressed together—either three or five layers, so the wood is marketed as three-ply or five-ply. Of course, some sort of adhesive has to hold those layers together. So the key to choosing an engineered wood is to ask about the adhesive and make sure it's low in VOCs.

With engineered wood, the portion you're going to see will be made of a really attractive, desirable wood. The maple, oak, walnut, or other attractive wood will be a thin veneer over potentially softer and definitely less expensive woods. There are benefits to engineered wood. According to the National Wood Flooring Association (see Resources, page 346), the layers are arranged so that the wood grains are running in different directions. This gives engineered wood more dimensional stability than solid wood, so it's a better choice for humid or wet environments, including basements, bathrooms, and kitchens. Also, by engineering a product, companies can produce more flooring from less wood, so it conserves resources. It also conserves dollars,

so engineered wood flooring costs less than solid wood.

LAMINATE FLOORING

Laminate flooring contains even less wood than engineered wood flooring. In fact, in many cases it's actually made from paper. According to the North American Laminate Flooring Association (see Resources, page 346), laminate flooring is "a rigid floor covering with a surface layer consisting of one or more thin sheets of a fibrous material (usually paper), impregnated with aminoplastic thermosetting resins (usually melamine). These sheets are . . . [then affixed] on a substrate. The product is normally finished with a backing primarily used as a balancing material."

The top layer of paper in a laminate flooring material will have a wood grain printed on it. Nowadays, it can look quite realistic. But laminate flooring *simulates* the look of solid wood. (You also can find laminate flooring that simulates the look of stone.)

Obviously, if you're considering laminates, you'll want to ask about the materials used in the manufacture of it, including adhesives. Some kinds of laminate flooring do indeed off-gas. But I know of some companies that are working to make laminates more environmentally friendly.

Volatile Organic Compounds

So what are volatile organic compounds (VOCs)? They're solvents, basically. They're gases that are emitted by a wide range of liquids and solids. You'll often find VOCs in paint, varnish, lacquer, glue, cleaning supplies, pesticides, and building materials.

One thing volatile organic compounds all have in common is they emit an odor that is quite easy to smell—hence the term *volatile*. They're airborne. They're also volatile in the sense that they ignite quickly. They're definitely not good for the environment. They contribute to the formation of ozone, which is a major air pollutant. They definitely are not good for the respiratory system. According to the U.S. Environmental Protection Agency, "VOCs include a variety of chemicals, some of which may have short- and long-term adverse health effects."

My friend Lou Alonso from ACT Environmental works with doctors to figure out what sorts of environmental factors—in people's home environments and work environments—are causing health problems. The people at ACT Environmental visit homes and offices and perform tests. The company has been doing this for nineteen years, so it has a pretty good handle on what might be the issues with indoor air quality. What's one of the main issues that Lou encounters over and over again? VOCs. People have a sensitivity to VOCs. They cause respiratory problems. They inflame people's allergies. They cause headaches. They cause all sorts of health issues.

If you can avoid VOCs altogether, that's the ideal and you should choose that path. If not—if you absolutely have to choose a paint that contains some VOCs, for example—then do everything you can to use the lowest levels of VOCs available.

BAMBOO

Bamboo has a very high environmental rating. In fact, I would say that bamboo is approaching a fairly dark shade of green.

Yes, it takes land to grow bamboo, and yes, it takes water to grow bamboo. But much of it is grown in China, a place where land is abundant and water does not come at great environmental cost. Bamboo also grows very, very quickly. It's a rapidly renewable resource. Bamboo forests are harvested every five or six years, and bamboo doesn't even need to be replanted. The parent plant will grow new culms in the same spot, which can be harvested again in another five or six years. Compare that with some trees used for solid wood flooring, which take a hundred years to mature. In that time period, you could have twenty harvests of bamboo.

Bamboo is not actually a wood. It's a grass. But it's strong. Some bamboo flooring is twice as hard as oak. That means there's less of a need to put a hard urethane finish on bamboo because it is, by its nature, very hard. It's like a hardwood but without all the problems that come with some of the other prized hardwoods: luan, teak, or mahogany. Those tropical rain forest woods are among the most environmentally damaging woods that you can buy, so you want to avoid those whenever possible. Bamboo is a great replacement for them.

One downside of bamboo—and one thing that can make it a lighter shade of green—is that it's similar to engineered wood flooring: Layers of bamboo are stacked and glued together. The other downside is it has to travel a long distance.

On the plus side, some breeds of bamboo release significantly more oxygen into the atmosphere than traditional hardwood trees. Bamboo does an excellent job of removing carbon dioxide from the air and releasing oxygen, so it helps improve the environment in that significant way.

Bamboo also resists moisture, so it can be much more durable in the home than many kinds of solid wood, particularly in very humid climates. Also, it has antibacterial and antimicrobial properties. You can find bamboo products and also bamboo flooring installers through the National Wood Flooring Association.

CORK

Cork flooring is made from the same material as wine corks and bulletin boards. Cork is actually the bark of the cork oak tree, and most of it comes from the Mediterranean, particularly Portugal, where national laws control the harvesting of cork. Because the bark can be peeled away from the tree trunk and branches about every nine years without harming the tree, cork is considered a rapidly renewable resource. The tree itself also lives as long as two hundred years, so a single forest can supply cork for generations.

Cork has been used for flooring for many, many years, but only recently has it been made into easy-to-install tiles and planks, which has helped to popularize it. Today, cork flooring is usually made from postindustrial waste from the wine stopper industry.

Cork flooring does have a warm feel to it. It gives, so it can be a good choice in a room where you're going to do a lot of standing or walking. That's because cork has millions of tiny air pockets within it. When you walk on cork, it compresses, then it springs back into shape.

Those air spaces also mean that cork has natural insulating properties. It doesn't transmit heat or cold easily. So if you're installing radiant floor heating (see page 240), that makes cork a poor choice of floor covering. But if you have a cold concrete slab under your home, cork can help to insulate the room from that cold in the wintertime.

The air within cork also helps it to absorb noise and vibration. You may have seen cork tiles in recording studios, for example. So cork can be a good choice if you want to reduce sound transmitted through the floors in a multistory house or condo or apartment building.

Cork is also naturally resistant to water, and then the finishes applied to it are designed to make it even more water- and stain-resistant. Plus, cork is repellent to termites, mites, mold, and mildew because it contains suberin, a naturally occurring waxy substance, so it can be good for people with allergies. That same substance also makes cork naturally fire resistant. The National Wood Flooring Association is a good source for cork flooring products and installers.

TILE

There are so many kinds of tile on the market today. Certainly, they're not all eco-equals. Some require a whole lot of water during the manufacturing process. Some require a whole lot of energy during the manufacturing process—particularly many ceramic tiles, which have to be fired twice in a high-heat kiln. In addition, some tiles have toxic chemicals involved in the glazing process. Tiles won't off-gas in your home. The environmental consideration has to do with the manufacturing part of a tile's life cycle, as well as the distance it has to travel to reach your home.

What other things can you look for in a tile? If you're looking at clay tiles, are they natural clay? Do they have natural fillers?

You can find many ceramic tiles that contain postindustrial—or, better yet, postconsumer—recycled materials. For example, some tiles include as much as 75 percent recycled glass from car windshields, bottles, and aircraft windshields. Others contain just as much recycled granite chips or granite dust or marble chips. You also can find concrete tiles that include postindustrial recycled carpet fibers. There are even tiles made using 100 percent recycled glass, including stained glass. Obviously, the more recycled content you can find, the more materials are taken out of the waste stream and kept out of landfills.

Another great option is to use reclaimed tile; it's not only 100 percent recycled, but you'll also be saving all those resources and all the energy that would have gone into manufacturing new tile. Reclaimed tile is available from a variety of sources in a wide variety of styles. European tile is actually the easiest to find. For instance, Pavé Tile & Stone (see Resources, page 347) offers reclaimed terra-cotta tile from Spain and France, while Cornerstone (see Resources, page 346) offers reclaimed tile from all over Europe. For tile that hasn't traveled around the world—or even halfway across the country—you can contact local architectural salvage firms or even search Craigslist.org.

STONE

It's becoming common to see travertine, marble, granite, slate, limestone, and many other natural stone materials in homes. So how do you choose a stone that's environmentally friendly? Clearly, it pays to do some research on where a stone comes from and how that quarry is operated. Are employees treated well? Is erosion a concern? Is water pollution an issue?

Unfortunately, there isn't a watchdog organization for stone—nothing akin to the Forest

Stewardship Council—but it should be easy enough to do a quick Google search for any quarries you're considering.

The type of stone also makes a difference. Softer stones, like slate and soapstone, are found closer to the earth's surface than harder stones, like granite and marble. So softer stones may involve less invasive mining practices and less energy to extract from the earth, along with lower emissions from the mining equipment.

Once again, buying local is a great way to go. Sourcing stone locally is certainly preferable to the energy expended to ship a very heavy product over great distances. Whenever possible, of course, I'd recommend the use of reclaimed stone. Again, 100 percent recycling—and conserving considerable energy and resources—is always the best choice.

CONCRETE

Concrete has become a popular flooring choice. A big benefit if you're building a new home with a concrete slab foundation is you don't have to purchase additional materials to cover the concrete. So you're conserving resources. Plus you don't need any kind of adhesive to attach a flooring material on top of that concrete.

If you're going to be installing radiant floor heating and the water tubes are getting set into concrete, then leaving that concrete bare—except for some sort of finish—also makes sense. You won't have anything between the heating surface and your room to act as an insulating barrier.

Concrete also retains heat well. So if you want to take advantage of passive solar, concrete flooring can absorb heat during the day in the wintertime, then release that heat slowly throughout the night, reducing your energy needs and your heating costs.

Also, with the huge assortment of finishes available, you don't have to live with ugly gray concrete. You can

- install colored concrete, which has the color mixed right into the material
- stain or dye concrete, even applying finishes that look like granite or other natural surfaces
- paint concrete
- have the concrete stamped so its texture mimics stone, brick, tile, or wood planks
- score concrete to simulate the look of tiles, even adding grout between the faux pavers

Of course, there are shades of green when it comes to concrete. One way to go greener is to choose concrete that has a fairly high concentration of recycled content in it. Concrete is made up of three key ingredients: cement, water, and aggregates such as rock, crushed gravel, and sand.

Limestone (one of the most abundant resources on Earth) is the main ingredient in cement. But fly ash, for example, can replace up to 30 percent of the cement in the mix. Fly ash is a by-product from coal-burning power plants. Waste products from steel mills and other manufacturing facilities—like slag cement and silica fume—also can be used. And, other recycled materials, such as crushed glass, plastic, and stone chips, can be incorporated into the concrete to create a sort of terrazzo look.

Using fly ash also can reduce CO_2 emissions during the concrete manufacturing process dramatically, and it can reduce the amount of water required to make concrete. Speaking of which, another thing to look for in concrete is one that is made using a dry—rather than a wet—process; it requires about half as much energy during manufacturing.

Also, if you're not stamping a texture into the concrete, you probably will want to polish it. You can find contractors these days who will employ more of a dry polishing technique, rather than using gallons and gallons of water to polish the concrete's surface.

Of course you'll want to use VOC-free (see page 302) finishes, too. Some chemical stains for concrete contain heavy metals, which can pose a hazardous waste problem during their application. Also, concrete floors are finished off with a sealer of some sort, either a colored or a clear coating or wax, and some of these sealers are more toxic than others.

LINOLEUM

Many people confuse linoleum with vinyl flooring. They're actually quite different. Vinyl flooring is made from polyvinyl chloride (PVC), one of the nastiest petroleum-based products around.

Linoleum is a natural product. It's made from renewable and even biodegradable resources: things like linseed oil, pine rosin, cork flour, wood flour, and limestone. The backing for linoleum is made from jute, a plant fiber—the same fiber that's used to make burlap bags and rope. In theory at least, you could throw old linoleum on a compost pile.

Linoleum also is quite sturdy. It lasts thirty to forty years usually—unlike vinyl flooring, which typically lasts only ten to twenty years. Now, linoleum does require more maintenance than vinyl, needing periodic waxing, but you also can sand it or patch it, if need be, which can extend its lifetime and keep more waste out of landfills.

Linoleum also is naturally resilient, so it's easy to stand on, which is one reason it's been popular for use in kitchens for decades. Plus, it's naturally antibacterial and it dampens sound.

You may have heard of Marmoleum. Marmoleum is a brand of natural linoleum from a company called Forbo (see Resources, page 346), which is likely the largest maker of linoleum in the world. Marmoleum is what I have in my kitchen. It contains no formaldehyde—unlike vinyl flooring—and has no VOCs in its manufacturing process. It's a durable material. Because it's organic, recyclable, and zero-VOC, Marmoleum is a great alternative to vinyl.

Marmoleum is a natural laminate that is also recyclable.

WALL-TO-WALL CARPET

Many people say carpet is very comfortable. You can go barefoot on it. You can lie on it. It tends to be warmer to the touch than a hard floor covering. I had carpet in my home and I was happy when we removed it. My wife, Rachelle, wanted to take it out, and I don't think I fought her even momentarily on that one because I liked the wood floors that were underneath. Plus, wood floors are much easier to keep clean.

If you really are a fan of carpeting, there are more heinous and more benign forms out there. I urge people to seek out the more benign forms. Most carpet fibers are made of nylon, acrylic, polypropylene, or polyester. In other words, they're made from petroleum. And then most of those carpet fibers are backed with synthetic SB latex, which contains styrene, a suspected carcinogen, or they're backed with polyurethane or PVC—again, petroleum products. On top of that, most carpet receives a toxic soup of chemical treatments: dyes, treatments to make it fire resistant, treatments to resist stains, treatments to prevent fungus from growing, and antistatic treatments. And then many installers glue the carpet into place using adhesives that are filled with VOCs.

So what are your other options? If you're really committed to carpet, you can install a carpet that doesn't contain all those toxic chemicals, and you can choose to tack it down

Sample Costs and Paybacks:
Bamboo Flooring versus Carpet

You know how I feel about carpet from a cleanliness and an environmental standpoint. But how does it compare financially with a greener alternative, like a bamboo floor?

Let's say we're considering carpet versus bamboo flooring for a 200-square-foot room.

Bamboo flooring materials range from about $4 to $6 per square foot. Then add another $4 per square foot for the installation. That brings it to $8 to $10 per square foot, installed. A bamboo floor should last twenty to thirty years if you clean it properly. And there's no real cost associated with cleaning it, since you can do it yourself with a mop.

What about carpet? Prices obviously vary depending on the kind of carpet you choose. But you certainly can find a good selection of carpet in the $2- to $4-per-square-foot range. Then you need to add another $0.70 per square foot for the installation, which brings the total installed cost up to $2.70 to $4.70 per square foot. Carpet should last five to ten years with proper cleaning. To keep your home as free from contaminants and allergens as possible, I recommend professional cleaning three times a year. That costs about $100 each time.

So, for our 200-square-foot room, we're looking at a price of $1,600 to $2,000 for the bamboo floor, installed. For carpet, we're looking at an installed cost of $540 to $940.

If you take really good care of your floors, the bamboo could last thirty years, while the carpet could last ten years. That means you'd have to install carpet three times to have it last as long as the bamboo. So now you're looking at an installed cost for carpet of $1,620 to $2,820.

Then you have to add in the cleaning costs over those thirty years. If you have bamboo, the costs are virtually nonexistent. But if you have carpet, you need to have it professionally cleaned three times a year. That's ninety cleanings over those thirty years, at a cost of $100 per visit. In other words, cleaning alone adds another $9,000 to the cost of carpet.

So now we're looking at $1,600 to $2,000 for bamboo versus $10,620 to $11,820 for carpet.

While there's clearly a higher up-front cost for the bamboo, the long-term costs are dramatically lower. You also will have a good-looking floor for the entire period, without the added hassle factor of shopping for flooring materials, moving your furniture, and dealing with installers two extra times. Plus, your home will be healthier without a toxin- and dust-magnet, and without potential off-gassing from the carpet materials. Healthy living definitely works out to be a better investment.

instead of gluing it into place. These days, you can find carpet made from natural fibers, including wool, cotton, silk, and other plant fibers, like jute, hemp, sisal (from the agave plant), and seagrass. Most of these natural fibers are considered renewable, but some have to travel great distances to reach the United States. And some involve some pretty resource-intensive agricultural practices.

Or you can find carpet made from recycled materials, including old used carpet (both wool and nylon) as well as recycled plastic soda bottles, recycled wool, and recycled cotton. For example, GreenFloors (see Resources, page 346) says a single square foot of its Recycled PET carpet keeps forty plastic food and drink containers out of landfills.

Now, one reason I'm still not a fan of carpet is because it's a trap for dust mites and toxins and allergens. You track an endless amount of gunk into your home on your shoes. You walk on grass outside and you get pesticides on your shoes. You get residue from animal waste. You get plain old dirt, dust, mold, and spores. If you walk through a parking lot, you get antifreeze and grease and other car-related gunk on your shoes. If it rains, you get the chemicals in acid rain. And then you wind up bringing all that stuff from outside, inside to your carpet.

At least when you have hard floors—like wood or tile or stone—you can easily wash all that residue off regularly. So if you do choose to have carpet, it's essential to have a professional come in and clean the carpet *at least* three times a year.

AREA RUGS

When we removed the carpet from our house and exposed the wood floors, we bought some area rugs to cover some of that space—to get the best of both worlds. With area rugs, you can take them outside and beat the dust out of them. You can use a good carpet cleaner outside and let the rugs dry in the sunshine. If you ever need to take the rugs to a professional cleaner—one that uses nontoxic cleaning agents, of course—you can easily do so.

With area rugs you have the advantages of carpet and then you have an aesthetic bonus as well with that wonderful border of wood that looks so nice around the rugs. It's for both aesthetic and environmental reasons that I'm a fan of rugs over wall-to-wall carpeting.

RECYCLED CARPET TILES

Modular carpet—also known as carpet tiles—is another way to enjoy the benefits of carpeting without the drawbacks. I'm very much in favor of this kind of carpeting, especially when it comes to the life cycle environmental cost of the material. Modular carpet contains recycled materials. It's recyclable. Plus, it's compostable.

The modular part of this carpet is really great. If you have a stain, you need only remove one or two squares. You can even wash them in the sink. If you have an uneven wear pattern in a hallway or somewhere, you just replace the affected tiles. You don't have to rip out and throw away the whole thing.

This kind of carpet also has a very low pattern. It doesn't have a long-pile design—or

Recycled carpet tiles are a great alternative to traditional wall-to-wall carpet.

worse yet, shag—so there isn't as much room for microbes and mites to hide inside it. It's not a dirt sponge. Also, each tile has its own padding built right in, so you don't need to install padding under it.

Interface (see Resources, page 346) is the big player in the recycled modular carpet scene, and I recommend checking out this company's product line if you're considering carpet at all. Rachelle and I have installed Interface's FLOR carpet tiles in her Pilates studio, and we love them.

OTHER RECYCLED FLOORING OPTIONS

I've mentioned a bunch of different recycled flooring options—and reclaimed flooring options, too—but there are more:

- **Recycled rubber.** Some of this flooring contains only postindustrial recycled content, but with a little research, you can find some that contains a considerable amount of postconsumer material. For instance, ECOsurfaces (see Resources, page 346) makes a rubber floor tile using tires that have been salvaged from landfills. The material is recyclable, and the company doesn't use any heat in the manufacturing process, so you don't have to worry about emissions from smokestacks. You can even find recycled rubber flooring that contains little or no VOCs, and it provides a non-slip surface.

- **Recycled cork.** There are also floor tiles made from a combination of recycled rubber *and* cork. A company called Capri Cork (see Resources, page 345) makes the Re-Tire Medley line, which contains recycled tires along with postindustrial rubber waste, virgin rubber, and postindustrial cork waste. It comes in a variety of color combinations and, like regular cork flooring, it's resilient and has sound-dampening qualities.

- **Recycled metal.** You can find shiny tiles that have been polished, as well as matte finishes and sandblasted, rough finishes. For instance, Eco Friendly Flooring (see Resources, page 346) has tiles made from 100 percent recycled aluminum or 100 percent recycled brass.

- **Recycled leather.** EcoDomo (see Resources, page 346) makes leather floor tiles that are made from 65 percent leather (which is recycled from postindustrial waste), 20 percent natural (not synthetic) rubber, and Acacia tree bark. These tiles are designed to be used as flooring, so they're durable, but over time you will see the signs of use. Much like a leather sofa, you can expect these leather floor tiles to develop a patina with age.

- **Palm trees.** At least one company has found a use for coconut palms that are too old and too tall to yield a sufficient number of coconuts. When these trees get to be about eighty years old, plantation owners just fell them and plant new ones. Until recently, there was no secondary use for the felled trees, but now Durapalm (see Resources, page 346) takes the trees, primarily from Asia, and turns them into flooring. Granted, the trees do have to travel a fair distance, and the product is not a solid wood. The company actually takes the hard outer part of the trunk and creates an engineered wood, but there are no toxic adhesives used in this product.

You can also find concrete tiles—an alternative to poured concrete or other kinds of floor tiles—that are made using fly ash, which again is waste from coal-burning power plants. For instance, Syndecrete (see Resources, page 347) cement-based tiles contain a considerable amount of fly ash, and the manufacturer says they're both half the weight and twice as strong as regular poured concrete.

COUNTERTOPS

Many of the same materials used for floors can also be used for countertops—in your kitchen, in your bathroom, anywhere you choose. This includes tile, stone, concrete, wood (especially butcher block), and even metal. Obviously, the same characteristics that make for a green floor also make for a green countertop.

Besides the materials I've already talked about, there are some very interesting recycled materials designed specifically for use as countertops, or that are primarily used for countertops these days. Among them are these:

- **Vetrazzo** (see Resources, page 347). I have this material in my kitchen. The countertop is made from 85 percent glass, and 100 percent of that glass is recycled from things like old traffic lights, car windshields, bottles, and plate-glass windows—including types of glass that currently are not being recycled for other uses. The different kinds of glass are used to create different color combinations. My counters have a green hue because they're made from recycled Coca-Cola bottles.
- **IceStone** (see Resources, page 346). A similar-looking material to Vetrazzo, IceStone is made from 100 percent recycled glass and concrete. It also has received the McDonough Braungart Design Chemistry Cradle to Cradle certification for being environmentally friendly throughout the entire product's life cycle (see page 321).
- **EnviroGLAS** (see Resources, page 346). This company offers several recycled countertop products, including EnviroMODE, which is made from recycled tubs, sinks, and toilets; and EnviroSLAB, which is made from recycled glass.

- **PaperStone** (see Resources, page 347). These countertops are made from paper and petroleum-free resins. PaperStone Original contains 50 percent postconsumer recycled paper, and PaperStone Certified, which is FSC certified, contains 100 percent postconsumer waste paper.
- **Armstone** (see Resources, page 345). This engineered stone countertop is made with various combinations of quartz chips, granite chips, and recycled glass, which always total more than 90 percent of the content.

Some of these materials are suitable for use as flooring, too. Plus, most of them are eligible for LEED points.

Countertops can be made with many recycled materials—like this one, which is made of 85-percent recycled glass.

CABINETS

Most cabinets these days are made from particleboard with some sort of veneer over it. And particleboard is problematic. The polyurethane used as a binder to hold together the bits of wood pulp usually off-gases formaldehyde, and lots of it. In fact, most formaldehyde off-gassing in a home is from the kitchen cabinets.

However, there are more environmentally friendly—and health-conscious—choices:

- It is possible to find formaldehyde-free (or nearly formaldehyde-free) particleboard, including particle board made from 100 percent recycled wood, like Arreis from Sierra Pine (see Resources, page 347).
- There's also formaldehyde-free particleboard made from wheat straw—an agricultural waste product. It's called wheatboard and is used for cabinets by such companies as Humabuilt and Greenline (see Resources, page 346).
- Some cabinets are made using FSC-certified plywood that's formaldehyde-free, instead of particleboard, such as

those from Breathe Easy Cabinets (see Resources, page 345).

- Another possibility is solid wood cabinets made from FSC lumber, like those from Grass Cabinetry and Muny Woodwork (see Resources, page 346).
- How about using salvaged wood for cabinets? You can find ready-made cabinets made from salvaged wood—including wood from dead and diseased trees—from firms such as CitiLog (see Resources, page 345).
- You also can find bamboo cabinets from companies like AlterECO and Henrybuilt (see Resources, page 345).
- Kirei Board (see Resources, page 346) is made from another kind of agricultural waste: stalks of the sorghum plant, which is grown for food. The stalks do have to be processed to make Kirei Board, but the company uses nontoxic adhesives.

As always, you'll want to check for VOCs (see page 302) in any finishes you choose, as well as in the glues used to make the cabinets.

 PAINT

Paints have changed a lot over the years. You may remember when the Federal Consumer Products Safety Commission (see Resources, page 346) banned the use of lead in residential paints. Architectural coatings were about

75 percent water-based and 25 percent oil-based in 1978. Some paints used natural oils, such as linseed oil, cottonseed oil, or safflower oil as a binder. But most used synthetic resins, resins that were derived from petroleum—that other kind of oil that has all of its attendant problems.

It took quite a while before the industry moved to water-based paints in a big way for indoor use. They first became commercially available back in the 1950s. But early water-based paints were problematic. They didn't work as well as oil-based paints.

Now, according to my friend Tim Garver from Dunn-Edwards Paints (see Resources, page 346), today's water-based paints actually outperform oil-based paints in many respects. They're breathable, so if there's any moisture on a wall when it's painted—or any moisture in the air, for that matter—water-based paints will dry just fine, whereas oil-based paints would likely crack and chip. Water-based paints also are more flexible, and they're less likely to fade or get chalky or yellow over time. So if you buy paint for inside your home today, it's going to be acrylic or latex. The two words are used interchangeably, but essentially it's a water-based paint.

Unfortunately, there's something in many paints—both oil- and water-based—that's a problem when it comes to indoor air quality. It's what causes that new-paint smell that gives people headaches: VOCs again (see page 302). They're included in paints to help them go on and adhere well. Once that paint actually is applied to a wall or some other surface, then the water and the solvents in the paint evaporate. That solvent evaporation is what releases VOCs into your home, affecting your indoor air quality. Tim points out that not all VOCs are horrible—some are toxic, others are not.

LOW-VOC PAINTS

The paint companies know VOCs are a problem. The EPA and the state air quality agencies know VOCs are a problem. Many areas have instituted legal limits for the amount of VOCs in paint, though not necessarily to improve *indoor* air quality. According to Tim, VOC limits were instituted because of the potential for *outdoor* air quality issues, specifically their potential to contribute to the formation of ozone.

Low-VOC paints have also become the standard for green building. For instance, the LEED for Homes Rating System follows what's called the Green Seal GS-11 standard. In Chapter 9, I discussed LEED extensively. Green Seal, (see Resources, page 346) is a different group. It's a nonprofit organization that has created a wide variety of environmental standards—for things like alternative-fuel vehicles, compact fluorescent lightbulbs, paper products, and, in this case, paint.

Green Seal's standard for paints and coatings addresses both a product's environmental friendliness and its performance. There's no point in buying something green that doesn't work. In the case of "interior topcoats," that means the product has to have good

- scrubbability, which is abrasion resistance

- hiding power, or opacity
- washability

Once minimum performance standards are met, a nonflat interior paint or coating (a gloss or a semigloss paint, for example) can have no more than 150 grams per liter of VOCs. A flat paint or coating can have no more than 50 grams per liter. Both kinds of coatings can have no more than 1 percent aromatic compounds. So how do you know if a paint or a coating meets this standard? Just look for the Green Seal on its container.

NO-VOC PAINTS

Low-VOC paints are good. In fact, they're good enough to get the Green Seal and LEED approval. But there's something even better. There are *no*-VOC paints. Paint companies worked on the formulas, and they came up with another way to have paint that would still do its job but without these volatile organic compounds in it, and what a good day that was.

I should point out that zero-VOC paints may contain a *small* amount of VOCs. The EPA allows paint that has no more than 5 grams of VOCs per liter to be labeled zero-VOC, and tints in the paint sometimes can add about another 5 grams even beyond that. So *zero* sometimes works out to be *more than zero,* but it's still much less than *low.*

The early no-VOC paints pretty much came in only white and various shades of off-white. But now EcoShield from Dunn-Edwards, for example, is available in any color that has what paint companies call a *light base* or a *medium base.* In the paint business, a color has a base, and then other tones are added to it.

Unfortunately, no-VOC paints haven't quite reached the performance levels of low-VOC paints when it comes to durability and *block resistance*—that is, the resistance of two painted surfaces to stick together. But Tim notes that demand for zero-VOC paints is increasing, so I'm sure paint companies will continue to work on their formulations.

You can find zero-VOC paints from such companies as Dunn-Edwards, AFM Safecoat, Benjamin Moore Paints, Frazee Industries, Sherwin-Williams, and Pittsburgh Paints. There's even a new line of no-VOC paint called FreshAire that's sold exclusively at Home Depot (see Resources, pages 345–47).

NATURAL PAINTS

In addition to low- and no-VOC paints, there's another category of green paints: natural paints. Rather than being latex or acrylic paints, these include

- **Milk paints.** The basic ingredients are milk protein, lime, and earth pigments. They're biodegradable, nontoxic, and odorless once they're dry. And they're available from companies like the Old Fashioned Milk Paint Company and the Real Milk Paint Company (see Resources, page 347).
- **Clay plasters.** They contain clay (sometimes mixed with sand, sometimes mixed with marble dust), and

they naturally absorb moisture and have antistatic qualities. They're available from such companies as American Clay (see Resources, page 345).

- **Clay paints.** These paints are made from natural clay, and they simulate the look of clay plaster at a lower price. American Clay also offers clay paints, and a company called BioShield Paint (see Resources, page 345) has a line of more brightly colored clay paints.
- **Inorganic mineral paints** (also called silicate dispersion paints). They use potassium silicate as the binder, and they don't actually form a film on a wall, like latex paint. Instead, they penetrate a wall's surface. They're also naturally antimicrobial. Inorganic mineral paints are available from such companies as Eco-House Natural Products (see Resources, page 346).
- **Soy-based paints.** These paints use soy in place of acrylic. For instance, the soy-based paints from Green Planet Paints (see Resources, page 346) contain less than a dozen ingredients, including marble, porcelain clay, mineral pigments, and soy-based resin.
- **Collagen paints.** Collagen, a protein, is extremely strong and has great elasticity, which are good qualities in a paint. Eco-Trend Collagen (see Resources, page 346) paint uses collagen from egg inner membranes. It's odorless, antimicrobial, and antifungal.

Repainting the Interior of My House

My office with freshly painted walls using zero-VOC paints

I began using low-VOC paints back in the early 1990s. As soon as they became available, I made the switch to no-VOC paints. In the beginning, my wife, Rachelle, used to complain about the durability of the paints that I "made" her use and also the limited color choices.

But now, finally, she's happy. We just finished painting the entire inside of our house with Dunn-Edwards' EcoShield. I'm happy to report that there's just absolutely no off-gassing at all. There's no smell. There are no headaches. I don't even get a headache from Rachelle complaining about this paint. She likes the colors and, considering this is the second time we've used it, I'm happy to report this paint has been performing very well. So going to this darker shade of green environmentally has made us both happier, thankfully.

- **Lime paints.** These are a basic whitewash, made with lime and water, and sometimes with pigments for color. Companies like Calcem and St. Astier offer lime paints. TexSton (see Resources, page 347) offers both lime paint and lime plaster.

These paints have far fewer ingredients—and far more pronounceable ingredients—than acrylic paints. In fact, some natural paints are so simple that you can make your own at home. If you're so inclined, you can find natural paint recipes online.

CLEANING

Most people would be outside with signs protesting a hazardous waste site near their homes, and I certainly would join them in solidarity. But the sad fact is, most hazardous waste sites are not *near* people's homes. They're *in* people's homes. They're under their sinks. They're in their bathrooms. They're in their closets.

Public enemy number one is in the kitchen. Under the sink, so close to where folks prepare their food each day, is all manner of toxic compounds. There are bug sprays. There are toxic drain cleaners. There are paint thinners. There are tile-cleaning compounds. There are oven cleaners.

If you read the label on one of your cleaning supplies and it says you should work in a well-ventilated area when using this product, that's a good tip-off that it's not the most environmentally benign product out there. If you work with some of the popular oven cleaners, tile-cleaning formulas, lacquer thinners, paint thinners, and so on, you know this to be true. They knock your head back when you smell them. You recoil from the scent.

These cleaning supplies contain corrosive ingredients like chlorine and ammonia and hydrochloric acid. They contain sodium hydroxide, which can cause chemical burns and blindness. They contain 2-Butoxyethanol, which can cause headaches and nausea. Many common household cleaning products are literally considered *poisons*.

SOAPS, DETERGENTS, AND GROUNDWATER

When you clean, some amount of your household cleaners winds up in the drain. But what goes down the drain in even larger quantities, in greater amounts to be sure, are all of your soaps and detergents. I'm talking about:

- hand soaps
- body washes
- dishwashing liquid
- automatic dishwasher detergent
- clothes detergent
- bleach or whiteners/brighteners
- liquid fabric softener

I developed a line of cleaners with ingredients that are all natural, nontoxic, and totally biodegradable.

So the questions become:

1. Are these products beneficial to the groundwater, or are they harmful?
2. Are they good or bad for a septic system?
3. Are they going to harm your plants if you have a gray water irrigation system?

Now, many people don't realize that *soaps* are made from fats and oils, whereas *detergents* are synthetic soaps. Detergents are made from chemicals.

Phosphates, which are commonly found in detergents, are not good for the ocean. They are not good for our waterways. They are not good for our groundwater. You want to choose

Certifications

Currently, there's no one single standard determining if a cleaning product is environmentally sound or not, but there are a handful of different certification processes that are relevant. Two of the ones that mean a lot to me are the Green Seal and the MBDC certification.

I talked about Green Seal in regard to paint. There's also GS-8: the Green Seal Environmental Standard for General-Purpose, Bathroom, Glass, and Carpet Cleaners Used for Household Purposes. Besides meeting normal performance standards, these products in their *undiluted* form cannot:

- be toxic according to the Consumer Product Safety Commission regulations
- contain any carcinogens, reproductive toxins, or mutagens (that is, ingredients that could cause "heritable mutations" or damage DNA)
- cause skin or eye irritation, including being corrosive
- cause skin sensitization (also known as *allergic contact dermatitis*)
- be toxic to aquatic wildlife, including fish, invertebrate organisms, and algae
- contain more than 0.5 percent phosphorus
- be combustible
- contain a whole list of prohibited ingredients, including 2-Butoxyethanol, phthalates, and heavy metals

a soap or detergent that doesn't have phosphates in it.

Fortunately, you can find nontoxic soaps and detergents without phosphates. You can find products that are biodegradable and nontoxic, like the laundry and dish soaps offered by Seventh Generation and the personal-care products from Hugo Naturals (see Resources, page 346).

WASHING YOUR CAR

Some people like to wash their car at home, but I take mine to a car wash. Why? Because when you wash your car at home, the detergents that you use and then hose off run into the ground and then they soak down into the groundwater. Or they run down into the gutter and then into a storm drain. Where I live in Los Angeles, the water that runs into the storm drains goes directly into the ocean. It doesn't get treated first. I certainly don't want harsh car-washing chemicals going out into the Santa Monica Bay.

Another major reason to use a car wash is because they use recycled water. No matter how careful you are at home, you're going to use more water than they will. The majority of the car washes out there have a water reclamation system. They just keep cleaning the water and using it again and again. Now that's water conservation!

But if you can't get to a car wash for whatever reason, or if the car washes in your area don't recycle their wash water, then there's a good alternative: a waterless car-washing product like Bayes Eco-Friendly Waterless Vehicle Wash (see Resources, page 345). It's nontoxic and it's biodegradable. It works on every part of your car. You just spray it on and wipe it off. The company says one 16-ounce bottle will wash five cars and save a tremendous 750 gallons of water compared with using the hose. So that's another option.

So, again, the Green Seal on a product means a lot to me. It's a real indicator of a product's friendliness to the environment at large and to your family's health and indoor air quality.

Another very good certification program for a wide variety of products—from cleaning supplies to office chairs—is the MBDC Cradle to Cradle Certification (McDonough Braungart Design Chemistry, see Resources, page 346). William McDonough and Dr. Michael Braungart founded MBDC in 1995 to promote Cradle to Cradle Design. It's cradle to cradle, as opposed to cradle to grave. As opposed to the take-make-waste paradigm that was a key part of the first Industrial Revolution, MBDC's goal is to create the "next industrial revolution," to help companies create new and much better products using what they call "eco-effective design principles."

The big addition with MBDC, compared with Green Seal, is an emphasis on a given product's entire life cycle, not just the manufacturing process. Each product needs to be designed with recycling in mind, and it needs to be either a biological nutrient or a technical nutrient. (If it's a combination of the two, it must

be easy to separate the parts at the end of the product's useful life.)

My Begley's Best All Purpose Cleaner has been certified as being a biological nutrient through this process. So as you can tell, the MBDC certification means a lot to me.

It's so important to pay close attention to the items you bring into your home. Your home is your sanctuary. It should be the place where you're safe, where you can relax and unwind, without getting headaches—or worse—from toxic cleaning products and toxic flooring materials and toxic paint and toxic cabinets. You deserve to live in a toxin-free environment, and so does your family.

Our planet deserves to be toxin-free, too. And you can make a big difference here. It's all about choices. So choose wisely, whether you're looking at wood for your floors, stone for your countertops, soap for your hands, or detergent to wash your clothes. All of these choices have ramifications inside your home and far, far beyond.

ED'S PROJECT

Starting a Cleaning Supplies Company

Using nontoxic cleaning products in your kitchen makes good sense.

A few years ago, I was looking for really good nontoxic cleaning products to launch a new company. I wanted to introduce my own line of environmentally friendly cleaning products—that is, products that are friendly to the earth, to the water, to you, to your family, and to your home's indoor air quality. I'm glad to say that I have met the right people who have developed the right formulas to make this stuff work. Today, I have the good fortune of having a company called Begley's Best (see Resources, page 345).

I have several products now:

- All Purpose Cleaner
- Glass and Surface Cleaner
- Spot Remover and Household Cleaner
- Spot Remover and All Purpose Cleaner in Concentrate

I use my cleaners and I use them often. Rachelle likes to remind me that I've gone so far as to drink the original formulation of Begley's Best, the Spot Remover and Household Cleaner, to prove to potential customers that it truly is nontoxic. Not only have I had labs verify this, but I'm living proof.

I've been able to eliminate all of the toxic traditional cleaners from my home. I clean my wood floors and my Marmoleum floor in the kitchen with Begley's Best Concentrate. Put a capful in a bucket of water, and it cleans the floors really well.

I use Begley's Best Spot Remover on my furniture and car upholstery and to remove stains from carpet and other fabrics, including clothing.

I use the All Purpose Cleaner to clean the bathroom, shower, sink, tile, and toilet. It's a good vegetable wash, too.

I use Begley's Best Glass Cleaner for all kinds of surfaces, like stainless steel. It's an antibacterial. It doesn't streak or leave a residue. It's got a little bit of alcohol in it, plus some coconut.

For the few things on which I can't use Begley's Best, I use other good, nontoxic cleaners. Jeffrey Hollender started Seventh Generation (see Resources, page 347) more than twenty years ago, and his wonderful company sells good products that I use. My line doesn't make recycled plastic bags; I buy the Seventh Generation brand. My line doesn't include a dishwasher detergent or dishwashing liquid; I buy them from Seventh Generation.

Eventually I would like to have my own dishwashing liquid and laundry detergent. I'm working on adding to the range of Begley's Best products right now. I want to develop really good formulas that are truly nontoxic and that clean clothes and dishes really well. I hope to be able to share these products with consumers soon.

15

BABIES & NURSERIES

Setting Up Your Home
for a Healthy Baby

Organic bedding is made from 100-percent organic-cotton fabric that is not treated with any chemicals.

WHEN I HAD MY TWO OLDER CHILDREN IN THE LATE 1970s, we used products that were as nontoxic as possible, but that was much tougher to do then than it is today. Often, I had to compromise. By 1999, when my youngest daughter, Hayden, was born, it was much easier to find nontoxic choices. So I was able to use nontoxic, zero-VOC paints for Hayden's room. I was able to use nontoxic cleaning supplies for her room and for the whole house. I even found nontoxic toys and nontoxic bedding.

Nontoxic everything has not only become more readily available these days, it's sought after by nearly everybody. So it's easier to make nontoxic choices, and that means it's much easier to set up your home for a healthy baby.

SETTING UP A NURSERY

An adult's bedroom environment is very important, but a baby's bedroom environment is that much more important because a baby is the most vulnerable, sensitive creature in the household. Children are far more affected by toxins in their environment than adults, in part because of their much smaller body mass and the fact that their small bodies are developing. Beyond that, small children tend to put everything in their mouths, so be sure those things are nontoxic, to say the least. Also, keep in mind that a baby often spends much more time in the nursery than an adult spends in his or her bedroom.

My friend Mary Cordaro, environmental consultant, educator, and healthy home products designer—of Mary Cordaro Inc.—(see Resources, page 347), is a fan of Sandra Steingraber, the famous scientist who wrote *Living Downstream*. Mary says, "I like to quote her usage of the words 'using the fetus as our benchmark.' Because if the fetus is safe among all the products that we make and use, then

that should be our benchmark. Not the adult hundred-and-whatever-pound male in a work setting, you know, declared by OSHA [Occupational Safety and Health Administration; see Resources, page 347]. Our benchmark for anything we produce or put in the home should be the developing fetus."

One of the reasons we make such a big deal about this is because the newborn baby isn't the only one to consider. Most people set up a nursery while they're pregnant. So a pregnant mother is being exposed—and her fetus is being exposed—to whatever materials are being used in that nursery. We know from very credible research studies that whatever a mother eats and breathes affects the fetus. So we absolutely want to take environmentally conscious precautions during pregnancy.

AVOIDING VINYL

One of the materials you absolutely want to avoid—particularly for a nursery, but really in every area of your life—is vinyl. Most of the time, when we use the word *vinyl,* we're really talking about PVC, or polyvinyl chloride. PVC is one of the *least* environmentally friendly materials around.

PVC off-gases. It's a source of volatile organic compounds, or VOCs, which I talked about in Chapter 14, "Decorating and Cleaning Your Home" (see page 302), as well as semivolatile organic compounds, or SVOCs. Mary has been extremely active in informing people about the dangers of SVOCs. And the problem isn't just when the vinyl is new. It off-gases for a long time. Also, as it becomes older, some of that vinyl turns to dust and then we breathe in those chemicals, which is really harmful. Mary points out that SVOCs—and also phthalates (see below)—bind onto regular house dust, too.

The chlorine in PVC is a big part of the problem. It leads to the creation of dioxin, a highly carcinogenic chemical that is a global problem.

When it comes to a nursery, PVC is often used in:

- mattresses and mattress covers
- pillows
- carpet and vinyl flooring
- plastic furniture
- toys
- children's car seats

Also, phthalates are used to make vinyl soft. They can be found in everything from beach balls and other toys to teethers. Japan and many European countries have already banned the use of phthalates because they've been shown to harm children's health.

It's possible to avoid vinyl in most areas of your life. Unfortunately, virtually all car seats are made with vinyl, but Mary suggests that you minimize your child's exposure to them. Don't store a car seat in the nursery or in the bedroom. Actually, it's best not to bring it in the house at all.

 ## THE MATTRESS

One of the most important things in the nursery is the baby's mattress. The baby is going to be right on top of the mattress for a good part of the time. And, as Mary says, "This is probably the most important thing in the bedroom because you can't wash your mattress. And so if it has any kinds of chemicals or pesticide residues or any other types of contaminants that aren't good for the body, you're stuck with them."

Again, your common, everyday mattress is likely to be made from PVC on the outside, and it's likely to contain phthalates. As of January 2009, the use of some phthalates has been banned for crib mattresses, but, sadly, the ban does not include all phthalates. The filling is likely to be made from polyurethane foam, which is petroleum-based and which often contains a toxic soup of chemicals, like formaldehyde and benzene and toluene.

Plus, one of the things that's particularly tricky about mattresses is they have to, by law, meet certain fire-resistance standards. Nowadays, a mattress literally gets torched and the fire has to be able to be extinguished within a certain time frame. How do most manufacturers make a bed fire resistant to that degree? They use chemicals.

For decades now, the most common fire retardant for polyurethane foam has been a family of chemicals called polybrominated diphenyl ethers, or PBDEs, especially pentaBDE. This nasty, toxic chemical leaches into the air

Sample Costs and Paybacks: Organic Mattresses

The kind of organic crib mattress that we're talking about—the kind that is filled with Pozzi Wool and then covered in organic cotton—is more expensive than your basic crib mattress.

A cheap synthetic mattress goes for as little as $50, but it will be really toxic.

As Mary Cordaro points out, many babies have a hard time sleeping on synthetic mattresses. The babies overheat and they fuss and cry and they're awake at night.

If you think about it, your baby is likely going to be sleeping in the crib for a couple of years. So is it worth a little more money for a healthy, happy, well-rested baby? And is it worth a little more money for you to get a good night's sleep, too?

An organic cotton and pure grow wool mattress for a crib is going to cost more like $250 to $400. Yes, there's a big difference financially, but the payback is immeasurable. And if you think about it over time, we're talking about less than 50¢ a day extra, at the high end. Plus, you get peace of mind and a healthy baby.

---

around the mattress quite readily. The U.S. Environmental Protection Agency (EPA) currently is studying PBDEs because they may cause liver toxicity, thyroid toxicity, and neurodevelopmental toxicity (see Resources, page 347).

Remember these chemicals don't go away. They don't dissipate. For obvious reasons, they're specifically designed to stay in the mattress to make sure it remains flame-resistant for its lifetime.

Here's more scary news: Now there are studies all around the world showing that these chemicals may be a possible cause of SIDS, Sudden Infant Death Syndrome. When the baby spits up or wets the bed, the growth of naturally occurring fungus combines with these chemicals to form some really toxic stuff.

So what's the alternative to a mattress made from synthetic materials and doused with toxic chemicals? The alternative is an organic mattress. It's possible to make a mattress that's fire-retardant without using chemicals. In fact, Mary's designed such a mattress, under the label The Mary Cordaro Collection, for cribs and beds. The key is in the materials selection.

Wool is the prime ingredient in making these organic mattresses flame-resistant. Wool is also resistant to moisture, mold, and dust mites.

Plus, it wicks moisture from the body and regulates the body's temperature and humidity. It keeps the baby warmer in the winter and cooler in the summer.

"There's a midwife I work with once in a while who's from Germany," Mary says. "And she would always put the babies who wouldn't sleep at night on wool because she almost always found—unless it was a medical issue or they were hungry or something—that they wouldn't sleep on their synthetic mattresses because they were too hot. And when they were put onto something that was wool, their body temperatures and the humidity would become regulated and they would sleep much better."

These mattresses don't use just any type of wool. They use Pozzi Wool™. It's organic, and it has a different label from that normal wool label you see. Then organic cotton fabric covers the tops of these mattresses.

Mary notes that there are some other organic mattresses that pass the flame test that don't have wool in them. However, these mattresses have a plastic cover on them. So that's a problem because it's petroleum-based and also because sleeping on plastic is not comfortable because babies can become hot and sweaty.

THE CRIB

The mattress has to go in a crib, so what should you look for in a crib? Certainly a used crib—a recycled crib—is a good idea. It's a good use of resources.

You also want to be careful what sort of finish the crib has. You obviously don't want to use an antique crib with lead paint on it. And you don't want some other paint or varnish to be off-gassing toxins in the nursery, in fact in the exact spot in the nursery where the baby is going to be spending the most time.

One way you can be especially certain of the finish is to buy a crib at an unfinished furniture store and then finish it yourself. Then you can choose your own zero-VOC finish or a natural oil finish or one of the other natural finishes I talked about in Chapter 14 (see pages 314–18).

You also want to buy a *solid wood* crib. It's important to avoid cribs that are made from plywood or particleboard because conventional plywood and particleboard contain nasty chemicals like formaldehyde (see page 314).

MOLD

Mary also suggests that you have your house checked for mold as a precautionary measure before the baby is born. You can find a list of certified bau-biologists at International Institute for Bau-Biologie & Ecology's website (see Resources, page 347). Mary is one, and she explains that the field of Bau-Biologie comes from Germany. *Bau* means building, and Bau-Biologie is focused on healthy, green homes and has specific standards to meet and follow. You can have a Bau-Biologist come to your home to perform an audit and troubleshoot to discover the source of any problems, then help you to detoxify your home.

"Mold is so prevalent now in our new building materials," she says. "If someone can afford to find a local Bau-Biologist to inspect their home . . . they spend time thoroughly investigating your house and find some of the culprits so that the pregnant woman and the new baby at least are not exposed to existing conditions in a home that could be toxic, like mold or high electromagnetic fields. Those are usually the major culprits."

Also, you certainly don't want to provide a good habitat for mold and bacteria to take hold in the future. One of the things new parents do that's a problem along these lines is use a humidifier in the nursery. "Humidifiers often are putting out way too much moisture in the room for the rate at which the materials in the room can dry," Mary says. "And so you can literally be feeding low levels of mold, especially if you have carpet." With a humidifier, you could be causing a problem more than solving one. If you absolutely need to add moisture to the room, at least limit the amount of time you're using the humidifier, and before refilling, clean out the water reservoir—where bacteria can grow—with hydrogen peroxide.

FLOORING

Flooring choices for the nursery—and for the whole house—are very important. You're going to be putting your baby on the floor in the living room and the den, and eventually your baby is going to be crawling all around the house. Also, you'll be feeding the baby in the kitchen or the dining area, and food will be spilling on the floor. There will be drool. There will be spit-up. There could even be—heaven forbid—leaky diapers. So flooring becomes a very important issue when there's a baby in the house.

Carpet, especially, becomes a big concern. As I mentioned in Chapter 14, you track all kinds of germs, pesticides, and nasty stuff into the house on your shoes, and that stuff gets trapped in the carpet. It's a catch basin. Then you've got a baby lying on the carpet and crawling on the carpet and drooling and more. So you're providing a nice fertile breeding ground for fungus and mold and bacteria to grow.

If you insist on having carpet, keep the old carpet instead of installing brand-new carpet to avoid new toxic chemical outgassing, and have it cleaned professionally with nontoxic cleaners well before the baby arrives. Also stop wearing shoes in the house. Better yet, get rid of the carpet. Get an easy-to-clean, no-off-gassing floor like hardwood or stone or tile or concrete.

Of course, if you put in hard flooring, you're probably going to want something soft for the baby to lie on. You can use a nice organic cotton throw rug or blanket—something you can throw in the washing machine regularly. Mary also recommends organic yoga mats; they're softer and provide a little padding, and you can air them out outside.

ELECTROMAGNETIC FIELDS

The other thing Mary is very concerned about is electromagnetic fields, or EMFs. In the case of a nursery, they're caused by any kind of electronic devices and anything that's wireless, including baby monitors.

If you want to look into the controversy surrounding EMFs, the Collaborative on Health and the Environment (see Resources, page 347) is a really good resource. As Mary points out, in general, the research has shown that our bodies are electromagnetic beings. And at the very least, these electrical frequencies cause a lot of stress on our bodies.

Even if you're still doubtful about the dangers, let's just say there's no proof that EMFs are *not* harmful. So from a precautionary standpoint, it couldn't hurt to be mindful of them and set up the nursery accordingly.

The key to avoiding EMFs is to keep electronic devices out of the room—TVs, DVD players, radios, clocks, and humidifiers. If you have to have something electronic in there, plug it in as far away from the crib as possible, or use battery-powered devices. The less you have to plug in, the better.

Radio frequency (RF) devices are a problem, too. That includes cordless phones and baby monitors. If you're going to use a baby monitor, please don't stick it in the crib. Leave it as far across the room from the baby as possible. And if you have a wireless router in your home, make sure the computer signal is too weak for your laptop in the nursery. If not, move the router further away from the nursery.

BATHING THE BABY

I talked about water filtration in Chapter 6, "Water Usage" (pages 105–110). Obviously, you want to bathe your baby in good, clean, filtered water. The skin is a giant organ that absorbs some of pretty much everything it comes in contact with. So you don't want your baby absorbing a whole lot of chlorine or chlorine by-products. For the same reason, skin-care and other personal care products are very important—for the baby and also the pregnant mother.

So what do you look for in terms of soaps and shampoos and lotions, both for mother and baby? Well, an easy approach is to read the list of ingredients and look for words you can pronounce. Ideally, look for ingredients you're familiar with, and the fewer ingredients, the better.

Stay away from products that have a long list of chemicals in them. Stay away from phthalates, parabens, and sodium lauryl sulfate.

Avoid fragrances and anything that's anti-bacterial. Look for organic, too, though some organic products are purer than others.

Mary recommends the Environmental Working Group's website (see Resources, page 347) as a source for the best personal care products for both mother and baby. It has a Cosmetics Safety Database that's really helpful because you can look up actual brand-name products and see how they score.

ORGANIC BABY CLOTHES AND BEDDING

Generally, you want to look for *organic* materials when it comes to both baby clothes and bedding.

Synthetic materials are usually petroleum-based thermoplastics such as nylon, acrylic, polyester, and spandex. These are man-made substances. They're made in a lab. They obviously increase our dependence on foreign oil, and they have a pretty serious carbon footprint.

Synthetic materials also don't breathe like natural fibers. They trap moisture up against your body. You don't want the baby to overheat, nor do you want the mom to overheat. Synthetic or synthetic-blend children's sleepwear may be treated with toxic flame retardant chemicals.

So, you want to look for organic clothing and bedding made from natural fibers, including:

- cotton
- wool
- hemp
- angora
- silk
- linen
- cashmere

Organic fabrics are made without the use of synthetic pesticides—and cotton is one of the most pesticide-laden materials in the world. Organic fabrics are free from the toxic mix of chemicals used to kill all kinds of pests out in the field. They won't be treated with toxic flame-retardant chemicals. They're also going to come from farms where an emphasis is placed on maintaining a healthy ecosystem and maintaining biodiversity. Plus, organic fabrics are made with less-toxic dyes than regular textiles.

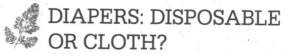 DIAPERS: DISPOSABLE OR CLOTH?

I get asked this question a lot: Should we use disposable or cloth diapers for our baby?

There's no one right answer to this question.

There's certainly some truth to the argument that in an arid climate like L.A., the amount of water used to wash cloth diapers doesn't make any sense. Of course, there's a fair amount of energy involved in washing them, too. You have to wash the diapers in hot water, plus you have to treat the used wash water as waste. You can't use it as "gray" water for your garden, because it's black water, containing human waste.

When it comes to cloth diapers, Mary says, "It's kind of like going back to the old days in a way, but there's now some improvements. Under the Nile (see Resources, page 347), for instance, is a children's organic clothing company, and they have a really good cloth diaper system."

Cloth diapers do last a long time—something like 100 to 150 uses. And the newer designs have straps that make fastening them a lot easier. It's not like you have to use old-fashioned diaper pins. But, obviously, using cloth diapers does take more work than using disposables. Washing and reusing diapers requires not just electricity and potentially natural gas but also human energy. You have to be committed to doing the extra work.

That's why I just wasn't getting any takers for cloth diapers when Hayden was born. Rachelle insisted on disposables. Thank goodness there were—and are—some better choices nowadays when it comes to disposable diapers. With Hayden, we used earth-friendly, biodegradable disposable diapers.

"Regular" disposable diapers are made from plastic. They're also made with wood pulp that gets bleached with chlorine, and they're treated with a variety of other chemicals. Biodegradable diapers are *not* made from plastic, which obviously does not biodegrade. Also, while environmentally friendly diapers may use wood pulp, that pulp *won't* be treated with chlorine, and it *will* come from FSC-certified wood.

Going biodegradable can make a tremendous difference. If you think about the sheer quantity of diapers that are taking up space in landfills today, it's astonishing. At last count, some 18 billion diapers are sold each year in the United States, and they account for around 2 percent of the country's municipal solid waste. That's considerable. It's enough to make some people lean toward cloth.

But again, I can see both sides of this argument, and people who have studied the cradle-to-grave aspect of the debate say it comes up even. There's no one good choice,

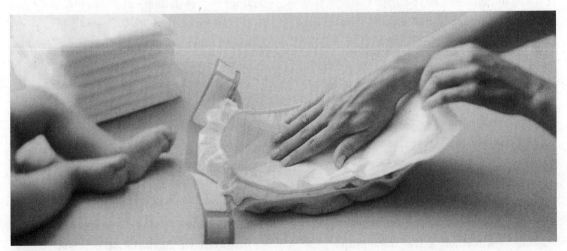

Flushable diapers have a plastic-free flushable diaper refill. You can flush, compost, or toss.

though Mary does believe that cloth diapers are actually a healthier choice for babies, assuming you use nontoxic laundry detergent, of course.

If you do choose to go the disposable route, there are two different kinds available nowadays:

- **Disposables that biodegrade in a landfill.** You can find these diapers from such companies as Seventh Generation, Nature Babycare, and Healthy Baby Diaper, which makes the Nature boy & girl diaper (see Resources, page 347). These diapers are fragrance-free, latex-free, and plastic-free, and they're made with chlorine-free wood pulp fluff. The Nature Babycare and the Nature boy & girl diapers also feature a back sheet that's made from corn, and they both have thinner designs, which use less material overall—a big plus. While there's some debate as to how long biodegradable diapers actually take to biodegrade in landfill conditions, some folks recommend doing it yourself using a composting toilet or worm composting.

- **Disposables that can be flushed down a toilet.** A company called gDiapers (see Resources, page 347) recently came out with a new type of disposable that's flushable and compostable. Actually, the disposable part is an insert that fits inside a pair of washable cotton/elastene "little g" pants. The baby wears the pants with a snap-in polyurethane-coated nylon liner to eliminate leakage. The liner is breathable and washable, and it's not made from PVC. Then the inserts themselves—the flushable/compostable pieces—are made from all-natural fiber on the outside that's water-resistant and breathable. It's filled with chlorine-free, tree-farmed wood pulp. Plus, the entire diaper is plastic-free and fragrance-free. According to gDiaper, the used diapers that are merely wet can go in the compost heap, whereas poopy diapers get flushed down the toilet. In case you're wondering if they're really flushable, they meet the Water Environment Research Foundation criteria for bowl and trap clearance. They've also received Cradle to Cradle certification from the MBDC (see page 320 for more about that certification).

BABY BOTTLES

At some point, whether or not you choose to breast-feed your baby, you'll need to use a bottle. So the question becomes: What sort of baby bottle should you use? The answer is easy: Always use a glass bottle.

The other choice, of course, is plastic bottles—both the disposable kind and the reusable kind. Clearly, reusable baby bottles are better. But the plastic bottles are petroleum-based, and many of the hard plastic ones are made from polycarbonate, which contains Bisphenol-A (BPA), which is now being linked to health issues ranging from problems with the reproductive organs to hyperactivity in children and even type 2 diabetes. So I would steer clear of polycarbonate, particularly for baby bottles. You can tell a bottle is polycarbonate by turning it over and looking inside the recycling triangle on the bottom. If you see the numeral 7 in there, the bottle is polycarbonate.

Plastic bottles also have been made from polyvinyl chloride, or PVC, which again is one of the most toxic plastics out there. So if you turn the bottle over and you see a numeral 3 in the recycling triangle, stay away from it.

"Polyethylene and polypropylene are less toxic," says Mary, "but there's still nothing definite. Some plasticizers may be getting into the food."

So the best choice for the bottle itself is glass, and then Mary says silicone nipples are generally better than latex or rubber nipples. Silicone nipples are less prone to house bacteria, and you can wash them in the dishwasher. They also last longer than the other options. Latex nipples decompose quickly, and rubber nipples can cause allergic reactions, plus they've been found to contain nitrosamines, a type of contaminant that's been linked to cancer.

I'm delighted to report that it's easier today to make environmentally friendly choices when you're readying your home for the arrival of a baby—and for the first few years of your baby's life—than it was just a few years ago. The best part is that those environmentally friendly choices also happen to be healthy choices. Healthy for the baby. Healthy for the pregnant mother. Healthy for the entire family.

Green choices and healthy choices are not always the same thing. But the fact that some green choices are also much healthier choices does make it easier to convince others of the value, and perhaps even the virtue, of following this kind of environmentally conscious path.

CONCLUSION

Remembering the Most Important Concepts

AT THIS POINT, MY HOPE IS THAT YOU ARE ENERGIZED by the possibilities before you. My hope is that you feel a sense of relief that you now have a road map, a guidebook, and a GPS to get you through your eco-journey. But if you take away only a few things from this book, please focus on the following:

- **Don't try to run up Mount Everest.** I've been doing these things since 1970. It took me fifteen years of conservation to save up enough money for solar hot water and twenty years to get solar PV electric. Take it slowly, get to base camp, get acclimated, and then continue the climb. As you save money, you can do more.
- **Conserve first.** Conservation is the number-one tool in your toolbox for saving money, saving energy, and saving resources. A kilowatt saved is always cheaper than a kilowatt produced.
- **Pick the low-hanging fruit.** Do the cheap and easy stuff first. Don't focus on the big, shiny objects such as solar panels and wind turbines right away. There are so many things each and every one of us can do right away that cost little or no money. A quick list of the best and easiest-to-do items follows.

FOR ALL YOU RENTERS AND APARTMENT DWELLERS

I want to speak briefly to the millions of renters and apartment dwellers throughout the country who e-mail me with questions. I certainly know how hard it can be to take on many of these projects described in this book when you don't own your own home or when you are at the mercy of a landlord or a home-owners' association. I was a renter throughout the 1970s, when I first embarked on this journey, so I know what you're going through.

Don't despair. There are many things you can do right now, today, that can lower your carbon footprint and help save you money. Here's a Top 10 list—and everything on this list is something I've done in the past, something I still do today, or something I have addressed with the addition of new technology in my home.

If you're a renter, this list is your low-hanging fruit:

1. **Get out of your car.** This is at the top of the list for me. Walk, ride a bike, take public transportation—if only a few days each month or one day a week. Every time you get out of your car, you're doing something to reduce your carbon footprint, save money, and reduce our dependency on Mideastern oil. I can't think of a bigger triple play!

2. **Choose the right rental.** Find an apartment or rental house that is close to your work, shopping, and other businesses. Find one with good windows and good insulation and other features that will ensure it's an energy-saver.

3. **Change your lightbulbs.** As soon as you move in, take out the incandescent lightbulbs and install compact fluorescent lightbulbs (CFLs) or LEDs (light-emitting diodes). Instant energy savings follow.

4. **Program the thermostat.** Reduce your heating and cooling bills right away with a programmable thermostat. At $50, this is something you can install and the landlord won't mind. When you move out, take it with you and put the old one back in.

5. **Make your place airtight.** Weather stripping is a cheap and easy way to ensure your rental is as efficient as possible.

6. **Unplug the phantom power devices.** Put in some power strips and make sure those big-screen TVs and computers aren't sucking you dry in standby mode.

7. **Change the air filter.** Changing the filter in your HVAC (heating, ventilation, and air-conditioning) system is regular maintenance that will save you some dough.

8. **Recycle and buy recycled.** This is a no-brainer, regardless of whether you rent or own.

9. **Save water.** Shorten your showers. Add aerators to the faucets. Run only full loads of dishes and laundry. All of these things will help.

10. **Use a fan instead of A/C.** Portable fans and ceiling fans, in conjunction with your programmable thermostat, can save you big bucks on your heating and cooling bills.

 ## WHAT THE FUTURE HOLDS

Based on all the fan mail I receive daily, I know there are plenty more topics that are important to you than I could possibly address in one book. There are many more areas throughout your home—and throughout your life—that you would like to make greener.

I'm often asked about things like solar heat for swimming pools and ways to reduce all the chemicals they require. I'm often asked how

I generate power using a stationery bicycle. I'm often asked about projects for kids, things parents and children can do together to get the whole family involved in a sustainable lifestyle. I plan to explore these and many other areas of interest in the future. In the meantime, I encourage you to stop by the *Living with Ed* website. I will put some of this additional information up there (www.livingwithed.net).

And just a couple of final thoughts.

Please take time to relax and reflect. Life comes at us so fast these days that we sometimes don't leave time to enjoy what's truly important. The words I try to tell myself are "Just slow down." Please do it. You'll be healthier and happier because of it.

And also remember, we're not alone on this planet. Everything we do impacts somebody else around us. By keeping our lives simple and efficient, we minimize our effect on others and the planet.

One of my favorite sayings, and one that I do my best to live by every single day, is:

Live Simply so That Others Can Simply Live.

ACKNOWLEDGMENTS

I suppose I played a small role in putting this book together, but the folks who did the *vast* majority of the work are: Sue Elliott, Greg Glass, and Cynthia Whorton. Their tireless efforts kept this project moving forward in spite of me. I am forever in their debt.

I'd also like to acknowledge all of my friends and business colleagues who contributed to the book: Lou Alonso, David Bergman, Steve Bilson, Buzz Boettcher, Craig Borland, David Chisolm, Rick Chitwood, Susan Colwell, Mary Cordaro, Jerry Dickson, Jim Gallman, Tim Garver, Stephen Gates, Duane Hallowell, Greg Hood, Chris Houchin, Lars Hundley, Jessica Jensen, Derek Kirkpatrick, Leslie Mackenzie, Pat O'Brien, Jason Pelletier, Bruce Ritchey, Barry Rosengrant, Randy Scott, Stephanie Thornton, Rob Wills, and Ellis Yan.

RESOURCES

Living Like Ed, www.livinglikeed.net

1 The Green Home Audit
ENERGY Guide
www.energyguide.com (energy resource)

Energy Star
www.energystar.gov (energy resource)

Low Impact Living
www.lowimpactliving.com/providers/
Environmental-Energy-Audits-Consulting/21
(green home audits, household impact calculator)

REAS Inc.
www.reasinc.com (green home audit)

Silicon Valley Power in Santa Clara
www.siliconvalleypower.com (green home audits)

2 Electricity
Department of Energy
www.energy.gov (energy resource)

Energy Star
www.energystar.gov (heating/
cooling maintenance checklist)

GreenSwitch
www.greenswitch.tv (remote-controlled switch,
payback calculator)

3 Lighting

1000Bulbs.com
www.1000bulbs.com (CCFL bulbs)

BestHomeLEDLighting.com
www.besthomeledlighting.com (LED bulbs)

BetterBulb.com
www.betterbulb.com (CCFL bulbs)

BuyLighting.com
www.buylighting.com (CCFL bulbs, LED bulbs)

Fire & Water Lighting
www.cyberg.com (lighting design)

Four Seasons Lighting
www.fourseasonslighting.com (LED lighting)

Home Depot
www.homedepot.com (CFL recycling)

Ikea
www.ikea.com (CFL recycling)

LEDLightBulb.net
www.ledlightbulb.net (LED bulbs)

Solatube
www.solatube.com (skylights)

TCP
www.tcpi.com (CFL bulbs)

4 Insulation

ACT Environmental
actenvironmental@sbcglobal.net
(environmental testing)

Bonded Logic
www.bondedlogic.com (cotton-fiber insulation)

Department of Energy
www.ornl.gov/~roofs/Zip/ZipHome.html
(insulation program)

Louisiana Pacific
www.lpcorp.com (TechShield radiant barrier)

Reflectix
www.reflectixinc.com (fiberglass-free insulation)

5 Windows & Doors

Energy Star
www.energystar.gov (energy resource)

National Association of Home Builders (NAHB)
www.nahb.org (windows and doors resource)

National Fenestration Rating Council
www.nfrc.org (energy-performance council)

Pella
www.pella.com (windows)

TerraPass
www.terrapass.com (carbon offsets)

T. M. Cobb
www.tmcobb.com (windows)

6 Water Usage

American Standard
www.americanstandard-us.com (toilets)

Brac Systems
www.bracsystems.com (gray water system)

Caroma
www.caromausa.com (dual-flush toilets)

EPA
www.epa.gov/watersense/pp/showerheads.
htm (showerhead, faucet, and faucet aerator
standards)

Falcon Waterfree Technologies
www.falconwaterfree.com (waterfree
urinals)

Kohler
www.kohler.com (toilets)

LifeSource Water Systems
www.lifesourcewater.com (whole-house water
treatment)

Maytag
www.maytag.com (washer)

Metropolitan Water District of
Southern California
www.mwdh2o.com (water-usage research)

Moen
www.moen.com (toilets)

Natural Home
www.naturalhome.com/Garden/2008-03-01/
Graywater.aspx (gray water legalities/
requirements)

Water for Life
www.waterforlifeusa.com (KYK ionizer)

WaterSense
www.epa.gov/watersense/

Whirlpool
www.whirlpool.com (dishwasher)

7 Solar Power

DSIRE
www.dsireusa.org (loan programs)

Energy Trust of Oregon
www.energytrust.org (rebate program)

Enphase Energy
www.enphaseenergy.com (microinverter
systems)

The Florida Department of
Environmental Protection Energy
www.dep.state.fl.us (rebate program)

Green Made Simple
www.greenmadesimple.com (rebates/tax
incentives resource)

Home Power
www.homepower.com (magazine)

National Renewable Energy Laboratory
www.nrel.gov (PVWatts solar energy calculator
creator)

New Resource Bank–San Francisco
www.newresourcebank.com/personal-banking/
solar-home-equity.php (solar bank loans)

New York State Energy Research
and Development Authority
www.nyserda.org (rebate program)

Photovoltaics: Design and Installation Manual,
by Solar Energy International staff
www.solarenergy.com

Power of the Sun
www.powerofthesun.ucsb.edu (*The Science of the
Silicon Solar Cell* film)

PVWatts
www.pvwatts.org (solar energy calculator,
financial calculator)

Real Goods
www.realgoods.com (*The Solar Living
Sourcebook,* solar panels, and supplies)

Solar City
www.solarcity.com (leasing program)

The Solar Electric House, by Stephen Strong
www.amazon.com/Solar-Electric-House
-Environmentally-Responsive-Energy
-Independent/dp/0963738321

Solar Fundamentals,
by Stephen Gates and Rob Wills
http://byelverton.net/solar/Solar_
Fundamentals.pdf

Stephen Gates
stephen@simplesunpower.com (solar system
installer)

Wainwright-Massachusetts
www.wainwrightloans.com/green.asp (green
bank loans)

8 Wind Power

American Wind Energy Association (AWEA)
www.awea.org/smallwind/smsyslst.html (wind turbines)

Bergey WindPower
www.bergey.com (wind turbines)

Choose Renewables
www.chooserenewables.com (wind maps)

DSIRE
www.dsireusa.org (loan programs)

EcoBusinessLinks
www.ecobusinesslinks.com/vertical_axis_wind_turbines.htm (wind turbines)

Enviro Energies
www.enviro-energies.com (wind turbines)

GreenMadeSimple.com
www.greenmadesimple.com (rebates/tax incentives resource)

La Crosse Technology
www.lacrossetechnology.com (wind speed meters)

Real Goods
www.realgoods.com (handheld wind speed meters)

Southwest Windpower
www.windenergy.com (wind turbines)

U.S. Department of Energy's Energy Efficiency and Renewable Energy
www.eere.energy.gov/windandhydro/windpoweringamerica/wind_maps.asp (U.S. wind maps)

9 Building & Remodeling

American Society of Interior Designers
www.asid.org (home improvement guidelines)

Building Works, Inc.
www.buildingworksinc.com (ICF research)

Build It Green
www.builditgreen.org (green building resource)

Cool Roof Rating Council
www.coolroofs.org (green roofing)

DSIRE
www.dsireusa.org (loan programs)

EarthCraft in Georgia
www.earthcrafthouse.com (green building programs)

Energy Star
www.energystar.gov (energy resource)

EPA
www.epa.gov/greenbuilding/tools/funding.htm (loan programs)

E-Space Systems
www.e-spacesystems.net (component building systems)

Forest Stewardship Council
www.fsc.org (wood certifier)

Freecycle
www.freecycle.org (nonprofit connection group)

Green Building Initiative of Northeast Ohio
www.thegbi.org/residential/featured-projects/northeastohio (green building programs)

GreenMadeSimple.com
www.greenmadesimple.com (rebates/tax incentives resource)

Green Roofs
www.greenroofs.com (green roofing)

Hickory and Catawba Valley Green Building Council of North Carolina
www.hickoryhba.com/index.html (green building programs)

Insulating Concrete Form Association
www.forms.org (ICFs)

Low Impact Living
www.lowimpactliving.com (green home audits)

Modern Earth Finance
www.modern-earth.com (small regional lenders)

My Green Cottage
www.mygreencottage.com (green home builder)

NAHB
www.nahbgreen.org (local/regional green building program list)

National Sanitation Foundation
www.nsf.org (green resource)

Regreen Program
www.regreenprogram.org (home improvement guidelines)

Structural Insulated Panel Association,
www.sips.org (SIPs)

U.S. Green Building Council
www.usgbc.org (green building standards source)

10 Garden & Compost

AGL
www.aglgrass.com (artificial grass)

American Rainwater Catchment Systems Association
www.arcsa.org (rainwater catchment promoter)

Clean Air Gardening
www.cleanairgardening.com (environmentally friendly gardening resource)

eNature
www.enature.com (native plants resource)

EPA
www.epa.gov/watersense/index.htm (List of Certified Irrigation Installers)

Gray Water Recycling Systems
www.reusegraywater.com/homepage (gray water systems)

HarvestH2O
www.harvestH2O.com (rainwater harvesting community)

Natural Home Magazine
www.naturalhomemagazine.com/garden/2008-03-01/graywater.aspx (article on legal gray water)

PlantNative
www.plantnative.org (native plants resource)

Quiet Garden Landscaping
www.quietgardenlandscaping.com (quiet gardening)

ReWater
www.rewater.com (gray water systems)

The Toro Company
www.toro.com (irrigation)

U.S. Environmental Protection Agency
www.epa.gov/watersense/index.htm (WaterSense program)

Watts Radiant
www.wattsradiant.com (rainwater collection systems)

Wild Ones
www.for-wild.org (native plants resource)

11 Heating Your Home

A. O. Smith
www.hotwater.com (water heaters)

Bryant Heating & Cooling Systems
www.bryant.com (boilers)

First Company
www.firstco.com (Aqua Therm furnace)

Hallowell International
www.gotohallowell.com (heat pumps)

Water Furnace
www.waterfurnace.com (geothermal products)

12 Cooling Your Home

Association of Home Appliance Manufacturers
www.cooloff.org (cooling load estimate form)

Cool-N-Save
www.coolnsave.com (A/C unit misters)

Department of Energy
www.energy.gov (energy resource)

Duct Blaster
www.ductblaster.com (electronic duct tester)

Hunter Fan Company
www.hunterfan.com (ceiling fans)

Trane
www.trane.com (HVAC)

Water Furnace
www.waterfurnace.com (geothermal products)

13 Heating Water

A. O. Smith
www.hotwater.com (water heaters)

Bateman Water Heating Engineering Inc.
1826 Colorado Blvd., Los Angeles, CA 90041, 323-254-4303

DSIRE
www.dsireusa.org (loan programs)

First Company
www.firstco.com (Aqua Therm furnace)

GreenMadeSimple.com
www.greenmadesimple.com (loan programs)

U.S. Department of Energy
www.energy.gov (energy resource)

U.S. Department of Energy's Energy Efficiency and Renewable Energy
www.eere.energy.gov/consumer (water consumption worksheet)

14 Decorating & Cleaning Your Home

ACT Environmental
actenvironmental@sbcglobal.net (environmental testing)

AFM Safecoat
www.afmsafecoat.com (zero-VOC paints)

AlterECO
www.bamboocabinets.com (bamboo cabinets)

American Clay
www.americanclay.com (clay plasters)

Armstone
www.armstone.com (recycled countertops)

Astier
www.limes.us (lime paints)

Bayes
www.bayescleaners.com (waterless vehicle wash)

Begley's Best
www.begleysbest.com (nontoxic cleaners)

Benjamin Moore Paints
www.benjaminmoore.com
(zero-VOC paints)

BioShield Paint
www.bioshieldpaint.com (clay paints)

Breathe Easy Cabinets
www.breatheeasycabinetry.com (formaldehyde-free cabinets)

Calcem
www.limepaint.com (lime paints)

Capri Cork
www.capricork.com (recycled rubber and cork tile)

CitiLog
www.citilogs.com (recycled cabinets)

Cornerstone
www.cornerstonesalvage.com (reclaimed terra-cotta tile)

Craigslist
www.craigslist.org (classified resource)

Dunn-Edwards Paints
www.dunnedwards.com (zero-VOC paints)

Durapalm
www.durapalm.com (recycled palm tree tiles)

EcoDomo
www.ecodomo.com (leather floor tiles)

Eco Friendly Flooring
www.ecofriendlyflooring.com (recycled aluminum tile)

Eco-House Natural Products
www.eco-house.com (inorganic mineral paints)

ECOsurfaces
www.ecosurfaces.com (rubber floor tile)

Eco-Trend Collagen
www.ecotrendlife.com (collagen paints)

EnviroGLAS
www.enviroglasproducts.com (recycled countertops)

Federal Consumer Products Safety Commission
www.cpsc.gov/index.html (consumer products resource)

Forbo
www.forbolinoleumna.com (linoleum, Marmoleum)

Forest Stewardship Council
www.fsc.org (certified lumber)

Frazee Industries
www.frazee.com (zero-VOC paints)

FreshAire
www.thefreshairechoice.com (zero-VOC paints)

Grass Cabinetry
www.grasscabinetry.com (solid wood cabinets)

GreenFloors
www.greenfloors.com (recycled carpet)

Greenline
www.gogreenline.com (recycled cabinets)

Green Planet Paints
www.greenplanetpaints.com (soy-based paints)

Green Seal
www.greenseal.org (environmental standards on paints)

Henrybuilt
www.henrybuilt.com (bamboo cabinets)

Home Depot
www.homedepot.com (zero-VOC paints)

Hugo Naturals
www.hugonaturals.com (handmade soaps)

Humabuilt
www.humabuilt.com (recycled cabinets)

IceStone
www.icestone.biz (recycled-glass and concrete countertops)

Interface FLOR
www.flor.com (recycled modular carpet)

Kirei Board
www.kireiusa.com (recycled cabinets)

McDonough Braungart Design Chemistry
www.mbdc.com (green certifications)

Muny Woodwork
www.munywoodwork.com (solid wood cabinets)

National Wood Flooring Association
www.woodfloors.org (consumer information on wood flooring)

North American Laminate Flooring Association
www.nalfa.com (flooring association)

The Old Fashioned Milk Paint Company
www.milkpaint.com (milk paints)

Pavé Tile & Stone
www.pavetile.com
(reclaimed terra-cotta tile)

PaperStone
www.paperstoneproducts.com (recycled paper
countertops)

Pittsburgh Paints
www.pittsburghpaints.com (zero-VOC paints)

The Real Milk Paint Company
www.realmilkpaint.com (milk paints)

Seventh Generation
www.seventhgeneration.com (nontoxic cleaners)

Sherwin-Williams
www.sherwin-williams.com (zero-VOC paints)

Sierra Pine
www.sierrapine.com (recycled cabinets)

Syndecrete
www.syndecrete.com (cement-based tiles)

TexSton
www.texston.com (lime paints)

Vetrazzo
www.vetrazzo.com (recycled-glass countertops)

Healthy Baby Diaper
www.natureboyandgirl.net (biodegradable
diapers)

International Institute for
Bau-Biologie & Ecology, Inc.
www.buildingbiology.net (certified Bau-
Biologists)

Mary Cordaro, Inc.
www.marycordaro.com (consulting/education
company)

Nature Babycare
www.naty.com (biodegradable diapers)

OSHA
www.osha.gov (safety and health resource)

Seventh Generation
www.seventhgeneration.com (biodegradable
diapers)

Under the Nile
www.underthenile.com (children's organic
clothing)

15 Babies & Nurseries

Collaborative on Health and the Environment
www.healthandenvironment.org (EMF studies)

Environmental Working Group
www.ewg.org (personal-care products)

EPA
www.epa.gov (Environmental Protection Agency)

gDiapers
www.gdiapers.com (disposable diapers)

PHOTOGRAPHY AND ILLUSTRATION CREDITS

Mike Agerton Ad Design: page 38

BCII: pages 10, 27, 31, 35, 36, 50, 56, 57, 67, 69, 71, 73, 75, 88, 115, 131, 132, 135, 136, 145, 149, 152, 153, 155, 187, 188, 190, 198, 201, 202, 205, 206, 213, 223, 256, 261, 278, 283, 284, 290, 299, 317, 319, 322

David Bergman: pages 42, 43

California Department of Water Resources: page 103

Cool-N-Save: page 270

Cotton Monkey: page 325

Ron Curtis & MrSolar.com: page 121

Wes Danskin, UGSG: page 92

EarthLED.com: page 48

The Energy Conservatory: page 20

Energy Star: pages 17, 86

Enviro-Energies, Ontario, Canada: pages 147, 160, 165

EPA: page 45

FLOR: page 310

Geothermal Heat Pump Consortium: pages 249, 251

Google: page 123

Gray Water Recycling Systems, LLC: page 218

Chris Guthrie, ETL: page 99

Hap Haven, U.S. Green Home: page 18

Hunter Fan Co.: page 34

Courtesy of Insulspan, Inc.: page 180

Jamie Krutz, as first published in *Smart Living* magazine: page 296

LifeSource Water Systems: pages 104, 107

Logix: page 178

Madison Gas & Electric (mge.com): page 46

Marley Engineered Products: page 242

Marmoleum Flooring: page 307

Milgard Windows & Doors: page 84

My Green Cottage: pages 54, 175

Designed, engineered and installed by Premiere Power Renewable Energy, Inc.: pages 124, 142

SKAR Advertising: page 245

Trane: page 237

USAIR.net: page 150

Vetrazzo: page 313

www.cleanairgardening.com: page 221

www.gDiapers.com: page 333

INDEX